MW00606843

CHARLES SIMEON
OF CAMBRIDGE

CHARLES SIMEON OF CAMBRIDGE

Hugh Evan Hopkins

WIPF & STOCK · Eugene, Oregon

Wipf and Stock Publishers
199 W 8th Ave, Suite 3
Eugene, OR 97401

Charles Simeon of Cambridge
By Hopkins, Hugh Evan

ISBN 13: 978-1-61097-813-2
Publication date 10/15/2011
Previously published by Hodder and Stoughton, 1977

TO

BOB HARLAND, GORDON MAYO,
HOWARD COLE, GEORGE BEVINGTON,
RICHARD SMART, ROY HENDERSON,
CLIVE COOPER, GLADYS CHOATE,
BOB HYATT, GEOFFREY HINTON,
JOHN ANDREWS, MIKE BISHOP,
PATTI SCHMIEGELOW,
STEPHEN MASLEN, CHARLES BONSALL,
GEORGE KENNY, WILL STEWART,

my colleagues over the years in the ministry of the Gospel, with gratitude and affection.

Acknowledgments

As a lifelong admirer of Charles Simeon and for very many years the proud possessor of a particularly handsome set of the twenty-one volumes of his works, I jumped at the idea that an up-to-date biography of the great man was long overdue and that retirement to Cambridge might provide an opportunity to attempt it.

No one can write about Simeon without frequent reference to William Carus' *Memoirs of the Life of the Rev. Charles Simeon* (London 1847) and Abner Brown's *Recollections of the Conversation Parties of the Rev. Charles Simeon* (London 1863), both almost unobtainable today. When not otherwise stated, quotations in the text will be from one or other of these books. I am, however, chiefly indebted to Canon Charles Smyth's *Simeon and Church Order* whose footnotes have sent me scurrying down all manner of fascinating passages in search of contemporary glimpses of what the 'Old Apostle' was really like. I could not have compiled this biography without the benefit of his meticulous researches.

I am deeply grateful to Donald Coggan, Archbishop of Canterbury, for his kind and warm approval of my typescript; to Michael Hennell author of *John Venn and the Clapham Sect,* for checking my history and making many helpful suggestions; to Max Warren, former Vicar of Holy Trinity Church, Cambridge, another lifelong admirer of Simeon, for his invaluable comments; and to Michael Rees, present Vicar of Holy Trinity, for the original suggestion that I should embark on this work and for his enthusiastic encouragement during the three years it has taken me.

Many others have contributed to making the writing of this book a pleasure, in particular the staffs of Cambridge University Library and King's College Library, and of the Cambridgeshire Libraries and Record Office, the Earl of Harrowby, the Simeon Trustees, the Archivist of the Church Missionary Society, the Principal of Ridley Hall, Cambridge, and the Reverend Robin Wilson of St Peter's Church, Colchester and the Reverend A. W. Adeney for the kind loan of letters.

My wife and family have borne patiently with my obsession, José and Margaret helping to decipher my writing, and Paul, a book ferret if ever there was one, saving me much time in looking up references.

Any personal views on the pastoral ministry which may have crept into the text of what I hope is an objective study of Charles Simeon, are the fruit of many happy years of service at home and overseas in the Church of England which we can thank God is so much more alive to its responsibilities today than it was when Simeon began his remarkable work.

Cambridge 1977 H. E. H.

Contents

CHAPTER ONE

Introduction to Cambridge

The four-in-hand with its smart bays drew up at the main entrance to the college. It was the wintry month of January when Richard Simeon Esquire of Reading, a rich and successful attorney, descended from his coach with his seven-year-old youngest son, Charles. While the footman held those precious horses, each bought at the price of a curate's annual income, the future Vicar of Holy Trinity, Cambridge, took a last loving look at them before being plunged into the harsh academic world of eighteenth-century Eton to begin his twelve-year stint in England's premier public school.

Fortunately he was a tough young man. He needed to be. He had lost his mother some years before and was thus to some extent prepared for the all-male atmosphere of Eton. But coming as he did from a comfortably affluent home, he was hardly conditioned for the rigours and economies which were thought to befit the training of the up and coming gentlemen of the day. School breakfast was not until ten when it consisted of half a pint of milk served in a tin can, and a penny roll and butter. Dinner followed at two o'clock. Everyday, throughout the school year, they had mutton.[1] It was said that the Eton flocks of sheep were particularly prolific. Be that as it may, the young scholars had little variety at their main meal, and with mashed potatoes as the only vegetable, they wielded their horn-handled knives and forks with little enthusiasm. Sunday's plum pudding provided the only variation. For those who had a private supply of loose coins there were ways and means of getting a little extra out of the kitchen staff, for it was a long wait till supper at six on left-over scraps of mutton which had to last till the modest night-cap of more milk and roll at ten p.m.

Sleeping accommodation for the new boys meant of course the notorious Long Chamber, the fifty-bedded dormitory of unhappy memory to so many old Etonians if their memoirs are anything to go by. It was the scene of many escapades, one of the more innocuous ones being that at which Charles' arch-enemy, Richard Porson, used to excel. It consisted of catching rats and mice with mutton-bones as bait, relics of which in enormous numbers were discovered years later under the floor-boards.[2] Fagging, with all its humiliation and petty sadistic undertones, was *de rigueur* from the first. Each small boy was adopted by one of the seniors who as 'master' would off-load on to his unquestioning fag the most trivial duties, though in those days when fops came to school with fanciful linen the unfortunate and fearful juniors did have the awesome responsibility of seeing that their bosses were kept in spotless array when the occasion required.[3] No doubt young Charles noted early on the attractions of this kind of vanity for he was to make a name for himself as a dandy when he became a senior. Meanwhile, the slightest slip-up on his part as a fag would result in his face being vigorously slapped or his hands mercilessly flicked with a wet towel at his 'master's' pleasure. Compensation for such and for worse injuries to the feelings of their small slaves had to wait until the seniors left college, when it was customary for them to slip a handsome pouch containing perhaps two pounds' worth of conscience money into their fags' forgiving hands.

Though the cane had not been introduced into Eton in Charles' time, the birch was frequently used, as one old Etonian neatly put it, to mark that part of the boys' anatomy 'which cherubs lack'. Some members of the staff were much addicted to using this form of punishment. It is recorded that as late as 1796 Dr Heath, the headmaster, flogged no less than seventy boys in one day with ten cuts each. Charles was there during what has been described as the 'absurd and barbaric rule'[4] of Dr Jonathan Davies who made no great name for himself during his eighteen years in office.

As Charles outgrew the days of fagging he began to show considerable athletic prowess. Mad on horses as he was, riding was his favourite pastime. Years afterwards it was said by a friend that if you could not find the Vicar of Holy Trinity, Cambridge, at the sick-bed of a parishioner you would be sure to discover him in the stables with his horses. He would spend hours grooming and exercising his precious charges once he was in position to have them, and a groom of his own, at Kings'. But while at school, cricket and other sports appealed greatly to him, and off the playing fields of Eton he was remembered for having entertained his companions in such home-made competitions as jumping over six chairs in a row, or snuffing out a lighted candle with his bare feet.

In spite of his ability at this kind of display, Charles was not particularly popular during his school days. For one thing he was bad-tempered, flying into a rage at the slightest provocation, a weakness which plagued him throughout his adult life, and must have made him many enemies at school. Nature had not provided him with handsome features. Indeed, through the ready and merciless wit for which school-boys have an unhappy knack, he soon acquired the nickname of 'Chin Simeon.'[5] A glance at Edouart's remarkable silhouettes in King's College explains the phrase (reproduced as end-papers to this book). It was probably to compensate for this that, unconscious that it would not go down very well with his fellow scholars, he began to develop the habit which clung to him throughout his life, of extravagance in dress and appearance. Richard Porson, who preceded Simeon to Cambridge, and eventually became one of the university's most renowned classical professors, delighted in calling him a coxcomb, a term he was particularly fond of using. Simeon suspected, rightly, though he could not prove, that it was Porson who was responsible for composing and circulating in the school some verses addressed 'to the ugliest boy in Dr Davies' dominions.'[6] The author had disguised his identity by writing with his left hand. It is hardly surprising that these two, who had nothing in common but their education, never became reconciled to one another. Porson in later life when at Trinity College complained that the Vicar of Trinity Church was 'a coxcomb in religion' as he had been in behaviour at school, while Simeon asserted, 'I never could make up my mind to agree with Porson in any matter of divine truth.'

Simeon showed no special academic talent at Eton. He worked hard and reached the Sixth Form. Greek was badly taught and he always regretted his poor grasp of it, but he did become a proficient Latin scholar. Indeed, in 1778 he was privileged to read a Latin speech in the presence of George III and the Royal Family with the Archbishop of Canterbury and the Prime Minister also present for good measure. The occasion was the triennial performance of the famous uniformed parade known locally as 'Montem.' Always captained by the senior King's Scholar, the procession was led by the appointed Marshal whose duties this year fell on Charles Simeon. Dressed in a blue military type coat with gilt buttons, sash and white trousers, bearing a sword and a gilt baton and wearing a cocked hat surmounted by a gorgeous plume, he looked very imposing. Behind him followed the band as they marched *ad montem* to Salt Hill where the festivities took place. The climax was a dinner at the local inn for the whole school of two hundred boys, paid for by funds raised from the onlookers en route. This survival of what was really in origin a medieval mummery, a never-to-be-forgotten break in the routine of the boys' life, used to conclude with a somewhat irreverent episode in which a Colleger, dressed as a parson, booted another dressed as a parish clerk down the hill to the uproarious amusement of the spectators. It is, however, recorded that the event this particular year was carried out with such realism that Queen Charlotte was not amused and prevailed on the college authorities to cut out the closing episode in future performances.

In spite of the clerical nature of the staff, it has to be acknowledged that religious education at Eton at the end of the eighteenth century was at a very low ebb. Chapel services were duly held but conducted mechanically and very much with an eye on the clock. Three times a day prayers were said in Latin. Preparation for Confirmation was non-existent, and religious instruction consisted of the whole school assembling every Sunday afternoon at two o'clock to hear a Fifth Former read four or five pages of *The Whole Duty of Man,* a book we shall hear more of in a later chapter. On Mondays different forms would gather to recite memorised verses of the Greek or Latin Testaments. That was about the extent of Christian teaching when Charles Simeon entered Eton. J. B. Sumner, who was to become the first evangelical Archbishop of Canterbury, complained that when he was on the school staff, some twelve years after Simeon left, he was hardly allowed to mention God or Christianity to his pupils.[7] W. E. Gladstone, looking back on his Eton days, recalled that 'the actual teaching of Christianity was all but dead, though happily none of its forms had been surrendered.'[8]

Things remained like this for many years. It is not surprising to read that Long Chamber, where the Collegers were locked in at night and left totally unsupervised, was 'a very undesirable, not to say, vicious place'[9] and sexual conditions there were 'a proverb and reproach.'[10] Charles Simeon declared that had he a son he would rather see him dead than committed to the Eton of his day. In 1827, much concerned for the welfare of his old school, he wrote to his friend Provost Goodall urging that more attention should be given to religious instruction: 'It is often with me a matter of regret that the atmosphere of Eton is so unfortunate for health of the soul; and that amidst all the attention that is paid to the poets and philosophers of Greece and Rome, scarcely ever by any chance is the name of our blessed Saviour heard.' It will be no surprise to those who know of the powerful influence Simeon had in later life, that the Provost promptly acted on his advice and a great change in the religious tone of the school was noted within two years.

This Dr Joseph Goodall was a lifelong friend of Simeon's. They had been contemporaries at school, and the story is told of an occasion in 1809 when they met again at a grand Election dinner one Saturday night. They began chaffing one another about the old days. At that time the Third Form was divided into four divisions, two of which came to be known as 'Sense' and 'Nonsense.' Those in 'Sense' had to turn English words into Latin while the members of 'Nonsense' were given verses to construct. In the course of their after-dinner merry-making Dr Goodall turned to his former fellow-Collegian and said, 'I think, Mr Simeon, that in our early days you were in the "Sense" and I was in the "Nonsense."' 'Just so, Mr Provost', Charles Simeon replied with the ready wit which from time to time used to lighten his seriousness, 'and there we have remained ever since!'[11]

We only get one glimpse of young Charles' own religious experience while at Eton. The occasion was a national Fast Day, during the apparently interminable American War of Independence, in 1776. Somehow the idea of the whole nation uniting to repent, fast and pray made quite an impression on the seventeen-year-old scholar who, looking back on those days, said 'I thought that if there was one who had more displeased God than others, it was I. Accordingly I spent the day in fasting and prayer.... But I had not learned the happy art of "washing my face and anointing my head, that I might not appear unto men to fast." My companions therefore noticed the change in my deportment and immediately cried out, "Woe, woe unto you hypocrites," by which means they soon dissipated my good desires, and reduced me to my former state of thoughtlessness and sin.' A fellow Etonian however, whose bed was next to Charles, and who had every opportunity to observe him, suggests he was being too hard on himself in this judgment. He recalls the fervour of Charles' observance of that particular day when he cut Hall and subsisted instead on 'one hard egg.' He maintains, moreover, that in spite of the way they tended to tease him, Charles did in fact sober down after this eventful commemoration moderating his dress and even keeping a private poor-box into which he made contributions when his conscience moved him. His later generosity to the needy had an early beginning.

Three years after this experience Charles left Eton and, as most of the King's scholars did, went up to Cambridge to begin a residence in that university town where he was to enjoy

The groves of Granta, and her Gothic halls,
King's Coll., Cam's stream, stain'd windows and old walls[12]

for fifty-seven years. Cambridge at the end of the eighteenth century was small, densely populated and pretty primitive. Encircled by the river, the built-up area extended no further than Magdalene College on the north, Emmanuel on the east and Peterhouse in the south. The two thousand or so houses and college premises were built so close together that of Trumpington Street, the present King's Parade, it was popularly but indelicately said that a man could quite easily spit across it. The cobbled streets and narrow alleyways were relieved only by the market place with its long-standing 'Hobson's Conduit' in the centre to remind the inhabitants of Cambridge's famous livery-stable owner who allowed his customers no choice but the freshest of his forty horses for hire.

Gas lighting was not introduced into the town until 1823, and even then street lights were opposed by dons and townsfolk alike on the grounds that the breaking of them might be too great a temptation for the less ruly element of undergraduate. There were no public conveniences of any kind, no pavements and no drains, the water running down the centre of the streets. In wet weather a brisk demand arose for the only umbrella in the place which was let out on hire by the hour from a shop in Benet Street.[13] Umbrellas were regarded in England as French fancies and like everything else at that time from across the channel, were suspect. Even in London, where they were first portrayed in a cartoon of 1784, they were only used in big houses to protect the gentry when entering their carriages in the rain. But this did not deter Charles Simeon from being ahead of the fashion, and he soon availed himself of one of these newly imported contraptions. To this day it has the distinction of being preserved in a glass case in the vestry of his church. This unwieldy looking object, which features prominently in his best known caricature, seems to have been almost as indispensable to him as his remarkable shovel hat.

Horseback was the only effective means of getting about. Telford and Macadam had not yet had the inspiration which was to revolutionise our roads and thus bring to an end the isolation of places like Cambridge. In Simeon's day the town was surrounded by open fields and marshy fens, only five or ten minutes' walk from the centre. Townsmen and gownsmen alike had no need to roam very far in their search for exercise or sport. They were happy with their swimming, cricket on Parker's Piece, boating to Grantchester or sailing to Ely, and of course endless opportunities to fish and shoot, snipe, partridge, pheasant, woodcock, plovers and hares being plentiful. Then of course they could always take a horse in the fresh air of the Gog Magog hills for four and sixpence a time, or twenty-five shillings if there was a foxhunt to add to the excitement. To the south and south-east of Cambridge in those days one could gallop for miles unhindered by fences or hedges. Simeon, who always revelled in the sunshine, was seldom so happy as when out on one of his horses. 'My rides have ever been of the greatest delight to me' he said when encouraging his young followers to take as much exercise as they could. 'I used often to see him,' remembered Dr Carlyon, 'when I was an undergraduate at Cambridge, riding to some milestone on the Trumpington road, or to the Gog Magog hills, a most remarkable figure, as erect on horseback as he was upright in his life and conversation.'[14] Apart from his regular daily rides Simeon kept himself fit by swimming. In his diary for May 28th 1784 he wrote, 'Went into the water and shall continue it at 5.' Even in the summer term the Cam can be cold at that sort of hour. No doubt he did not want an audience. He also knew that by making an early start he would be well out of the way before the barges bringing coal and wine from King's Lynn for the college cellars would be stirring up the mud as their horses waded chest deep in the middle of the stream.

The town was dominated then as now by 'The Freshman's Landmark', 'King's Chapel, the finest I ever saw . . . the most capital piece of architecture indeed' as Parson Woodforde wrote of it three years before Simeon went up. The buildings of King's College itself in addition to its Tudor masterpiece consisted of Old Court on the north, now used as university offices, where he had his rooms as an undergraduate, and the imposing Gibbs' Building which divides the two great lawns. It was in this Fellows' preserve that Simeon resided for the greater part of his life. The present screen facing King's Parade had not yet been erected, and the forecourt of the college was at that time a mass of old cottages and shops right up to the main street. To the west of the Gibbs' Building the grass expanse was divided by a path which led down to the old two-arched bridge with its brick gateway. In 1818 this bridge was in imminent danger of collapse. The story of its replacement, involving as it does our young freshman who had in the intervening thirty-nine years clearly become a dominant personality in the college, is worth recording here. The bridge was on the point of being pulled down and rebuilt on its old site when Simeon intervened and suggested that it be moved to the present position nearer Queens' College. The King's authorities agreed to his plan but only on condition that Simeon himself contributed the sum of £700 towards the cost.[15] This was a lot of money in those days and one can justifiably enquire what was Simeon's particular interest in such an alteration. The answer seems to be that it just meant easier access from the stable where he kept his two horses across the river to the Backs where he could exercise them. So he readily agreed to this considerable expense, and the work was done the following year.

But we must return to the nineteen-year-old scholar from Eton who on January 29th 1779, together with just two other freshmen, Joseph Goodall, and Simeon's lifelong bugbear, William Moore, of whom we shall hear later, entered King's College.[16] In this strange new world he found waiting to see to his domestic requirements a bed-maker, a gyp or male servant, and a coal carrier, with a shoe-black and a hairdresser available when required to attend to his personal appearance. This latter gentleman was much in demand for the use of wigs and the curling and powdering of hair did not go out of fashion until after Pitt's tax on hair powder in 1795. It was said that at Oxford, in rather earlier days, George Whitefield and John Wesley did without these vanities in order to save the hairdresser's fees to give them to the poor.

Charles' first breakfast must have made a good impression on one who became known as fond of his food, having been on pretty short commons throughout his Eton days. If Trinity College is anything to go by, he would, according to a contemporary, have started the day with 'toast, muffins, crumpets, eggs and two inches of butter' (George Eliot's Amos Barton remembered Cambridge as the place where 'there are able mathematicians and butter is sold by the yard'). On top of this would follow at choice, ham, cold chicken, beef steaks with ale, tea or coffee, and honey, marmalade and anchovies to complete the menu.[17] This sounds a fairly substantial meal but it had to last till 'dinner' which in 1792 was moved from one o'clock to a quarter past three. This meal was quite an occasion, everyone dressing in white waistcoat, white silk stockings and wig, or with hair freshly combed, curled or powdered. After dinner the men would be free to relax until compulsory evening Chapel at five-thirty, after which they would normally retire to their rooms until taking tea and light supper last thing. In King's on Sundays there was a special evening meal laid on for the benefit of those clerical Fellows who had been riding out into the country taking duty in the local churches. This supper, which was never very popular, became known as 'Neck or Nothing', the only dish that the kitchen provided being cold mutton.[18]

Eighteenth-century college life was marked by the existence of three classes of undergraduates. At the top of the social scale came the noblemen who went by the name of Gentlemen- or Fellow-Commoners. They were men of means and some breeding whose presence in Cambridge had little connection with any academic interest. They threw their weight about the college courts adorned in purple, green black or even rose-coloured gowns with trimmings of gold and silver lace, and caps with conspicuous tassels. They expected to attract a respect which they little deserved. Arthur Pendennis of Thackeray's novel is an example of such a gentleman of fortune of that day, with his special orders for port and sherry to be sent up from London (and charged incidentally to his widowed mother's account), his velvet waistcoat and smart shooting jacket, not to mention his new horse on which he so delighted in showing off. John Byng took a very dim view of these wealthy and undisciplined layabouts. When staying a night at 'The Cock' in Eaton Socon in May 1794, he records 'observing from our window, with dread and detestation, the outrageous behaviour of some Cambridge bucks, who were abroad on a route of dissipation. The waiter was shock'd! At length off they went in their gigs and tandems, at 9 o'clock to drive 19 miles to Cambridge; arm'd with broomsticks more to encourage than to repel insults: but I sadly fear discipline is lost in our schools and that our young men start blackguards and democrats.'[19]

Men like this were strongly resented not only by traditionalists such as the author of the *Torrington Diaries* but even more by the other two classes of undergraduate, the pensioners and sizars. The former provided the bulk of the students while the latter, who were often also known as 'hounds', were the poorer men who had to have special terms and who got their name from their daily allocation of rations. For them college life was far from the care-free extravagant experience of their more privileged colleagues. They very naturally envied their affluence and the easy-going honours that came their way; but even more they felt sore about the fact that they often had to swell their own meagre resources by carrying out such duties as transcribing manuscripts for these 'Empty Bottles'[20] who refused to take their academic work seriously.

Charles Simeon entering Cambridge as a pensioner and a King's Scholar sounds rather more grand than it really was. King's was a very small college and far from distinguished at that time for intellectual prowess. Their total complement in Simeon's day was a Provost, some thirty-five Fellows and only about fifteen undergraduates, all from Eton.[21] Any incentive for them to study hard was weakened by the fact that college statutes allowed the scholars to take their degrees without any examinations. They were then free to go on and become Fellows after three years' residence, always assuming that they did not marry. It is not therefore surprising that at the end of the eighteenth century King's College had attained the dubious reputation of being 'the grave of genius'.

Throughout the university, as a matter of fact, few dons at this time were genuine scholars and little original research was undertaken by anyone. In 1802 for instance, neither the Regius nor the Lady Margaret professors of divinity gave any lectures at all, and the professor of Greek gave only one in the whole academic year.[22] Those few lectures that were given were in Latin which, as attendance was in no way compulsory, discouraged an audience, which in turn discouraged the lecturers who disliked holding forth to a deserted auditorium. A situation of this sort easily lent itself to abuse by the lazy dunce and the unscrupulous playboy, but even a conscientious, hardworking student had little to encourage him. When Simeon started at King's the only public lectures that he was expected to attend consisted of one on the *Ethics* of Aristotle and another on Pearson's treatment of the Apostles' Creed.[23] The actual teaching of undergraduates, such as it was, was in the hands of tutors (known today as supervisors). It covered a wide range of subjects of which mathematics was given priority. But the standard required as late as 1799 for a pass degree in Maths only demanded 'a competent knowledge of the first book of Euclid, vulgar and decimal fractions, simple and quadratic equations, and Locke and Paisley,'[24] the last for their basic philosophical background. We need to disabuse ourselves of any idea of the Cambridge of Simeon's day teeming with intellectuals. The average candidate for an ordinary degree was a pretty ignorant young man whose education so far had left him ill-equipped in elementary mathematics and uselessly knowledgeable in Latin.

There were, as we shall see, some brilliant scholars whose names are still mentioned with respect, and the fact that so many undergraduates were hoping to go on to ordination meant that due emphasis was also placed on the Classics, Ancient History, Philosophy, Moral Science and even Poetry. The BA degree could be taken after ten residential terms, but the normal examination for it consisted merely of reading a Latin essay on a mathematical or philosophical question and then being cross-questioned on it *viva voce* by three opponents, also in Latin. Although theology had no place in the undergraduate curriculum, when it came to the MA degree Divinity was an essential subject. Examination in it comprised a somewhat formidable system of two hour public disputations, again in Latin. But one seldom hears of any scholar being 'plucked' though there were frequent references here and there to the horrific nature of the Latin employed. And there were in those days ways and means of getting round the somewhat lighthearted examiners. The incumbent of Great Massingham, for example, one Cock Langford by name, besides being known as 'the greatest fop imaginable' and meeting his end on the dance floor, was specially noted for the way he got his MA at Trinity College in 1769. Apparently he was asked as a test question whether the sun went round the earth or the earth round the sun. After some thought he came out with the original comment, 'Sometimes the one, sometimes the other.'[25] For this brilliant piece of temporisation it seems, they awarded him his degree.

We have to envisage Charles Simeon trying to find his feet in this somewhat bizarre academic setting. For a conscientious young man like him it must have taken some sorting out. Though he was not particularly gifted, we have no reason to doubt that in spite of little encouragement from those who were meant to be responsible for his intellectual development, he devoted himself to his studies with reasonable concentration. All unknown to him he had an eminent contemporary, born in the same year as himself, who similarly went on to great things largely unaided, and with whom in later years Charles was to find so much in common. This was William Wilberforce, a Fellow-Commoner of St John's College. Speaking of his dons he once said, 'Their object seemed to be to make and keep me idle. If I occasionally appeared studious, they would say to me, "Why in the world should a man of great fortune trouble himself with fagging?" '[26]

There was plenty going on in the town to distract the undergraduate Simeon. A few years before he went up the Vice-Chancellor had complained that they were 'much pestered with lewd women who swarm as much in our streets as they do in Fleet Street or Ludgate Hill'.[27] In 1793 the Proctors were taken to task for not dealing severely enough with the local prostitutes, most of whom lived in the small village of Barnwell with its sixty-five very sub-standard dwellings.[28] As late as 1810 Isaac Milner, President of Queens', in his capacity of Vice-Chancellor, had reason to deplore the 'breaking of lamps and windows, shouting and roaring, blowing of horns, galloping up and down the streets on horseback or in carriages, fighting and mobbing in the town and neighbouring villages; in the daytime breaking down fences and riding over cornfields, then eating, drinking and becoming intoxicated at taverns or ale-houses, and, lastly, in the night frequenting houses of ill-fame, resisting the lawful authorities and often putting the peaceable inhabitants of the town into great alarm.'[29]

Much of this disturbance was the work of the Fellow-Commoners who were a law to themselves. No doubt Charles, who was to become very much a 'loner' as he grew older, was glad to withdraw to the seclusion of his rooms when this sort of thing was going on for he was by nature a man of peace. It is very possible that the peculiar practice of fitting a second outer door to an undergraduate's room, known as 'the oak' for it was always extremely substantial, originated in these days of violence. Certainly no student who has experienced the peace of retreating to the privacy of his own quarters and 'sporting his oak' lightly values the security and freedom from interruption that this facility to this day provides for him.

But Charles was not by nature a recluse and was always very ready to enjoy himself, certainly in his early days as an undergraduate. No doubt he would have frequently patronised the two coffee-houses which were particularly popular just then. One of these, Smith's, was opposite the Round Church and the other at the Rose Inn in the market place. Here he could read the *Spectator* or the *Daily Post*, and other papers were available. The student fascination for endless discussion and the airing and trying out on their friends of newly acquired ideas could be enjoyed at leisure over tea or coffee. It would be in such a setting that he acquired his reputation for being something of a fop. Meeting another gownsman with a similar love of dress, he challenged him to a competition as to which of them could produce the most imposing display. Simeon was eventually declared the winner on the grounds of having been discovered wearing two watches on two rich gold chains, one on each side.[30]

Even after the spiritual experience which, as we shall see, so fundamentally altered his way of life, late in his first term, he enjoyed visiting Newmarket for the races, an activity which it only slowly dawned on him might be called in question. He was also extremely fond of dancing, at which he was supposed to be something of an expert. It was some little time before he came to see anything wrong in attending the country balls with which the wealthy entertained their friends. One memorable occasion he and a companion, lured partly by the prospect of a good game of cricket when they got there, travelled part of the way to a dance on a Sunday evening as they could not reach their destination on the Monday alone. In those days it was a bold man who broke the Sabbath like this whether he was religious or not. Anyway, in the course of a long ride they stopped off at a friend's house where refreshments were served in the form of tankards of a beverage a good deal stronger than Charles expected or to which he had been accustomed. When he remounted he was too far gone to know whether he was coming or going, and might well have come to a bad end had not his horse, familiar perhaps with his master's youthful idiosyncracies, been inspired to turn in at an inn. Here the innkeeper took charge of the situation and looked after the young man overnight until he was sufficiently recovered to resume his journey. That was a party that Simeon never forgot, the more so because on the way home in solemn mood, the landlady of an inn where they rested said in all innocence to him, 'Have you heard that a gentleman of Reading (his own home town) has been killed by a fall from his horse while drunk?' 'Why not me?' was the question that bothered him for the rest of the journey back to Cambridge.[31]

It was possibly this incident more than any other that led Simeon, years later, to record in typically exaggerated though sincere evangelical phraseology, 'Never can I review my early life without the deepest shame and sorrow. My vanity, my folly, my wickedness, God alone knoweth. If I be found at last a prodigal restored to my Father's house, God will in no ordinary measure be glorified in me; the abundance of my sinfulness will display in most affecting colours the superabundance of his grace.' But this is anticipating. At the moment we are leaving Charles Simeon as a lively athletic young man with a touch of vanity saved at present by an engaging light-heartedness, an intelligent and moderately intellectual but spiritually unenlightened undergraduate settling into his rooms in Old Court, King's. Soon, however, any thought of settling down was to be out of the question. He was in for the surprise of his life.

CHAPTER TWO

A Christian at King's

It was but a moment's walk for Charles from his rooms in Old Court across to the chapel, but at seven o'clock on a winter's morning even that glorious shrine in which Wordsworth imagined

> Every stone is kissed
> By sound, or ghosts of sound, in mazy strife

could be uninviting. There was no music at that hour of the day to lure anyone to worship. It was not the fear of the Lord but of entrenched authority that dragged men from their beds, often with just a long surplice flung over their night attire, mustering 'with all the reluctance of a man going to be hanged' as a contemporary of Simeon's remembered it.[1] What chance the worship of Almighty God when, to quote a Cambridge parody of Gray's Elegy,

> Each morn, unchill'd by frosts, he ran
> With hose ungarter'd, o'er yon turfy bed,
> To reach the chapel e'er the psalms began.[2]

Such an unwilling congregation would not mind the chaplain hurrying through Mattins or Evensong at break-neck speed, but Simeon, whose fondness for the Prayer-Book liturgy never deserted him, complained that in King's the services were almost always 'very irreverently performed'. Even a hundred or so years later some Cambridge college chapels were accustomed to the reading of Mattins in ten minutes dead. When one earnest Christian undergraduate approached a Professor who had just finished a particularly hurried service with the request that he might in future perhaps read the prayers more slowly, he was withered with a look. Stopping in his tracks in the cloister, the don turned upon the young man and cured him of any desire to go on attending chapel when he was taking the service with the words 'May God forgive you this impertinence'.

The system of compulsory attendance twice daily at college chapels lay at the heart of the Anglican monopoly of the university. The colleges were, in fact, clerical clubs, their combination rooms being staffed almost entirely by ordained men. Holders of any office and all applicants for a degree had to acknowledge that they were members of the Church of England. To prove it the Test Acts insisted on a man attending communion whatever his personal religious beliefs, a practice scorned by Simeon and condemned by William Cowper who had no time for those who make

> the symbols of atoning grace
> An office-key, a picklock to a place.

In such an ecclesiastical world as this, the ordinary student had to make the best of things, though compulsory worship had a soul-destroying effect upon many of them. In later years Simeon wrote, 'I am far from considering it a good thing that young men in the university should be compelled to go to the table of the Lord: for it has an evident tendency to lower in their estimation that sacred ordinance, and to harden them in their iniquities.' Not only did the undergraduates object to the 'clocking-in' process with eagle-eyed college porters actually walking up and down during the service on the lookout for absentees; but the fact that hardly any of the Fellows, who after all were almost all clergymen, attended chapel themselves made matters worse and caused much offence. William Wordsworth, a late contemporary of Simeon's, 'looked in vain for the presence of any of those who ate the bread of the founders .... He felt that there was something like hollow mockery and profane hypocrisy in this.'[3]

Not until near the end of Simeon's life, in 1834 in fact, was there any serious agitation or revolt against this highly unpopular college tradition. Even then, when it was proposed in the House of Commons that these regulations be lifted, in the Lords, Lord Palmerston failed to get adequate support for his argument: 'Was it either essential or expedient that young men should be compelled to rush from their beds every morning to prayers, unwashed, unshaved and half-dressed; or in the evening from their wine to chapel and from chapel back again to their wine?'[4] On a lighter note, a few years later a society was formed in Trinity College 'For the Prevention of Cruelty to Undergraduates' with the express purpose of drawing attention to the contrast between the compulsory attendance of gownsmen and the voluntary abstention on the part of dons. Volunteers made out a score-card and marked the number of times their seniors attended, and then offered a prize 'for general regularity and good behaviour in Chapel' to the one who came out top. It happened rather naturally to be the Dean, William Carus, who later became Charles Simeon's biographer; he was, however, disqualified by virtue of his office. The scores of the other seniors, which proved to be far from complimentary, were published weekly in a broadsheet accompanied by typically acute undergraduate comment. The results of this good-natured but desperate protest were meagre, and the rules remained in force for another thirty years.

The situation would have been more tolerable had academic and religious life in the late eighteenth-century university not been at so low an ebb. There was a glaring inconsistency between the pious regulations in force and the daily practice of those whose duty it was to enforce them. As an extreme example of the casual attitude of so many dons to their duties, the notorious Richard Watson became Professor of Divinity in 1771 after getting a DD only 'by some adroitness'. Previously he had held the chair of Chemistry of which subject he had 'never read a syllable nor seen a single experiment'. After making a study of this new subject he eventually succeeded in suggesting ways and means of improving the manufacture of gunpowder,[5] surely a unique accomplishment for any Bishop of the national church. In 1782 he cornered the Bishopric of Llandaff while living for the most part in Westmorland. It was a matter of much concern to the more conscientious President of Queens', Isaac Milner, that after his election this new Regius Professor of Divinity neither gave a single lecture nor visited Cambridge while retaining his lucrative appointment.[6]

It is tempting and would not be difficult to enlarge on the academic negligence and religious indifference in Cambridge during Simeon's days, for examples are legion. There were, no doubt, many splendid exceptions, but we have seen enough to realise the kind of conflict that an undergraduate would be faced with when as a freshman he discovered himself in a world where anything goes, little was expected of him, and few of his seniors either worked hard enough or were devout enough to win his or anyone's respect.

Charles had been three days in residence when he and his fellow King's Scholars received the customary note from the Provost requiring their attendance in chapel at Holy Communion in three weeks' time. He was never to forget the date, February 2nd 1779, when the porter brought him this devastating piece of news. He had only just come up and had been busying himself with such mundane matters as getting his rooms in order, stocking his lockers with madeira at twelve shillings a bottle, and a crate of 'Black Strap' port at sixty shillings a dozen, all stored away in sawdust next to his coals. His furniture had to be sorted out as well, though the grey curtains for which Old Court was renowned he inherited from his predecessor.[7] And there were also his coachman and two fine horses to be settled into their new quarters. Altogether a busy time.

As a freshman, or 'Nib' as he found himself called, he had to make the acquaintance of the man who had rooms above him, being a year senior. He was known as his 'Chum'. From him Charles would learn the college customs, and be duly warned amongst other things not to fraternise with or even raise his cap to any of the golden-tasselled Fellow-Commoners whom he might encounter. They were better ignored by a pensioner such as him. So, while still hardly knowing his way about the college, let alone the town, out of the blue came this unexpected summons. Thoughts of religion were far from his mind at the time. What he had seen so far and gathered from his fellow-students neither commended chapel worship nor the serious study of divinity. But somehow this was different. It had the nature of a personal intrusion on his soul, or what he had of a soul. It struck him as a direct challenge to his integrity. Still at heart the gay, easy-going and rather conceited Charles, humbug he never was nor would be.

His first reaction was to try to dodge the issue, to get out of it if he possibly could, for he was far from feeling in the mood for quite so serious an activity as going to Holy Communion. 'Satan himself was as fit to attend as I' was how he put it years later. But finding that he could in no way be excused, he began to look for some guidance. His father's advice would have been of little value. Christian friends he had none. Everything around him was still new and strange, unusual and bewildering. He had no idea what to do and time was short. The only religious book he had ever heard of in his nineteen years was a once popular seventeenth-century devotional writing called *The Whole Duty of Man.* George Whitefield is said to have so strongly disapproved of it that he made one of his Georgian orphans throw it in the fire.[8] William Cowper blamed it for not helping him in his depression, calling it crossly a 'repository of self-righteousness and pharisaical lumber.'[9] This was the book of which Samuel Johnson complained to Boswell 'Sunday was a heavy day to me when I was a boy. My mother confined me on that day, and made me read *The Whole Duty of Man* from a great part of which I could derive no instruction.'[10] Charles bought himself a copy and plunged into it, not surprisingly with little result. He then turned to a book by Bishop Thomas Wilson which he found much more helpful, *Instruction for the Lord's Supper*. In a state of spiritual panic lest the day when he must go to communion catch him still unprepared, he made himself quite ill with his studies, his prayers and his acts of fasting. He became so obsessed with a sense of unworthiness that he said, 'I frequently looked upon the dogs with envy' (most Fellows at King's in those days we are told sported a dog), wishing he had their mortality and they his immortal soul.

He does not record in his somewhat scanty memoirs how the dreaded compulsory communion went. He was at that point far from having achieved any peace of mind, and was still engrossed in his amateur theological researches. Fortunately for him, he persevered with Bishop Wilson's book for another two months which brought him to Lent and Holy Week. He spent hours trying to reconcile his sense of guilt with the mystery of the sacrifice of Christ as portrayed in the communion service of 1662. He had had no evangelical training to throw light on the subject. There was no one he knew to whom he could turn. The skies seemed brazen overhead and when he looked down it was only to see his horrific reflection as a sinner beyond hope. In this frame of mind he suddenly came upon a phrase to the effect that 'the Jews knew what they did when they transferred their sin to the head of their offering'. Like a flash it came to him, 'I can transfer all my guilt to Another! I will not bear them on my soul a moment longer.' Looking back in happy retrospect over the years, he recorded later, 'Accordingly I sought to lay my sins upon the sacred head of Jesus; and on the Wednesday began to have a hope of mercy; on the Thursday that hope increased; on the Friday and Saturday it became more strong; and on the Sunday morning, Easter Day, April 4th, I awoke early with those words upon my heart and lips, "Jesus Christ is risen today! Hallelujah! Hallelujah!" From that hour peace flowed in rich abundance into my soul, and at the Lord's Table in our Chapel I had the sweetest access to God through my blessed Saviour.'

Charles Simeon had begun his new life as a conscious Christian. He had been thoroughly converted. It was for him a peak experience such as Thomas Carlyle envisaged when, referring to a similar turning point in the life of Oliver Cromwell, he wrote in his most lyrical fashion: 'Conversion . . . certainly a grand epoch for a man; properly the one epoch; the turning point which guides upwards, or guides downwards, him and his activity forevermore. Wilt thou join with the Dragons? Wilt thou join with the Gods?'[11] Some twenty-five years afterwards Charles confided to his friend Arthur Young, the great agriculturalist, to the latter's apparent surprise, that for all that time he had never doubted of his future salvation. Seeing that it had come to him in so strange and unpredictable a way, and had not depended on his virtue, his devotion or his piety, there is nothing particularly presumptuous in such a claim.

At the end of his life, in a private letter not intended for publication, he wrote with transparent sincerity, 'The light of God's countenance then first visited me, and in his great mercy he has never wholly withdrawn it from me during fifty-six years. I was then enabled by his grace to set my face towards Zion, and though I have had much to lament and mourn over, and for which to be confounded before God, yet, blessed be his name, I have never turned my face away from Zion!'[12] His was a life-time commitment. He made a special note in the margin of his massive study Bible against Deuteronomy 26.3, 'That thou mayest remember the day when thou camest forth out of the land of Egypt, all the days of thy life . . .' 'So must I, and God helping me so will I, the Easter week and especially the Easter Sunday, when my deliverance was complete, in 1779.'

It is convincing proof of the reality of Charles' conversion that there was so clearly no human influence at work. No one had tried 'to win him for Christ.' No earnest believer had button-holed him and suborned him into making a decision about which he might have second thoughts later. Indeed, it was this total loneliness of his experience which was to influence his personality for the rest of his life. He was driven into an aloneness with God where, as we shall see, he found comfort and encouragement and the power to remain faithful to his newly-discovered Master for over half a century. In his last year, writing to a friend about the assurance which he had always had, he said, 'I stamp on the Rock of my salvation, and never find it shake under me; and whilst this is the case I never feel anxious about any little blast that may blow around me.'

In fact, the blasts he was to receive were far from being little ones. Many another convert would have given up if over a period of three years he could, like Simeon, find no one else with whom to have fellowship and to share the joys of his new life. It was a great deprivation. For lack of kindred spirits to talk to, he tried to make the most of the church and chapel services available, such as they were. Though he did not share the contemporary craze for keeping diaries, he did jot down some of his experiences during these vital months. We can thus trace the ups and downs of his spirit as he writes: 'At Evening Chapel not so much wandering as usual . . . prayer tolerably fervent in and before Morning Chapel, and received the Sacrament so, but after Chapel found a lassitude . . . At

Evening Chapel sad wanderings and coldness; at night I seemed almost to sleep over my prayers such was their weakness . . . Evening Chapel very fervent. At night very devout and penitent.' We see him struggling with the new demands that his faith was beginning to make on his way of life and the uncertain feelings that worried him so much.

On Sundays he attended Great St Mary's, the university church, little dreaming of the many occasions on which he himself would have the privilege of mounting that pulpit to address the Senate and undergraduates in years to come. But at the time of which we are writing Sunday was not a very inspiring day. In 1780 Charles says, 'Had no devotion at St Mary's . . . the preacher did not keep my attention well.' Only once does he mention having gone to Holy Trinity church. On this occasion he stayed on to receive Holy Communion and found himself one of only three communicants. In the year of his death he saw a very different Holy Trinity: 'Yesterday I preached to a church as full as it could hold, and partook of the Lord's Supper in concert with a larger number than has been convened together on such an occasion in any church in Cambridge since the place existed.' Then referring to that first visit of his he remarks with the heavy wit with which he used to make wry comments from time to time, 'So greatly has the Church of England been injured by myself and my associates.'

But going to church and chapel did not satisfy the overflowing heart of the new convert, who, as he said, from the time that he found peace with God himself wished to impart to others the benefits he had received. There was precious little scope for a freshman, however soundly converted and however earnest a Christian, to embark on evangelism in the setting of late eighteenth-century King's. He would have been quickly written off as of unsound mind had he followed his natural inclinations and started preaching to his fellow undergraduates. But he did find one outlet for his zeal which though unusual aroused no adverse comment. He invited his personal servant or gyp, Hollis, to evening prayers in his rooms on Sunday nights when he read to him and any others who joined them, and led them in prayers from the Prayer Book. Hollis must have been an exceptional person for Henry Kirke White, the poetical genius of St John's College whom Simeon later befriended, claimed that gyps as a whole were a menace. In a letter to his brother Neville in 1805 he says 'This place is literally a den of thieves; my bedmaker, whom we call a *gyp* from a Greek word signifying a vulture, runs away with everything he can lay his hands on, and when he is caught, says he only borrows them. He stole a sack of coals a-week, as regularly as the week came . . . Tea, sugar and pocket-handkerchiefs are his natural perquisites . . . There is no redress for all this; for if you change you are no better off; they are all alike.'[13]

When the Long Vacation of 1779 came, Charles returned home a different man. The reaction of his father and brothers was mixed. They were all strangers to any kind of 'enthusiasm', but were intelligent level-headed men. His brother John became a Fellow of All Souls', Oxford, having studied law, and went on to be made a Master in Chancery, and eventually one of the Commissioners in charge of the private property of King George III. He ended up as Member of Parliament for his home constituency of Reading and was created a Baronet in 1815. The youngest brother, Edward, known as 'Ned', became a successful merchant and rose to a directorship of the Bank of England. Charles' eldest brother, Richard, was already a sick man. When his now fanatically religious brother from Cambridge wanted to establish family devotions in the ancestral home, it was he alone who supported him. Charles had, however, to restrict himself to conducting prayers for the servants. John and Edward were careful to keep out of the way. There is an affectionate letter extant which John wrote to Charles some three years later in which he gently but firmly takes him to task for trying to convert his family to his own way of thinking. Charles had written a long and earnest plea which has not survived, and his eldest brother explains its effect on them: 'We laughed and looked serious alternately under the apprehension that you should lose that valuable gift called common-sense . . . It is natural for young people to be zealous in anything new; and therefore I trust that in the common course of things your zeal will slacken a little.'

This was not the kind of reaction that Charles had hoped and prayed for but he had to accept it. All three brothers remained very good friends in spite of their differences, and in the end Charles was able to say that both of them 'lived to embrace and honour the Saviour whom I had commended to them.' His father, with whom Charles was never able to relate happily, proved quite indifferent to his new aspirations. It was a matter of real concern that he did not get on better with him. 'I was always so unhappy,' he said, 'in his company that I could not put on sufficient ease and cheerfulness.' He often reproached himself for not trying harder 'to bear with him, and feel for him and try to win him'. He found it a great trial that his father felt so strongly about the evils of 'Methodism' as he called it, that he demanded that his son should renounce his friendship with William Cadogan, Vicar of St Giles in their home town of Reading. This in all conscience he could not do, though he did agree not to preach in his church. 'Unhappily my poor father retained his prejudices to the last; but I have never entertained a doubt but that I did right in obeying God rather than man,' he wrote to a clerical colleague.

It was out of these personal strains and stresses in his relationship with his father that Charles was able to preach with conviction that while we must always 'obey God rather than man' in such a situation, 'if you do it with petulance and disrespect, you sin against God: for no conduct on the part of your parent can absolve you from the duty of honouring him.'[14] It cannot have been easy for him to come to this conclusion, when he remembered how old Mr Simeon had so strongly disapproved of the way he disposed so freely of his money to the poor that he had left Charles' share of the parental estate in the hands of trustees lest he should ruin himself by his Christian generosity. Yet in spite of all this, when Richard died in October 1782 and Charles was on the verge of his Cambridge career, he offered to give it all up and go and look after his ageing father 'to render his few remaining years as comfortable as I can'. He even got as far as packing up his books ready for the move when the events related in the next chapter took place and altered all his plans. His father's momentous intervention on his behalf in spite of his son's 'Methodist enthusiasm', showed that he was prepared to help him to a life of ultimate fulfilment. And though the old man never changed his views in these matters, to Charles' great joy he was fully reconciled to him personally before his death.

Three years residence at college passed quickly for Charles, swept along as he was by his new-found faith. With few lectures to attend and no examinations to concern him, he could very easily have slipped into the indolence that ruined so many other King's Scholars from Eton. It was such Kingsmen as these that the pamphleteer R. M. Beverley had in mind when in 1833 he composed his candid but mischievous open *Letter to his Royal Highness the Duke of Gloucester, Chancellor, on the Present Corrupt State of the University of Cambridge*. Referring to the 1820s he said, 'If ever gothic grandeur was thrown away, it is on this fraternity who fatten ingloriously in gothic apartments; who take degrees, by a particular charter, without any examination: who are privileged to be ignorant and nurtured to be useless.'[15] But, though a Fellowship waited for Charles automatically at the end of his studies, he was not a man to waste his time. He had ordination in view, the only possible destiny for one who had been so wonderfully delivered from doubt and despair.

It was, however, exceptional for a young man in those days to take ordination as seriously as Charles did. For most it was a social or cultural matter, a way of life, a case of taking up a respectable profession rather than responding to any kind of challenge. Jane Austen, who told her sister that her new novel, *Mansfield Park*, which she wrote in 1811, was to be a complete change of subject from her other ones and deal with ordination, had a large number of friends and relations in holy orders as well as her father and two brothers. She therefore knew what she was writing about within the limitations of her times. When the question of Edmund Bertram being ordained is discussed, Mary Crawford considered it likely to lead to his surrendering his manhood. Fanny Price, on the other hand, to her great credit far from thinking it an effeminate calling saw it as a career that would draw out the best in a man. It is interesting, incidentally, to read in her private correspondence of how the authoress, who was by way of being a sincerely devout person, in 1809 wrote 'I do not like the Evangelicals', but by 1814 her views seem to have changed. Writing then to her niece about her admirer who was showing signs of becoming 'earnest', she interestingly comments 'As to there being any objection from his goodness, from the danger of his becoming even evangelical, I cannot admit that. I am by no means convinced that we ought not all to be Evangelicals, and am at least persuaded that they who are so from reason and feeling must be happiest and safest . . . Don't be frightened by the idea of his acting more strictly up to the precepts of the New Testament than others.'[16]

Charles did not long keep up his diary, nor did he ever find it easy to lay bare his soul or share his more intimate feelings. One of his curates, Matthew Preston, said of him, 'Mr Simeon was not ordinarily communicative, never obtrusive, on subjects of personal feeling in religion. These he regarded as matters between God and the soul, not lightly to be divulged.'[17] So we do not know a great deal about the inner workings of his heart as the day of his ordination drew near. But we do know that he was quite at a loss as to how he should set about finding a curacy where he could happily serve his Lord. He even thought at one point of putting out an advertisement in these terms:

> A young clergyman, who felt himself an undone sinner, and looked to the Lord Jesus Christ alone for salvation, and desired to live only to make that Saviour known unto others, was persuaded that there must be some persons in the world whose views and feelings on this subject accorded with his own, though he had now lived three years without finding so much as one; and if there were any minister of that description he would gladly become his curate and serve him gratis.

So it was in a very different spirit from that of many of his contemporaries that Charles Simeon, who had entered into his Fellowship on 29th January, was ordained deacon on the strength of this appointment on Trinity Sunday, 22nd May, 1782, by the Bishop of Ely in his Cathedral. He was still only twenty-two years of age. For the last few months he had been attending St Edward's church where he found the ministry of Christopher Atkinson the most in harmony with his new convictions of all the clergy in the town. He had hoped that by regular attendance in his congregation the incumbent would befriend him and provide something of that fellowship he so much lacked. But this was slow in coming and he was too shy to introduce himself. In the end, just a few days after his ordination, they met face to face and found themselves to be indeed brothers in Christ. Charles had been invited to a tea-party in Atkinson's rooms in Trinity Hall. There he was introduced to John Venn ('a man after my own heart') and Henry Jowett and some other like-minded gownsmen. When he discovered that they also were committed Christians he greeted them with great delight: 'Where have you been living that I did not know you?'

One thing led to another and it was only a week or two before Charles was drawn into a deep fellowship with them all and particularly with John's father, the great Henry Venn. Formerly Rector of Huddersfield he had recently accepted the living of Yelling, a small village some twelve miles away where the elderly saint could recover from the exhaustion that led him to give up his busy parish. No less than six times during that summer, sometimes on horseback along the many bridle paths that still cross these fenlands, and sometimes on foot, Charles would call upon him. They were men of like spirit. 'My soul is always the better for his visits,' wrote Venn to a friend. 'Oh to flame, as he does, with zeal and yet be beautified with meekness!'[18] The young ordinand's opinion of his veteran friend was no less warm: 'In this aged minister I found a father, an instructor and a most bright example; and I shall have reason to adore my God to all eternity for the benefit of his acquaintance.'

Since, though he had been ordained deacon, Charles had not yet found a curacy, when Christopher Atkinson invited him to take charge of his church, St Edward's, for the summer months, he jumped at the opportunity. So this young Fellow who still had another nine weeks to run before getting his BA found himself preaching from the venerable narrow oak pulpit with its plain linen-fold embellishment, from which the great Reformer Hugh Latimer used to address Cambridge and the Protestant world in 1529. To be in that sacred tradition, a son of the Reformation standing where one of its greatest prophets had proclaimed the gospel, was an inspiration to the young minister. The parish for which he was now temporarily responsible was quite small and covered the quarters of all the local butchers. Charles threw himself into the task with all his energies, conducting a couple of weddings though still a deacon, and visiting the neighbourhood from door to door. 'I am come to enquire after your welfare. Are you happy?' he would say as they answered his knock.[19] Disarmed by his friendly approach and surprised out of their anti-clerical prejudice, the parishioners began to wonder what had hit them. On his very first day, returning from a service along the narrow St Edward's passage, he heard a violent quarrel taking place between a man and his wife whose door was standing open. In he went, and before long, as a crowd of passers-by gathered to watch, he had them both kneeling on the floor as he led them in prayer.

But it was in his preaching ministry that the young locum made his mark during that summer duty. Henry Venn felt he must tell his friends of what was happening in that small church. 'In less than seventeen Sundays he filled it with hearers – a thing unknown there for near a century.' The news reached John Berridge of Everton, the peripatetic evangelist who found the Church of England so restricting. He was so thrilled that he wrote off to John Newton in London telling him that St Edward's 'is crowded like a theatre on the first night of a new play.'[20] Indeed, the congregation began to overflow the pews, crowd the aisles and even the sanctuary, not to mention invading the privileged Parish Clerk's precious seat. No doubt it was this unprecedented and disturbing experience of being dislodged from his place of honour that led this dignified gentleman to greet the Vicar on his return from holiday with a sigh of relief. 'Oh sir, I am so glad you are come; now we shall have some room!'[21] Crowded congregations were by no means to be Charles Simeon's normal experience when in due course he began his own ministry. But these three summer months were a wonderful start to his life's work.

CHAPTER THREE

Minister of Holy Trinity Church

From time to time during his student days Charles had passed the high wall from behind which emerged the ungainly tall transepts and low chancel of Trinity church. 'I had often said within myself, "How should I rejoice if God were to give me that church, that I might preach the gospel there, and be a herald for him in the midst of the university!" But as to the actual possession of it, I had no more prospect of attaining it than of being exalted to the see of Canterbury.' So testified Charles Simeon as he looked back over thirty years to the remarkable events of November 1782. The ambitious day-dreams of the new young convert who, as we have seen had no church in view where he could look foward to working in fellowship with and learning something of the disciplines of his ministry from a like-minded rector, did in fact come true. It was possibly the most unusual, most unlikely and most irregular of all appointments in the strange history of patronage in the Church of England. The circumstances were unique. For one thing, Simeon was still only a deacon recently ordained and not yet qualified to administer Holy Communion. He was a totally inexperienced and untrained young man of only twenty-three who in normal times would have served as a curate for a number of years. By no stretch of the imagination could he be described as ready for so important and demanding an office as vicar of one of the town's leading churches.

Yet, by a stroke of what some would call coincidence, but he and in due course thousands of others came to believe to be divine providence, the incumbent of Holy Trinity church died. This was just when Charles' summer vacation stint at St Edward's was coming to an end. With all the brash boldness and self-assurance which led him into many a difficulty in his relationships with people in those early days, and apparently blissfully forgetful that he had not yet been a curate nor even taken his BA, Charles wrote to his father, who knew the Bishop of Ely personally, and asked him to put his name forward for the living. On the face of things there would seem to be hardly one chance in a thousand that his Lordship would even contemplate such a thing, with its blatant tones of favouritism. But without any hesitation, in a matter of only a week or two, the offer came to Charles as he waited anxiously in his rooms wondering what God had in store for him now that his time at King's seemed to be ending. For reasons which are hard to fathom, he had been allowed to jump the queue. The obtaining of livings by men of his views was next to impossible in those days, so great was the fear of the spirit of 'Methodism' on the part of bishops and patrons. Worthier veterans and greater saints had long been kept waiting for a church of their own. James Bean as late as 1808 drew attention to this difficulty in his *Zeal without Innovation* in which he stated that 'almost the whole of the clergy called evangelical are in the dependant and precarious condition of curates.'[1] This was a problem about which, ever thankful for the remarkable way in which things had worked out for himself, Charles was to take action in days to come. Meanwhile, to his delighted surprise and with little idea of what was coming to him, not that that would have made him hesitate one instant, here he was in office.

Though history does not seem to have been a subject that ever caught Charles' imagination, for he was one who tended always to look forward rather than backward, yet he must have been solemnly aware when he entered Holy Trinity church for the first time as incumbent that there had been evangelical saints of no mean distinction in that pulpit before him. At the end of his life he was to refer to them in what he called 'my dying testimony.' In 1610 a 'Memorial' was addressed to one Richard Sibbes, 'public preacher', signed by the minister, churchwardens and twenty-nine parishioners of Trinity church, inviting him on account of 'the extream straytnes and div'se other discomodities' which at the time limited his sphere of preaching, to become lecturer at their expense. Sibbes gladly accepted this invitation and immediately made the church a spiritual centre for students as well as townsfolk. A gallery had to be erected to accommodate the large numbers that this very able, devout and popular lecturer used to attract 'at 1 of the clocke' on Sunday afternoons. After five years he left to become preacher at Gray's Inn, but in 1633, Puritan though he ever remained, he was recalled by Charles I to succeed Thomas Goodwin as vicar of Holy Trinity, a post he only lived to hold for two years.[2]

Meanwhile, the lectureship was taken over in 1624 by Doctor John Preston, the Master of the newly established Puritan college of Emmanuel.

This eminent divine had declined the Bishopric of Gloucester in order to be free to minister at the heart of the academic world in Cambridge. He and Simeon had the same idea. The sum of £80 a year was raised to go with the post of lecturer, and it is recorded that the largest subscription to this, of £1, came from the celebrated carrier Hobson. The chosen preacher was provided with an 'hower-glasse', costing ten pence, to ensure that his eloquence did not allow the lecture to encroach on divine office or the catechising of children. Dr Preston's addresses were so popular that the churchwardens had to make a ruling that seats be kept for those who had subscribed until the bell stopped tolling, after which 'such others as shall be lyked of by such as shall keep the dore' could be admitted.[3]

As far as Charles Simeon was concerned, these two men had pioneered a trail which he was hoping to follow. But at first he was far from being the well-known preacher much in demand. The simple fact was that he was not wanted. The parish had become attached to the former vicar's curate, the Reverend John Hammond, and as churches often do, they petitioned the bishop to appoint him. After all, they knew him and he knew them. Who was this unknown, unheard of young King's scholar with the Eton accent and affected manner? What did he know of the working man's way of life sheltered as he was in the ivory tower which his fellowship and rooms in King's College had provided for him? He was unwelcome enough as an academic, but rumour had it that he was badly tainted with 'Methodism' into the bargain. His Lordship of Ely, however, did not think on quite these lines. Not apparently averse to private approaches from a mutual friend, he seems to have strongly disapproved of parishioners having any say in who should become their minister. He turned down their application straight away, and on 9th November appointed Charles Simeon to the living at £40 a year.

The next day the new minister preached for the first time in Holy Trinity church. The churchwardens and the vestry, or Church Council, were infuriated. Their first reaction was to encourage all the regular pew-holders to fix locks on their pews so that, while staying away from the services themselves in protest, no one else could be admitted to their empty seats, thus leaving the preacher with a sea of vacant places before him. So those who did in fact wish to attend and had no proprietory pews of their own, and were too Christian to join in this disgraceful boycott, had either to stand in the aisles or sit on benches in obscure corners of the church. When Simeon had further seats provided at his own expense, the irate and frustrated wardens showed their total lack of Christian grace by throwing them out into the churchyard. Holy Trinity church, Cambridge, was in for a whole pack of troubles.

It is perhaps an appropriate point at which to pause and see what the charge which he had so unexpectedly inherited was like. The population of the parish when Simeon went there was about a thousand. In the earlier days of his ministry when public health was a secondary consideration and medical facilities were negligible, the births and burials recorded in the parish register more or less cancel themselves out. Infant mortality was such that some eighteen out of thirty deaths in the year were very young children. Few well-to-do people lived near the church. 'My parishioners in Trinity parish are very poor church folks' he told his undergraduates. In the petitions which were made from time to time in protest against their new minister, some seventy members were literate enough to record their signatures but as many as twenty had to do with making their mark. These poorer working men and women seem to have valued their church highly, even though when attending a service they often had to make do for accommodation on the benches in the darker corners of the building reserved for 'the lower orders' for free. It was one of the joys of Simeon's old age that when in 1835 it was possible to enlarge the chancel of Holy Trinity and make other alterations he was able to say 'There are fixed benches in all the aisles with backs to them so that the poor sit as comfortably as the rich.'[4]

The mainly artisan congregation was joined in due course by paupers from the 'Parish House' who were bound by Rule 6 of their institution which ran 'Every pauper shall attend Divine Service twice on the Sabbath Day, and those who refuse to comply with this order shall not be allowed any dinner on that day.' From where all these less privileged church-goers were accustomed to sit, the Holy Table and the painting of the risen Jesus with Mary Magdalene which hung against the east window, were invisible. But the then all-important pulpit surmounted by its heavy sounding board could not be missed. In that dominating position the preacher was able to survey his people, keeping a special eye not so much on the devout poor as on the easy-going well-to-do church members within their high box pews. Who knows but that, as George Eliot describes in *Amos Barton*, a nurse might have smuggled in some bread and butter to keep her hidden child quiet, or perhaps the father of the family be having his customary snooze. It took all sorts to make up Charles Simeon's congregation, once the initial opposition had died down.

Even when no spirit of hatred and dissension infected the church and no large empty gaps showed in the nave, an act of Anglican worship in the late eighteenth century was not by any means the inspiring activity that it can be today. For one thing, there was very limited scope for music. Choirs were rare, and a band in the gallery as pictured by Hogarth was the exception rather than the rule. In a town church the people normally left the singing to the parish clerk who may, or may not, have been gifted with a tuneful voice. While he was struggling through what John Wesley, referring to the metrical Psalms, called 'the miserable, scandalous doggerel of Hopkins and Sternhold'[5] to the best of his ability, as like as not the people would be talking, whispering or gazing about them. It was with the greatest difficulty that evangelical Anglican clergy got their congregations to take a leaf out of the Methodist books and stand up and praise God 'lustily and with a good courage'.

Charles Simeon was greatly concerned about all this. He made the most of the wave of hymn-writing which followed the Wesleyan revival, and produced for his church his own selection of psalms, and no less than three hundred and forty hymns which he had privately printed at Cambridge. Amongst these some twenty-five or thirty are favourites still today though less than a dozen of the tunes he used are familiar now. In August 1793, somewhat desperate about the state of the singing in Holy Trinity, and at this age always ready to pick up tips from others, he wrote for help to his friend Thomas Haweis who was rector of a small rustic village in Northamptonshire. He was known to have a well-trained and gifted choir. 'I have been so charmed,' he said, 'with the singing at Aldwinkle that I have determined to leave no stone unturned in order to accomplish something of the kind in my own church. I have therefore ordered a barrel-organ which will cost me not less than £200 or rather £250, including all expenses, and another of a smaller construction that will cost £40, to teach my people in private.'[6] He went on to ask if he could borrow some of the 'sweetest and most select tunes' that Haweis had himself composed which he intended to add to others he had. The barrel-organ would then include a selection of some sixty tunes in all.

These remarkable instruments were at that time just beginning to be used in churches and chapels where their main function was to provide voluntaries and anthems beyond the powers of local musicians. Oblivious of any difficulties they might create, Charles decided to be well in the fashion, and naïvely expected that a barrel-organ would be the answer to all his musical problems. In a subsequent letter, when Haweis had tactfully but firmly pointed out that with its lack of flexibility or adaptability it was far from a good teaching instrument, and that there was no substitute for even a moderate small choir, Charles admitted 'I have not, indeed, any scientific acquaintance with music, nor any taste to boast of, but perhaps sufficient for this purpose. I intend to have a barrel [*sic*] on purpose for teaching so that I myself, ignorant as I am, shall be able to act as well as if I were a professional man.' When Charles Simeon once made up his mind about something neither modesty nor other people's advice could deter him. In this case history does not relate how the machine improved his services or for how long it remained in use. According to a local newspaper it cannot have had a very prolonged life for in 1839, in a series of articles on parish church organs in Cambridge, we read 'At Trinity church (where is the worst organ and in the worst order) may sometimes be heard three pedals cyphering at once, without seeming to excite any great sensation in the congregation.'[7] And this was just after the church had been renovated.

But at least in March 1794 Simeon succeeded in persuading Dr John Randall, who had been organist of King's since 1745 and became the university Professor of Music ten years later, holding both offices till his death in 1799, to perform the opening ceremony. We do not know much about the standard of musical accomplishment in the university at that time. The surprising readiness of the professor to associate himself with such a mechanical and new-fangled form of music-making as a barrel-organ may possibly be explained by the appearance in the local paper of an advertisement. This offered for sale 'A collection of 60 Psalm tunes harmonised by the Professor of Music, Dr Randall, published in association with the introduction of the barrel organ into Trinity church.'[8] The Professor of Music received no stipend and depended for his livelihood on the fees of the very few students who required his help,[9] so no doubt he was glad of the publicity that this unique occasion provided.

It is hard to imagine how, in conditions such as these, Simeon's curate, Henry Martyn, was able to state, albeit with typical conscientious scruples lest his feelings were getting the better of him, 'At times during the service I had a joyful sense of the divine presence, but as it was chiefly during the hymns, I think these affections suspicious.'[10] Perhaps the congregation had made a special effort after the dedication of the organ when Simeon had urged them to try a bit harder in their singing:

> It is much to be regretted that, in our worshipping assemblies, the greater part of the congregation never join in this part of the service [the praise]; they seem to think that they are not interested in it, and that it may well be left to those few who may have studied music as a science . . . Yes, my Brethren, let me hope that many of you will unite your endeavours: . . . let not one be silent; and while we are united in

singing the high praise of our God, may God himself come down in the midst of us, and fill the house with his glory![11]

Music may not have been Charles Simeon's strong point. Where he really broke new ground was in the way he conducted the spoken parts of a service. We can picture him, dressed in his voluminous white surplice with hood and black scarf, being led with all due dignity to his place by the sexton in a gown adorned with gold lace. There he would kneel in prayer while a hush came over the people. Instead of the prayers being rattled off at speed, they began to hear them actually being prayed. To Charles this part of a service was sacred. 'Never do I find myself nearer to God than I often am in the reading-desk,' he said.[12] He did everything he could to bring reality to the time-honoured phrases of the Book of Common Prayer which for so many and for so long had become hackneyed and meaningless. He made a special point of reading as clearly and as distinctly as he could, and expressed the hope that the younger John Venn in his new living in Hereford would remember that 'it is in *pauses* in which almost the chief excellence of reading consists.'[13] Josiah Pratt, who became secretary of both the Eclectic Society and the Church Missionary Society, recalled that when he was a young man attending a service at St Mary's, Birmingham, he was enormously impressed 'by the earnest manner in which the service and especially the *Venite Exultemus* was read by the Rev Charles Simeon who had recently entered the ministry,' and was on that occasion officiating for the minister.[14] Another who frequently went to his services noted not only his clear articulation but specially how 'he prayed the prayers'[15] as if that was uncommon. Young and new to the practice of leading an act of worship, Simeon was himself so intensely aware of the presence of God that he was able to diffuse the whole congregation with a feeling of solemn devotion.

Although he particularly made a name for himself for his sermons, he never allowed preaching to displace the importance of worship. In 1823 he prepared an address to be delivered at the opening of the new church of Holy Trinity, Cheltenham, in which he made it abundantly clear that a church building is primarily a House of Prayer: 'Those who make light of the Prayers, and regard them only as a kind of decent prelude to the Sermon show that "they know not what spirit they are of": since all the preaching in the universe will be of no use without prayer . . . A congregation uniting fervently in the prayers of our Liturgy would afford as complete a picture of heaven as ever yet was beheld on earth.'[16] On another occasion he repeated the thought, 'The finest sight short of heaven would be a whole congregation using the prayers of the Liturgy in the true spirit of them.' In the same vein, his divine calling was so real to him and he was so conscious of God being with him in a service that he used to say that when he was pronouncing the benediction, 'I do not do it as a finale, but I feel that I am actually dispensing peace from God and by God's command.'

This was the reality which Charles Simeon hoped and prayed and worked to establish as he led his people in worship. But it must have seemed a long time coming for, as we have seen, the atmosphere around him was positively volatile when he began his ministry. It was not simply a case of people being prevented from coming to church. There was the more delicate and extremely trying matter of the former curate, John Hammond, who was to be very much in evidence for another five years. Frustrated in their attempts to have him made vicar, the parishioners promptly elected him to the lectureship which still existed after more than a century. This appointment was at the disposal of the laity and carried with it a remuneration of £80 a year raised by public subscription, twice the income of the incumbent. Whoever held it had the right to conduct a service and preach on Sunday afternoons and on market day whether the minister wished it or not.

It is hard to imagine what kind of a relationship if any Simeon was able to establish with Hammond who, though only the lecturer, had the effrontery to sign himself in the parish registers as 'Minister', a practice he only corrected to 'Officiating Minister' three years later, no doubt after having had words with the true incumbent. It must have been galling in the extreme for Simeon, bursting with zeal and a love for souls, flattered perhaps by the remarkable success of his preaching at St Edward's, to have a meagre apology for a congregation at Morning Prayer and then to know that at the afternoon service the pew doors would be unlocked and his so-called colleague have unrestricted access to those for whom he himself had been solemnly given the 'cure of souls' at his ordination and appointment. It was hardly to be expected that Charles Simeon took this limitation of his ministry lightly. Within a few days of his taking up his post, however, he received letters of encouragement and advice from veteran evangelicals who were delighted to hear that so earnest a man had gone to so important a sphere. John Thornton, for example, the wealthy Christian merchant and most generous benefactor to all good causes, wrote from his home at Clapham: 'Watch continually over your own spirit, and do all in love; we must grow downwards in humility to soar heavenward. I should recommend your having a watchful eye over yourself, for generally speaking as is the minister so are the people.'

John Newton reassured his young friend and brother in the faith, 'The Lord has chosen for you, and on him therefore, you may confidently rely for all that patience, fortitude and meekness of wisdom which you will need especially in a place where so many eyes will be upon you, so many tongues ready to circulate every report to your prejudice, and so many ears open to receive them . . . Particularly the spirit and conduct of our Lord in the days of his humiliation furnish the best model. His manner, his gentleness, his patient attention to the weakness and prejudices of those around him, we cannot imitate too closely.'[17] And so, encouraged by the sympathy and support of such veteran Christians as these, and relying on being able to make frequent visits to his dear friend at Yelling, Henry Venn, Charles settled down to what it was going to mean to be an unwelcome minister.

On 28th September, 1783, he was ordained priest by the Bishop of Peterborough in the Chapel of Trinity College, of which the Bishop was also Master. Strengthened by this further commitment to the service of his Lord, Charles looked around for a field of wider opportunity as one act of worship on a Sunday hardly absorbed his boundless energies. He thought he would try holding a Sunday evening service and lecture for 'instructing the poor who could not easily attend Divine Service in the earlier parts of the day', as his friend Henry Coulthurst had successfully done at the Round Church. He asked the Venns for their prayers. But he ran straight into a storm. The churchwardens simply shut and bolted the church doors against him. He tried again a year later, but was greeted with a solemn manifesto signed by the two wardens, three overseers and fifteen other members of the vestry. In this document they could not bring themselves to acknowledge him as anything but 'The Sequestrator.' They claimed that 'preaching a third time on Sundays in the parish church of Trinity is contrary to custom . . . is unnecessary, unprecedented, attended with great inconvenience to the parishioners and detrimental to the church as the greater part of the congregation come from many parishes in and out of the town of Cambridge.'[18] They went on, quite incorrectly, to state 'the said sequestrator is not incumbent consequently can have no right to go into the church whenever he thinks fit; therefore . . . the church wardens do lock the church doors and refuse the sequestrator admittance.'

It is interesting to notice in this unpleasant manifesto the reference to people attending Holy Trinity from far and near after Simeon had only been there eighteen months. While the local parishioners were still up in arms against him and the vestry positively hostile, he had begun to build up a following from those who valued his message from further afield. At first Simeon's presentation of the gospel, which was so much in accord with that of Wesley and others of his persuasion, resulted in a greater welcome to him from those outside the Church of England than from those within. In May 1783 he told John Venn about the first Youth Group that he had been able to get together at Trinity: 'On Sunday last I met in a private house in my parish about a dozen young people, at their earnest request; they were all dissenters.'[19] This was some encouragement to him. John's father, hearing of all this, was able to pass the good news on to Rowland Hill in London that 'Mr Simeon's light shines brighter and brighter. He is highly esteemed, and exceedingly despised; almost adored by some; by others abhorred.'[20]

The mixed reception to his ministry remained. This was not entirely due to disagreeableness on the part of the church officials. He was still a very young man and there were certain awkwardnesses about him of which he was probably quite unaware at first. But they struck those who did not know him well and made them, while appreciating his earnestness and sincerity, hesitate to go along with him in full commitment. Thomas Dykes, who went up to Magdalene College in 1786, and who was happy to attend Holy Trinity church, spoke of his first impressions that Charles Simeon was

> one of the most unlikely persons to become extensively useful that he had ever known. He saw in his young friend much zeal, but not according to knowledge; he heard him preach the most crude and indigested discourses, containing ever and anon some striking remark, but abounding in incorrect statements and in allusions offensive to good taste. He also perceived an apparent affectation of manner, a fastidiousness about personal appearance, an egotism and a self-importance which seemed likely . . . to neutralise any good effect which might be produced by his ministry, especially among persons trained to academic modes of thinking.[21]

These of course were still early days. By the grace of God and through the faithful advice of his friends, one of whom he told Venn in a letter instead of complimenting him on a sermon as he had hoped, had pointed out its deficiencies, Simeon, as his friend Dykes came to realise, was able in due course to overcome most of these failings. They do not seem to have handicapped him as much as his friends feared. As he matured it became possible for the Venns to write to each other, 'Our dear friend

Simeon came over to see me; very much improved and grown in grace; his very presence a blessing,' and 'He appears indeed to be much humbled from a deeper knowledge of himself. He is a most affectionate friend and lively Christian.' By learning to accept his unpopularity Simeon became gradually less aggressive. He says that he found great comfort and assurance in the passage of Scripture which runs 'The servant of the Lord must not strive', and he used to repeat it to himself 'hundreds of times.' In a letter to a very close friend, Thomas Lloyd, he showed something of what the months of strain and humiliation were teaching him: 'They who are most earnest in prayer for grace, are often most afflicted, because the graces which they pray for, e.g. faith, hope, patience, humility etc. are only to be wrought in us by means of those trials which call forth the several graces into act and exercise.'

After five years John Hammond, brazen to the end, wrote to the vestry offering his resignation as 'minister [*sic*] and lecturer.' Simeon, more relieved than he dared to express, had hoped that he would now be elected to the post, but it was not to be. One of the parishioners had a son who won the day over the signatures of sixty members, so the Reverend Butler Berry of Trinity College became lecturer and the dichotomy in Simeon's direction of church and parish had to continue until 1794. However, in 1790 to his great joy there was a change of churchwardens, the new men no longer standing in the way of him starting an evening service. Now he could preach twice a Sunday, his curate when he eventually could appoint one reading the prayers for him. Sunday evenings in Trinity church were by no means always a haven of peace and quietness. Simeon never quite knew what was going to happen next. In December 1792 for example he had to suspend his service for a few weeks owing to the disturbances in the town associated with panic in some quarters. Levellers and republicans, affected by ideas from the revolution in France, were threatening to overthrow the constitution in England. On this particular occasion for two nights running, bands of loyalists paraded through Petty Cury and Market Hill looking for offenders. One, Musgrave by name, a draper of some note, who had opposed an address of loyalty to George III from the citizens of Cambridge, was seized and forced to sing 'God save the King' there and then in the street. A notorious republican living beside the church who had publicly stated that he thought all churches should be pulled down and the stone used to repair the highways, had all his windows broken.[22] With this sort of thing going on Simeon warned his congregation: 'Much as I wish all men to feel an attachment to the King and Constitution, I think every sober-minded person must join me in disapproving such a method of showing it.'

Unable to visit his parishioners in their own houses because they were so embittered against him, Simeon invited the faithful few to meet him for prayer and Bible study in a private room in the parish on a week-night evening. This room soon grew too small so he took the only other place he could find large enough for the purpose. This happened to be situated in a neighbouring parish. To encroach on another's domain in this way was a highly irregular act, for Anglican clergy work on the principle that each parish priest is responsible for all the people within his own parish boundaries and does not intrude elsewhere. But Simeon, after asking Henry Venn what else he could do and being assured of his prayers, carried on, though he promised that he would give it up if there was any strong protest. In fact none came from the parson concerned so he took this as a sign of divine favour. Thus this weekly meeting was enabled to flourish, and for very many years became a centre of fellowship in Christ which the lonely and much misunderstood young minister found an invaluable spiritual stimulant.

Out of this, as Simeon explained in an address to the Eclectic Society in London,[23] there gradually arose a system of group meetings which show something of the pattern of John Wesley's classes. Long before the days of Church Councils or Lay Synods he organised a team of twelve laymen whom he called stewards and committed to them the management of the church finances and any matters of charity and relief that would come their way. These stewards were individually also members of the six other 'societies' into which his faithful followers found themselves divided according to their status and condition, senior men and senior women on their own, with juniors in a mixed group.[24] A collection for alms was taken at each meeting. Simeon himself went the rounds visiting each society in turn once a month thus getting to know his people in a very intimate way. It gave them a chance to see another side of their minister than the austere and rather forbidding preacher who tended to strike awe into their souls as he leaned over his pulpit cushion and gesticulated to make his points. In due course he had as many as a hundred and twenty people linked to each other and to him like this in a warm fellowship which was always ready to welcome newcomers.

In close association with these groups of Christian laity meeting for Bible instruction and fellowship, Simeon organised the pastoral side of his parish work through a 'Visiting Society'. He described the work of this body in a sermon preached at one of its anniversaries: 'Its design is to find out the modest and industrious poor in a time of sickness, and to administer to them relief for their bodies, and at the same time instruction for their souls.'[25] He divided the parish into areas and appointed a man and a woman church member to be responsible for the homes in their particular district. These two would keep on the look out for cases of distress and special need, and be authorised to give them assistance at their discretion. Once a month the visitors would meet together under the chairmanship of Simeon himself, and report on what they had been able to do, and be advised in cases of special difficulty. In his usual meticulous way, Simeon saw to it that accounts of expenditure were duly examined and the records, he tells us, were kept open for inspection at any time. In this very up-to-date manner he was able to supplement the worship of God in church on Sunday by pastoral care during the week. The gap that can so easily develop between parson and public was thus firmly bridged, and the Christian laity given responsibility not just for the business side of church life, but also for the spiritual welfare of their neighbours. Simeon seems to have been the pioneer in this particular field, and was able to keep these District Visitors going for over fifty years. His example was soon followed by John Venn at Clapham and later by Thomas Chalmers in Glasgow. What became a widespread Victorian church practice in which the Christian paternalism of leisured gentry was devoted to a very good cause, had its origin in the narrow cobbled streets and meagre housing conditions of late eighteenth-century Cambridge.

There came a sad time, however, if we may look ahead for a moment, when Simeon's trust of the laity led him into great difficulty. It was in the year 1811, when he had worn himself out to such an extent that he lost his voice and had to take a long break from the pressure of parochial work. When he began his 'society' or group meetings in the parish room he had made a special point of always being personally present. But after a while this proved too much of a tie, and the prayer meeting which he had instituted during the crisis of fear arising from the Napoleonic war situation, began to meet without his guiding or restraining presence. Its leadership got into the hands of a group of self-assertive men some of whom started to fancy themselves as itinerant preachers, speaking at meetings outside the parish. Simeon regarded this as quite out of order, even had they been qualified to do it properly. When he raised objections great feeling was aroused. In his absence a petition signed by over forty dissident members was sent to the new Bishop of Ely, Dr Dampier, who was known to be unsympathetic to evangelicals and to Simeon in particular. They made their chief complaint the evening lecture-service to which some parishioners still took exception after all these years, particularly one or two who had aspired unsuccessfully to become church-wardens.

When their minister returned from his sick leave to deal with the situation, it was almost beyond even his powers to restore the confidence and fellowship that had previously marked their parish life, at least of recent years. He had always been a stickler for everything being done 'decently and in order.' Though in his own early days he had occasionally wandered round the countryside looking for an opening where he might preach, he soon left these excesses of his exuberant youth. When he was reminded of this one day he cried out with some embarrassment, 'O spare me! spare me! I was a young man then!' He was essentially loyal to his church, his bishop and his fellow clergy, and felt he simply must stop these extremists from his own congregation behaving in this way.

The first thing he did was to dismiss one of his stewards who, without his authority or encouragement, had taken out a licence as a preacher. He then decided to close down the weekly meetings for the time being, suggesting that a number of smaller house-groups be held instead. While the parish as a whole was prepared to stand by their minister, the disgruntled minority turned down this suggestion of smaller meetings. He hesitated to excommunicate those who refused to accept his authority and so the dispute dragged on for over a year. 'Many trials have I met with from relations, from my parish, and from the world;' he wrote in his memoir, 'but in all of them I was enabled to rejoice, yea, frequently to "rejoice and leap for joy"; but this greatly oppressed my spirit, not only because I was wounded in the house of my friends, but because the state of my people's souls, of some at least, was as bad as would not consist with any hope of their final salvation.' In spite of this great setback arising after thirty years of faithful ministry, Simeon still believed in the principle of lay groups with lay stewards in responsible leadership under the minister, whereby, to use his quaint metaphor, 'the coachman' (himself) could use 'the reins' to guide the church in the direction he believed God wanted it to go.

When in 1794 Simeon was at last elected to the lectureship associated with Holy Trinity, believing that 'it was unprofitable for one minister to labour three times a day in the same church', he used to leave the afternoon service to his curate and go out to one of the surrounding villages. In this way he found that his body and mind would be refreshed by the ride and his spirit be uplifted in the further proclaiming of God's word in churches where he was more than welcome. Men and women who wanted to share in the outstandingly evangelical ministry at Holy Trinity had been finding their way there, for there was next to no spiritual life in the places from which most of them came. We need to remember that though five out of every six Englishmen at the end of the eighteenth century lived in the country, village church life was woefully neglected. There was hardly a resident parson in any parish round Cambridge. Services had to be conducted by university clergy who would trot out of town on Sunday morning and do a round of several churches, galloping back at speed in order to be in time for hall in college at four o'clock. There is a well-known tale told of an aged Cambridge divine called Field who made a name for himself by the way he carried out his Sunday duty. He was responsible for the villages of Hauxton, Newton and Barrington. He used to ride to Hauxton first. The church could be seen from the Newton road so if a congregation of any kind had assembled there he arranged for the parish clerk to put his hat on a pole specially kept in the porch, and waggle it. When Field saw this signal he was ready to turn down the road and take a service. If no hat appeared he went on to Newton where he knew that there would be two old ladies expecting him. Turning his pony loose in the churchyard he began the 'Dearly Beloved' exhortation as soon as he entered the porch, and then continued with the service as he put on his robes.[26] If it was wet or very cold as likely as not the name of Dr Drop would be mentioned as having done duty, a convenient way of disguising the fact that the service had been cancelled.[27]

There was a complete change when Charles Simeon came on the scene. He soon showed the villagers that he was made of different stuff and would carry out his duties in a conscientious and spiritual manner. He devoted each Sunday afternoon, while his curate took Evening Prayer, to this special ministry. Soon he made many friends as far away as Potton, Everton, Haddenham, Wilburton, Lolworth, Stapleford and of course his favourite spot, Yelling. On these visits he found it a great help to repeat his Cambridge sermon extempore as thereby he found he could achieve greater 'familiarity and homeliness of style.'[28] In this more informal and intimate approach his preaching benefited from the closer contact with the listeners which enabled him to remember how human they were. When Henry Venn had to go to London for three weeks he asked Simeon to take his afternoon service for him in Yelling. Such a crowded and attentive congregation gathered that, having stayed the night, he held an extra service very early on the Monday morning before riding back to King's at six a.m. It is said that 'The Archdeacon of Yelling' as his friend John Berridge of Everton quaintly called Venn,[29] was not over pleased with quite such enthusiasm as young Charles was showing. Perhaps he feared that at his advanced age he would be expected to keep it up on his return.

At Wrestlingworth, always a particularly poor village, Simeon was made welcome by the curate, Joseph Crowder, whose twenty-four years in that subordinate capacity is commemorated on a tablet in the church. It says that he was one whose concern for the temporal well-being of his people was no less than that for their spiritual good. This is very likely a reference to the bread famine of 1788–9. In Cambridge a subscription list was opened to which Simeon handsomely contributed. But as no one was doing anything for the peasants in the villages round about, he offered to organise what relief he could for them. This proved a great success, the more so as he kept his eagle eye on those concerned with carrying it out. Every Monday he would ride out into the countryside to see for himself that the local bakers in the twenty-four villages on his list who had received a subsidy, were being honest in selling their bread to the poor as arranged at half-price. When news of this piece of practical Christian caring reached the ears of the town and university, men began to take notice of the work of the new man at Trinity church whom so many were inclined to write off as an oddity. In January 1795, during a particularly severe winter, Simeon was one of the sponsors of a further relief scheme during which nearly £1000 was subscribed, a very large sum in those days. The collection for this cause in Trinity church was no less than £36. Some 7000 poor people benefited from this effort, the money being spent on bread, coals and blankets.[30]

Throughout his ministry Simeon was greatly concerned for the underprivileged and deprived families around him. He once expressed the belief that 'the poor in a time of health are happy because their minds and habits are fitted to their state.' Such a view does not imply complacency on Simeon's part; it would have been shared by many if not most middle-class Christians at that time. He met many examples of the contented and godly poor and could imagine no other way of life for them. But when sickness struck down the wage-earner of a family, then indeed his heart went out to them in their distress. He would at once put all his energy into rallying his people and calling on them to be generous. He reminded his laity that it was their responsibility to tackle this kind of situation, and right well they did it. He was happy to learn too that Wilberforce and others were facing the problem of poverty in the country as a whole by launching a 'Society for Bettering the Condition and Increasing the Comforts of the Poor.'[31] Simeon did his share by helping to get a Provident Bank established in Cambridge and preached a sermon on the occasion of its opening.[32] He also gave much support to the creation of a School of Industry in the town and commended it as rendering 'the lower orders of people more intelligent, more useful, more prosperous and more happy through learning "habits of industry" of economy, of subordination to men and of piety to God.'[33]

This last phrase shows how Simeon's concern for the condition of the poor never reached a point of working towards any reform of the social or political order. He was a child of his day, a conservative through and through, and read his Bible inevitably through blue-tinted glasses. 'There is no need of throwing down all distinctions in society,' he preached.[34] Indeed, isolated in a largely academic and non-industrial world, he seems to have been totally unaware of any agitation for change in the structure of society. Nor did his study of the Scriptures lead him to see this as in any way a legitimate aspect of working for the kingdom of God. Very few Christians did at that time, certainly within the Church of England. But he wanted at all costs to make the poor as happy as he could which meant that spiritual comfort had to accompany any practical relief. Little though he realised it, his acts of charity did in fact make more impression on the public at large than any number of his prayerfully and carefully prepared sermons. But then he prayed too for God's blessing on those in distress, and people soon realised that he really cared for them whoever they were and whatever their need.

Amongst the most needy of all those to whom Simeon had to minister were the unfortunate victims of our as yet unreformed judicial system. In his attitude to prisoners he shared something of the spirit of the Vicar of Wakefield who it will be remembered had a particularly soft spot for them, even though they delighted to pull his leg at times. To his wife and family who did not share his concern he used to say 'These people, however fallen, are still men, and that is a very good title to my affections.' It might have been Simeon speaking. 'Men', or 'souls' as he more readily might have expressed it, they had to be visited. Quite apart from what he did in the local gaol, Simeon paid no less than nine visits to Newgate to preach to its unfortunate inmates. His sermons there do not appear noticeably different in structure and composition from those he delivered in Holy Trinity. But the interesting thing is that he should have been invited to go all that way so often for this purpose. One cannot help wondering who invited him. It might have been his friend Fowell Buxton who began his reforming activities about 1814. Or possibly it was Elisabeth Fry herself, whose incumbent and special confidant at King's Lynn was Simeon's former Kingsman friend, Edward Edwards. He was soul-consultant to most of the Gurney family several of whom he managed to steer from their Quaker inheritance into the Church of England.[35] He would have certainly been able to assure Elisabeth that Charles Simeon would deliver her protégés a faithful word.

In Cambridge, amongst those condemned to death in Simeon's time was a chimney sweep by the name of Grimshaw. He was accused of stealing and had his house on Newmarket Road pulled down in the course of a search for stolen articles.[36] Arthur Young tells of getting a letter from a Cambridge friend referring to the unfortunate man's hanging on March 28th, 1801. It read, 'Your friend Simeon was not wanting in his visits to him. He told an acquaintance of mine "that he found Grimshaw's conversation delightful; that he had grace to die; and that the sooner he was executed the better, for fear this grace should evaporate."'[37] When Henry Venn asked Simeon to call on a parishioner of his in gaol he found that he had already done so and had begun to point him to heaven. 'Oh, I have been with him several times,' he was able to say, 'and have good hopes he will go from the gallows to glory.'

On another occasion Venn and Simeon drove together in a post-chaise to visit a man from Henry's former parish of Huddersfield whom he had known some twenty years before. It says much for the faithful pastoral work of Simeon's elderly father-in-God that when the felon saw his one time Rector he fell on his neck in gratitude for his care and concern. In this case the man's life was spared through the intervention of Mr Pitt who in 1784 had just been made Member of Parliament for the university.[38] Not so fortunate was the wretched man of whom Simeon wrote to John Venn that same year, who was hanged for stealing a watch. Though one hesitates to use the word wretched when reading what was the result in his case of the visits made by the vicar from Trinity church: 'The Lord . . . had given him so strong a faith that death had entirely lost its sting; not a fear disturbed his breast. He addressed the people for near half an hour—humbling himself, exalting Christ, exhorting them to faith and repentance; and declaring the full assurance which he had of entering into glory. After which I harangued them on the same scaffold for a few minutes on the nature of that religion which could give such serenity and joy in death. He then commended his soul into the hands of Jesus and launched into eternity without a doubt, without a sigh.'[39] Young parson and hardened criminal standing together at the foot of the gallows praising the Lord for his mercy must have been a never-to-be-forgotten sight for all who, after the custom of the day, had come to stare at their latest public execution.

Right from the start of his Christian career Charles Simeon, who later became accustomed to dealing with large numbers and addressing full congregations, was at heart a man who cared for individuals. We have seen him with condemned criminals. He was frequently to be found beside the many beds of sickness of that unhealthy age. When it came to working among gownsmen, each man as we shall see was treated as if there was no one else around. Even in his first year in orders, in the course of doing duty for a friend, his interest in the ones bore wonderful fruit. One day, while waiting to conduct a funeral, Simeon wandered amongst the gravestones noting the different epitaphs. When he came across the words

> When from the dust of death I rise,
> To claim my mansion in the skies,
> E'en then shall this be all my plea—
> 'Jesus hath liv'd and died for me,'

he at once looked about him to see if there was anyone near with whom he could share the message on this tombstone. Sure enough there was a young woman, obviously in great distress, whom he called and showed the verse with its promise of eternal hope. Not satisfied with doing that, he took her address and made a point of calling on her next day when he was distressed beyond words with the squalor in which he found she was living. There was practically no furniture. An old woman, far gone with asthma, her mother, lay on a rickety bed and she herself was sitting on a box while two small dirty children were trying to warm themselves by the few embers in the grate. She had come to the end of her tether, having just been refused help by her sister who could certainly have done something to relieve their suffering. Simeon knelt down and prayed for them but soon was so overcome by the tragic scene that his tears began to flow as well as theirs. The next evening and the following one he visited them again. On the last occasion the woman spoke to him with a smile on her face and a lighter heart: 'Now, Sir, I will tell you what the Lord has done for me; when you called me in the churchyard I had been there five hours . . . I thought God had utterly forsaken me and left me and my children to starve . . . At the instant you spoke to me I was going to drown myself.' And she went on to explain how she was trusting now in the Lord that he would take care of them all. Simeon kept closely in touch with the family, got the children sponsored through school and frequently visited them. Once he stayed there so long that he arrived late at a party in his friend's house, an engagement he enjoyed much less than the time spent with his new and grateful convert.

CHAPTER FOUR

Simeon in the Pulpit

The best-known picture of Charles Simeon, though often called a caricature, is in fact a fair and faithful representation of a remarkable man. Though only some five feet eight inches tall he was accustomed to 'bearing himself so well he seemed taller'.[1] A determination to carry on whatever might face him in the way of opposition from man or the devil marks his whole appearance as he tucks his huge umbrella under his arm and sallies forth from King's to Holy Trinity church. He is meticulously dressed in his short black coat, breeches and gaiters, black gloves, white ruffled shirt and voluminous preaching gown trailing behind. He appears every bit as Sir James Stephen says 'destined to wage irreconcilable war with the slumbers and slumberers of his age',[2] or as the veteran Henry Venn told him at the outset of his career, 'Thou art called to be a Man of war from thy youth.'[3] It requires a more careful look at the picture to detect the loving creases at his eyes which tell of a kindly heart under the overriding severity of the whole portrait. He is on his way to conduct the worship of his people who had been very difficult but whom he was growing to love, and for whose eternal good he had spent many early hours preparing his sermons for the day.

Not 'six feet', as the saying goes, but more like ten feet 'above contradiction' Charles Simeon would soon be towering over his congregation from the high pulpit which dominated the south side of the church. It was just such a pulpit at Blunderstone that so impressed the young David Copperfield when he was not looking out of the window at a stray sheep—'I don't mean a sinner, but mutton—half making up his mind to come into the church.' Dickens fans will remember that when his eyes came to rest on the preacher he could not stop himself thinking 'what a good place it would be to play in, and what a castle it would make, with another boy coming up the stairs to attack it, and having the velvet cushion with the tassels thrown down on his head.' But children standing on the pews to see what was going on were not likely to distract Simeon from delivering himself of the burden of his message. He had been sent to declare God's Word. There was no question of contradiction. It was not a matter of argument. His church members would not have dreamed of questioning the teaching of this learned and devout apostle. They went to church to hear him. To a degree that he himself would hardly have approved, it was not so much the service or even the sacrament, but the sermon that accounted for the crowds that in due course filled his parish church.

Preaching of Simeon's standard was rare indeed in those days. For one thing, many of the clergy were spiritually and educationally unfitted for the responsibility of expounding the Bible. They had had no training whatever for their ministry. It was ignorance as much as laziness that drove the eighteenth-century parsons to take into their pulpits what George Crabbe's Dissenting Minister so scathingly called

> Some low-prized stuff they purchased at the stalls,
> And more like Seneca's than mine or Paul's.

Printed volumes of sermons by eminent divines were in great demand at the time. Sterne talked about publishing, for what they were worth or more likely were not worth, two volumes of his sermons which he expected would more than double the profits he had made on his very popular *Tristram Shandy*.[4] Parson Adams of Fielding's *Joseph Andrews* had the same ideas in 1742, but he found his prospective publisher too full of orders to accept the nine volumes of manuscript that he had so carefully carried in his saddle-bags all the way to London.

It is not easy to envisage an age when the publishing and reading of long and generally tedious sermons was something of an industry. Dr Johnson, who himself claimed to have written forty sermons for others to deliver, believed that no self-respecting library should be short of such collections. The most popular of them all were the works of Archbishop Tillotson the golden-tongued seventeenth-century preacher whose sermons Parson Woodforde quite unashamedly repeated to his people word for word.[5] The Archbishop's fame was such that it is said his wife was offered no less than £2000 for the copyright of his sermons after his death.[6] Most readers of his works, however, were more likely to have left them half-read like George Eliot's love-sick Caterina. They tucked her up on a sofa near the fire with a copy of Tillotson because her headache prevented her from going to church. But it was heartache she was suffering from poor girl, and archiepiscopal logic and eloquence were no cure for that.

As we come to consider Simeon's own ministry in the pulpit it is helpful to remember how few of his contemporaries were able to share his view of preaching as a noble vocation, carrying with it the prophetic note, 'Thus saith the Lord.' He did not, however, come by his reputation as a preacher easily. No one trained him. No books on the subject were to come to his notice for many years. He freely admitted at one of his Conversation Parties that for the first seven years of his ministry he had been floundering and 'did not know the head from the tail of a sermon'. He found it very much a case of hit or miss at a rather dodgy, inattentive target at first. But with kindly advice from the touch-lines by one who had been through it all himself, Henry Venn, and with the assurance of his and of others' prayers, he carried on in all his youthful ardour. In his precious little pocket Bible, acquired in 1825, he made a special mark in the margin of Jeremiah 20.9 showing how his fellow-feeling with the great prophet, 'His word was in mine heart as a burning fire . . .', still coloured his outlook after forty years. He ended his pulpit ministry as he had begun it.

Simeon believed that his task was to let the Bible speak, and in doing so he was to act as an interpreter. The deep things of God which he discovered in his long hours of personal Bible study were to be expounded in such a way that his hearers, who may not often have read and seldom understood the passages concerned, would be left in no doubt of their meaning and application. Hence his reiterated advice about giving a text 'its just meaning, its natural bearing and its legitimate use',[7] and the need for a preacher 'to ascertain from the original and from the context the true, faithful and primary meaning of every text.'[8] Let the point of a passage, he would say with a quaint homely illustration, come out naturally 'like the kernel of a hazel-nut; and not piecemeal, and after much trouble to your hearers, like the kernel of a walnut.' 'My endeavour is to bring out of Scripture what is there, and not to thrust in what I think might be there,' he explained to his publisher. And to a bishop who had accepted an early edition of his printed sermons he stated 'I never wish to find any particular truth in any particular passage. I am willing that every part of God's blessed Word should speak exactly what it was intended to speak.' In this way he could be as certain as it was possible to be that the message given would really be the word of God and not a human composition however devoutly put together. This was the principle that inspired all his preaching and made him, in the words of a distinguished admirer, Daniel Wilson, Bishop of Calcutta, as an expository preacher 'unquestionably one of the first of his age—as a divine, one of the most scriptural.'

Simeon had been preaching for ten or twelve years according to his own convictions before he came across the work which was to help him clarify his thoughts about sermon preparation, and encourage him to create what in fact became a kind of unofficial school of Biblical exposition. Canon Smyth has reminded us that he was 'almost the first man in the history of the English pulpit since the Middle Ages to appreciate that it is perfectly possible to teach men how to preach, and to discover how to do so'.[9] What led him to that point was his discovery of Jean Claude's *Essay on the Composition of a Sermon*. Claude was a seventeenth-century divine of the French Reformed Church who over a period of forty years had gained a considerable reputation for his preaching ability. What he had to say appealed to Simeon's methodical mind, and was in tune with his own ideas. For example, of sermons that did not give 'the entire sense of the whole text' Claude commented, in Robinson's translation, 'Preachments of this kind are extremely disgustful'.[10] So Simeon proceeded to republish the essay with his own editorial comments which included as a matter of interest, calling the Frenchman's anti-establishment views 'an odd farrago.'[11] But he so valued his explanation of how sermon composition should be carried out that he had it bound up with his own works as an epilogue occupying over a hundred pages.

It is difficult to realise today that Claude's suggestion that a sermon should be constructed in three main divisions, an Introduction (or Exordium as it was grandly called), a main Discussion, and an Application or challenge at the end, was in fact largely original.[12] The introduction was intended 'to prepare the hearer's mind and insensibly to conduct him' to the matter in hand. To preach a sermon which launched his listeners straight into the subject without any preliminary was, he said, to treat them 'as the angel did to Habbakuk when he took him by the hair of his head, and transported him in an instant from Judea to Babylon.'[13] This Exordium was not to be used as a trick to catch the attention of the congregation by referring to 'the persons of the hearers, or the circumstances of times, places, general affairs or news of the world',[14] which is a more modern practice. Claude was assuming, it seems, that the preacher could in those days count on his people preferring to be drawn away from mundane considerations rather than to hear a discourse relevant to their everyday concerns.

The main substance of the sermon would itself need to be subdivided for the sake of clarity and simplicity, about which Simeon like his tutor was very emphatic. 'A sermon should be like a telescope' he said. 'Each successive division of it should be as an additional lens to bring the subject of your text nearer, and make it more distinct.' In the preface to his bound volumes of sermons Simeon urged the importance of unity of theme, perspicuity or insight in the arrangement of the exposition, and simplicity of expression. He stressed that crossed lines, tangled thoughts, involved arguments and multiplicity of themes should be avoided at all costs. He was very conscious that many of his own people, and possibly most of those whom his young ordinand friends would ultimately be addressing, were simple-hearted folks with the minimum of education. He could not bear to think of anyone preaching over their dear heads, and would have agreed with Charles Haddon Spurgeon when he reminded his pupils that their divine calling was to feed sheep and not to pasture giraffes. Simeon's own analogy was to ask the young men, if they were faced with having to fill some narrow-mouthed glass vessels with water, whether they would do so from a large pail full to overflowing or from a tea-kettle with a nice spout. When it came to a congregation of dons and undergraduates he stuck to the same principle: 'Most of my sermons before the University have given satisfaction from their plainness, clearness and simplicity; for it is a mistake to suppose that men of science will not be pleased unless the sermon be abstruse or profound.'

Most of what Simeon taught is today accepted homiletical practice, but even in December 1821 it was still fresh in people's minds as an article in the *Christian Observer* contributed anonymously by Simeon himself bears out. This was headed *A Dialogue between Diaconus and Pastor on the subject of the Ministry*, and included the question 'Can you give me any hints for making my sermon?' To this the reply reads: 'Yes: Reduce your text to a simple proposition, and lay that down as the warp; and then make use of the text itself as the woof; illustrating the main idea by the various terms in which it is contained. Screw the word into the minds of your hearers. A screw is the strongest of all mechanical powers . . . when it has been turned a few times scarcely any power can pull it out.'

Here we may refer in greater detail to the many volumes of sermon outlines, or *Skeletons* as he at first liked to call them, that Simeon published. It all began in 1796 with a hundred sample sermon notes to illustrate the points of Claude's Essay with which they were bound up. By 1801 these had grown to an edition of five hundred, now called *Helps to Composition*, and published interestingly enough by the University Press. In his preface he gratefully acknowledges his indebtedness to the university for their patronage. A mutual friend told Joseph Farington, the painter and diarist, that Simeon had told her that these first five volumes had involved him in seven thousand hours of work. His shrewd comment on this was, 'He appears to live by rule, noting the manner in which he passes his time',[15] which was very true.

By 1819 Simeon was able to issue another edition, but this time not through the University Press. There were now seventeen volumes in all to which, after the fashion of the times, he gave a rather grand title, *Horae Homileticae*. By some stretch of his imagination he said he derived this term from the Greek of Acts 20:11. The reception of this work was so cordial that he went on and compiled more until in 1832 he was able to complete an edition covering the whole Bible from Genesis to Revelation. In twenty-one volumes there are no less than 2536 sermon outlines, an immense work possibly without parallel in religious publishing. His only possible rival in this field was Parson Davey of Lustleigh in Devon who in 1781, when he found that it would cost him £2000 to have his sermons printed professionally, bought a modest printing press of his own, and helped by his maid proceeded to run them off and publish them in twenty-six octavo volumes.[16] The crowning moment for the author of *Horae Homileticae* was his being received at court by William IV to whom he gave a presentation copy. He also personally presented a similar beautifully bound and gilt-edged set of the full twenty-one volumes to each of the Archbishops, and sent one to all the chief libraries in Europe and America, and to each of the Cambridge college libraries. Simeon never did anything by halves.

Thirty-two men had been fully employed in the printing of Simeon's *magnum opus* which took sixteen months.[17] The work was magnificently typeset, and the proof-reading which occupied endless hours of Simeon's time at the end of his life, was like everything else that he did, meticulous. He was delighted that the publishers did not hesitate, for instance, to correct a colon to a semi-colon where needed. Each volume sold at ten shillings and the total proceeds eventually amounted to £5000, a prodigious sum in the book world of those days. In fact it was twice the amount that Boswell received in his lifetime for his famous biography.[18] But Simeon did not enrich himself on these profits. In a letter to his publisher he mentions how his royalties had become 'the actual property of three societies. If God be honoured and my fellow-creatures benefited, it is all I want.' This was his special contribution to raising the standard of Biblical preaching in the Church of England. 'If it leads the ignorant to preach the truth, and the indolent to exert themselves, and the weak to attain a facility for writing their own, and the busy and laborious to do more and with better effect than they otherwise could have done, I shall be richly repaid for my labour. My prayers for God's blessing on it will, I hope, ascend as long as I am able to pray at all.'

The publishers and author may have been rather optimistic when they advertised these outlines as 'peculiarly adapted to be read in families', for even fully developed Victorian family prayers would have found them a little heavy going, children and servants not having quite the vested interest in Biblical exposition that the average ordinand could be expected to show. In Cambridge itself the news that he was engaged in such a vast enterprise gave the undergraduate wits something to work on. In 1818 they produced a skit entitled *Cambridge Besieged, written by a saint—as a deep tragedy to be performed by serious Christians at the next meeting of the Bible Society.*[19] 'Mr Simeon,' it declares, 'that great Goliath of our armies fires away his minute guns, and publishes his speeches and sermons with great effect.' Among the *dramatis personae* they included '500 Skeletons', and there was a satirical sermon on Alexander the coppersmith by a Mr Moan which was divided, à Charles Simeon, into nine subdivisions, one for each letter of the character's name.

Clergy and would-be clergy must have been Charles Simeon's chief readers, and some even to this day are to be found delving into this treasury of devoted Bible study in a hopeful attempt to let the Simeon who lived before the railway was dreamt of speak to a generation brought up on thoughts of supersonic speed. The author realised that it was expecting a great deal to ask anyone to wade right through the twenty-one books though he did whimsically point out that 'if the readers will peruse one discourse every day of his life, the whole will occupy him exactly seven years.' Charles Smyth in referring to the 'Procrustean bed on which Charles Simeon had sought to stretch sermon composition', points out that however avidly clergy of his day may have clutched at his proferred instructions, the fact was that it really took a Simeon in person to clothe them 'with flesh and skin and features.' The dry skeletons 'could not but seem artificial and repugnant to those who had never heard their author in the pulpit.'[20]

One J. C. Philpot, who seceded from the Church of England to become a strict Baptist in 1835, said that one reason why he did so was because of the way Anglican evangelicals composed 'their sermons out of Simeon's dry and marrowless skeletons' which he called 'patent crutches.'[21] The Christian Press were kinder in their comments. The *Eclectic Review*, referring to the 1819 edition, felt that it would indeed fulfil its author's hopes: 'To the influence of his high character and unremitted exertions in the peculiarly important sphere allotted to him we ascribe, in a higher degree than to any other individual, the progress of evangelical sentiments among the clergy of the established church. Although not a Professor of Divinity in the university of which he is so bright an ornament, yet to his instructions and advice, as well as to his writings, many hundreds of the younger clergy are ready, we doubt not, to acknowledge themselves indebted for the most valuable assistance they ever received in preparing for the duties of their sacred office.'[22] The *Christian Remembrancer*, whose readers would very likely not be a hundred per cent behind Simeon, had the whole work before it in 1834. Mentioning how the author had the gift of getting honour and respect from those who did not entirely share his views, they attributed this to his depth, sincerity, breadth of sympathy, charitableness and humility, virtues of which those who sat under him in person were well aware, but which not every reviewer would have had the insight to recognise in these sermon notes. One cannot help wondering for how long clergy of evangelical outlook continued to find the *Horae Homileticae* ideal for their purpose. One of Simeon's staunchest followers, a man who deserves a biography to himself, Francis Close, the Dean of Carlisle, in 1861 published a volume of eighty sermon outlines himself, with an introductory essay *On the Composition of a Sermon*, rather strangely without making any reference to Claude nor even to the one at whose feet he had spent four years learning these very lessons.

To a modern reader the Preface is the most valuable thing that Simeon wrote. Much of it is devoted to the contemporary conflict which still agitated the evangelical world between the Calvinist and the Arminian views of free grace and free will. We shall be seeing later what attitude Charles Simeon adopted in this controversy. Where a reader's heart begins to warm to this prolific preacher is when he leaves the field of disagreement and declares, whatever people may think about him refusing to take sides, that he has only one real anxiety in presenting his work to the public, and that is, 'Does it uniformly tend

TO HUMBLE THE SINNER
TO EXALT THE SAVIOUR
TO PROMOTE HOLINESS?

If in one single instance it lose sight of any of these points, let it be condemned without mercy.'[23] This was the ultimate touchstone by which he would have all his sermons judged, and no preacher could aim higher than that.

But high as his aim was, and outstanding as his final achievement became, Simeon's ministry in the pulpit got off to a somewhat shaky start. The impression given by the new young Minister in the 1780s was very different from that which the 'Old Apostle' (as Thomas Fowell Buxton christened him in a letter to his family in 1831)[24] imparted half a century later. In those early days Charles Jerram, who used to attend Trinity church as a student, speaks of the Vicar being 'animated, zealous and energetic', but he was worried about certain peculiarities of manner, movement and facial expression which disconcerted those who did not know him well, though they played a part in helping to rivet attention on the speaker.[25] Another contemporary of that time had to acknowledge that his impassioned earnestness frequently 'approached the grotesque', but said 'never did he address an audience in a cold, lifeless or formal manner.'[26] Some of the aspiring clergy in his congregation noticed a change for the worse when he gave up using a written manuscript and confined himself to those tiny sheets of notes some 1½ by 3 inches in size.[27] It appears that as a result he often floundered and repeated himself, and Jerram in all honesty had to admit that much as they admired him 'we all deplored this transition from one mode of preaching to the other' for it left him 'confused and embarrassed' at times.[28]

People's chief complaint at the onset of Simeon's work was not his lack of expertise in the pulpit but his vehemence in preaching the gospel. Some of his parishioners actually wrote to the bishop about it, and his Lordship was not too pleased with Simeon's explanation. It seems that he was in some danger of becoming like Trollope's Mr Slope who always 'had an anathema lurking in his eye'. John Williamson acknowledged in his memoir that 'he occasionally wielded the terrors of the law and presented before his hearers a sinner riven with the thunders of the Almighty's vengeance'.[29] At other times he would drive home his point with particularly dramatic actions. Once his text was 'Will a man rob God?' (Malachi 3:8). With much deliberation he repeated it. Then, looking round on the congregation, he said in tones that only Simeon could muster, 'You have all robbed Him;' and pointing with his finger in various directions, said 'You! and You!! and You!!!'[30] An unforgettable but admittedly disturbing approach.

It may well be that Simeon had been unduly influenced by the advice he got early on from the earnest but eccentric evangelist John Berridge of Everton. In 1794 he had written to him, 'When you open your Commission, begin with ripping up the audience, and Moses will lend you a carving knife, which may be often whetted at his grind-stone. Lay open the universal sinfulness of nature, the darkness of the mind, the frowardness of the tempers, the earthliness and sensuality of the affections', and much more in the same tone. 'When your Hearers have been well harrowed, and the clumps begin to fall, (which is seen by their hanging down the head), then bring out your CHRIST . . .'[31] Over the years Simeon grew out of this kind of thing, and was able to warn his young ordinand friends against the immaturity of those 'preachers who act like butchers: they cut at sin as if they did not feel any mercy for sinners'. In his prime during the eighteen twenties the *Christian Observer*, trying to account for Simeon's success as compared with the ineffectiveness of so many clergy who preached basically the same message, felt it was because 'in a hard and unfeeling manner . . . they constantly overwhelm their people with a black and appalling catalogue of their transgressions . . . Accustomed to hear the threatenings of Scripture constantly brought forward, and seeing their minister apparently unconcerned in denouncing them, an audience grows hardened under rebuke.'[32]

But there was no doubt about the power of his preaching. It was in no way weakened by his growing sensitivity to people's feelings. In his diary for 1804 Arthur Young, who had been converted through reading Wilberforce's *Practical View* when deeply depressed about the death of his daughter, records, 'I have been at Trinity church thrice today. In the morning a very good sermon by Simeon, a decent one by Thomason, and in the evening to a crowded congregation, a superlative discourse by Simeon (on Acts 4:12), vital, evangelical, powerful and impressive in his animated manner.'[33] John Stoughton has a similar recollection. He felt that Simeon's sermons far from having the slow penetrating force of the dew came down like 'hailstones and coals of fire.' 'I was struck with the preacher's force, even vehemence. He spoke as one who had a burden from the Lord to deliver – as one who, like Paul, felt "Woe unto me if I preach not the gospel".'[34]

Matthew Preston remembers hearing from a friend in Scotland about a sermon on ministerial duties and faithfulness in which Simeon used the illustration of a lighthouse-keeper who had gone to sleep on his job. A ship lay wrecked on the shore; dead bodies were floating about; widows and orphans were wailing their hearts out. He imagined the offender being brought before an inquiry and when asked why the light had gone out, replying that he was asleep. 'Asleep!' 'The way in which he made this "Asleep" burst on the ears of his audience who were hanging in perfect stillness on his lips, contrasting the cause with the effects, I remember to this day.'[35] The same writer was present when, after preaching a powerful and intense sermon in a church in Edinburgh, Simeon rose from his knees and called out 'No music', actually ordering the bemused organist to desist from a somewhat light-hearted voluntary which the speaker felt was out of keeping with the devotional tone of his address.

Later in his career, at a time when John Shorthouse in his novel *Sir Percival* remembered Simeon as an aged veteran winning all hearts with his 'courteous manners' and 'humorous quaintness', he had not lost his passion in the pulpit. He unashamedly told a friend that he would preach 'with my tongue, my eyes and my hands,' a truth amply demonstrated by the famous silhouettes preserved in King's College. Abner Brown remembers sitting next to a married undergraduate and his family in Trinity church and overhearing their small daughter, intrigued by the antics of the demonstrative man in the pulpit, whispering to her mother, 'O Mama, what is the gentleman in a passion about?' Dean Howson of Chester recalled to Bishop Moule an incident that occurred one day when he was attending one of Simeon's services. The veteran saint kindled into intense enthusiasm as he spoke of his Master. He lifted his hands and his face lit up and the great listening concourse was strangely moved as he cried, 'That He might have the pre-eminence! And He *will* have it!—And He *must* have it! And He *shall* have it!'[36] As his curate Carus wrote in his Memoirs, 'The intense fervour of his feelings he cared not to restrain; his whole soul was in his subject and he spoke and acted exactly as he felt.'

The portrait of Charles Simeon at the age of forty-nine in King's College hall shows a kindliness in his eyes and expression which must have been very winning even from a distant pulpit. Having learned it himself the hard way, he never tired of telling his young friends that in presenting the gospel they must show an attitude 'which expresses kindness and love, and not that which indicates an unfeeling harshness.' 'Let your preaching come from the heart,' he would say. 'Love should be the spring of all actions and especially of a minister's. If a man's heart be full of love, he will rarely offend. He may have severe things to say, but he will say them in love.' And from that point he went on to give illustrations of how Jesus demonstrated this winning tenderness in his approach to people. Towards the end of his life he wrote to a clergyman who had asked for help with a touch of the whimsy that broke to the surface from time to time: 'In relation to all these matters, take counsel *not of fear* but *of love*. Whatever be the number or quality of your counsellors always put love in the chair, and give him a casting vote.'

William Cowper, remembering how John Newton used to condemn 'angry and scolding preaching', expresses the spirit that made Charles Simeon the winning evangelist that in his maturity he became, in his good Evander who

> with a smile
> Gentle and affable, and full of grace,
> As fearful of offending whom he wish'd
> Much to persuade, he plied his ear with truths
> Not harshly thunder'd forth or rudely press'd,
> But, like his purpose, gracious, kind and sweet.

Francis Close illustrated something of what this passion and loving concern cost Simeon when he mentioned in his obituary sermon in Cheltenham Parish Church:

> Never shall I forget one remarkable instance which I myself witnessed, of his affectionate concern for the souls entrusted to him. He was preaching upon those striking words: 'All day long I have stretched forth my hands unto a disobedient and gainsaying people' (Rom. 10: 20, 21). And after having urged all his hearers to accept the proffered mercy, he reminded them that there were those present to whom he had preached Christ for more than thirty years, but they continued indifferent to a Saviour's love; and pursuing this train of expostulation for some time, he at length became quite overpowered by his feeling, and he sank down in the pulpit and burst into a flood of tears, and few who were present could refrain from weeping with him.[37]

The modern parson is sometimes heard complaining of the fatigue of preaching weekly to the same congregation. Before ten years have passed he will start talking about being 'preached out' and needing a move. Such an idea would have been anathema to Charles Simeon. His remarkable achievement, unparalleled by any other local incumbent before or since, was to hold the attention of undergraduates and townsfolk alike preaching twice a Sunday for over fifty years. Declining a lucrative preferment in order to remain at his post, he continued his preaching ministry with unabated zeal until age and infirmity necessitated him having the support of a high stool in the pulpit. This phenomenon is only explained by the fact that he made a lifelong habit of devoting the first four hours of each day to prayer and concentrated Bible study. Joseph Farington was told by his friends the Offleys in London, who were full of anecdotes about the distinguished Cambridge clergyman who stayed with them from time to time, that one Saturday night he had asked for pen and ink to take to his room as he would be up by four o'clock next morning to finish the preparation of his address.[39]

The six-inch thick quarto volume of *Brown's Self-Interpreting Bible* which he acquired in 1785 was his constant companion throughout his whole career. He was so thrilled with it that he ordered forty copies from the publishers to give away to impecunious clergy who could not afford the luxury of such an aid to Bible reading. The copious marginal references to parallel Scriptures, and the editor's introductory remarks, together with the fruit of his own study which he wrote in the neatest of hands on almost every page, provided Simeon with the material on which to work. 'He was not a technical scholar, and his exegesis of the Greek text was sometimes disconcerting' says Charles Smyth,[40] but this never seemed too serious a handicap. Daniel Wilson tells us that to his knowledge behind most of Simeon's sermons there lay not less than twelve hours of study. Simeon's assiduous study of the Scriptures was inspired by his deep sense of the authority of the Word of God. He believed that he was handling truth, that he was, to use Cowper's phrase, 'the messenger of truth, the legate of the skies.' He would have been happy to know that the great pulpit in Ghent Cathedral with its Baroque ornamentation and remarkable double staircase is known as the *Chaire de Verité*. It was in the confidence that he had been called to be God's messenger, that week by week he mounted his rather more modest pulpit. 'As earthly kings are represented by their ambassadors, and speak by them in foreign courts, so the Lord Jesus Christ himself speaks by his ministers; they stand in his stead; they speak in his name; their word is not their own but his; and must be received "not as the word of men but, as it is in truth, the word of God".'[41] Armed with this inner assurance, and warmed by a burdened and caring heart, Charles Simeon carried on regardless of opposition or indifference. No one has ever demonstrated more effectively to future generations of preachers what it means to be a messenger of divine truth.

CHAPTER FIVE

In the Academic World

As soon as Charles Simeon was awarded his Fellowship he moved from his rooms in Old Court to the much more recent and stately Gibbs building where for the next thirty years he had a spacious room on the ground floor of the staircase nearest to Queens'. There was no question of his living out for by the university regulations his fellowship precluded him from marriage. In his mind there was no doubt where his priority lay between being married, and working among students which he felt to be his special calling. His comment on this point was frank and revealing: 'I should hate the university above all places as a married man; but the singular way in which I have been called to my present post, and its almost incalculable importance, forbid the thought of my now leaving it: therefore I think I shall never marry. Again, in my present situation I am quite a rich man, and almost as free from care as an angel; but if I were to marry, I should instantly become a poor man (reducing my income one half, while I doubled my expenditure): therefore I think I shall never marry. Again—there are but few married people truly happy in each other in comparison of those who are unhappy; and fewer still who are truly happy in their children (one who turns out ill depriving his parents of all the comfort they might feel in the others)—therefore I think I shall never marry'.

This apologia, written when he was well past forty, the age at which many Fellows used to surrender their Fellowship and independence, marry and settle down in a living, sound untypically cold-blooded and cynical. It is a sad commentary on the unhappy state of family life as Simeon saw it in Cambridge in particular, in the houses he used to visit, or in the experience of anxious fathers and mothers who would turn to him in their troubles, or in the lives of the many young men from loveless homes who came up to college. In a letter to Robert Noble, who became a Christian while at Sidney Sussex College and went on to serve God in South India for twenty-four years, Simeon wrote: 'Had I married I must have resigned my fellowship, and with it, probably, my usefulness. I remained, therefore, unmarried for the sake of my Lord's work. I have felt it a great sacrifice, *but I have never regretted it*; and if, to be more useful as a missionary, you determine on a life of celibacy, God can and will support you, and you will be blessed in the deed!'[1]

It will be seen that Simeon did not look on celibacy as a more spiritual or sublimated way of life than the married state, but simply as making him more free for his particular work. As we shall discover later, though he lived in a masculine world he was by no means lacking in appreciation of feminine society, but romance was not to be allowed to cross his path. He had made up his mind. By deliberately refusing to be entangled in the distractions of family life he was free to cultivate his devotional life with nothing to distract him—no household chores, no shopping, no gardening and of course no washing up such as occupies a fair proportion of the time of his modern successors in the married ministry. He had his own servants. His bed would be made, his meals provided, and only his precious horses remained for him to concern himself about though even they had a groom in charge of them.

Simeon was not a don in the accepted sense of the term today, for he had no academic work for which he was responsible, and no teaching or lecturing to do. This set him completely free for the study of the Bible, the pastoral care of the parish, and the evangelism of undergraduates, more than a full-time job for a healthy man. To gather the spiritual strength that he needed he made a practice of devoting the early hours of each day to prayer and Bible reading. While his fellow Fellows slept on, Charles Simeon was disciplining himself to rise before dawn. Being as fond of his bed as the next man, this did not come easily to him, so he decided to fine himself half-a-crown, which he would give to his bed-maker, every time he overslept. After a while it dawned on him that she was doing rather well under this arrangement and the temptation to treat her poverty as an excuse for his laziness had to be resisted. So he altered his tactics and the day came when he decided that he would throw a guinea into the Cam if he offended again. Only one golden guinea thus rests in the mud by King's bridge for he had cured himself for the time being, and became a little more sensible when the need arose in later years.

In 1812 Simeon had the opportunity to change his rooms moving to the top floor of the staircase to the north of the main archway. Here a magnificent suite was to be the scene of his labours for the rest of his life. On one side the front room, marked by a large semi-circular window, looks out at the handsome court which separates the college from the town. At the back a similar window faces the wide green expanse of lawn which spills over into the river, with a gentle curtain of yellowing willows and stately elms rising to the skyline. A very narrow and steep staircase ascends out of his bedroom to an attic where his personal servant used to sleep. And from this room a small glazed door opens on to the leads where it is still possible to walk on the roof behind the stone balustrade, which is what he used to do whenever the weather permitted. From that secret vantage point he could see his church, his parish and his college spread out before him, and bring them all to God in his prayers day by day. 'I now have a solitary oratory on the roof, a walk where no eye but that of the Supreme can behold me,' he wrote with enthusiasm to his former curate, Thomas Thomason.

To this day one can see the rows of old-fashioned hat and coat pegs which lined the passages to his rooms erected for the benefit of his many undergraduate visitors, and also the substantial shoe-scrapers which he insisted that they used to save spoiling his carpets with the yellow gravel of the college paths. All the way down the broad two-storied flight of stairs still runs the iron handrail which the college authorities placed there in the days when the Old Apostle was getting infirm. It was known for years afterwards as 'The Saint's Rest'. Charles Simeon's new headquarters were more than adequately equipped for the operations planned in the seclusion of his prayer-times.

Doctor William Cooke was Provost of King's during the first fifteen years of Simeon's life as a college Fellow. He is portrayed in Orde's drawing, *A School of Athens,* presiding over the election of a professor from a most unpromising looking group of candidates.[2] It shows him up as a victim of the deficiencies of contemporary academic standards though in fact he seems to have taken his duties more seriously than many of his colleagues. Certainly when he was appointed Vice-Chancellor he addressed the university with some conviction on the low state of education at the time. But he does not seem to have been sufficiently convinced of his own diagnosis to give much support to the one or two who wanted to do something about it, such as instituting annual university examinations in addition to the tests set by colleges and the Senate House degree examination which came at the end of an undergraduate's three years.[3] Such reforms needed more vigorous introduction than it seems he could provide.

For seven years from November 1788 Simeon held various college appointments such as two turns each as second, and first, Dean of Arts and later as Dean of Divinity. In his capacity as Dean he was responsible for ensuring the discipline of the college. His powers to deal with offenders included gating (confining them to college precincts for a period), forfeiting their food allowance, or such impositions as making them learn five hundred lines of Virgil or the first book of the Iliad by heart.[4] The highest compliment that was paid him was his appointment in 1790 as Vice-Provost at the age of thirty-one after only eight years as Fellow. In this office, which he held for two years, he had a chance of showing what kind of a disciplinarian he was by the firm manner in which he dealt amongst other things with a recalcitrant Fellow who, after being rusticated, insisted on returning to college without permission. This gentleman had made a great nuisance of himself by getting drunk and threatening the local inhabitants with a loaded pistol. In company with his friend Dr Glynn, famous for his scarlet cloak and three-cornered hat,[5] Charles Simeon ran the dangerous offender to earth in the Bull Inn. He succeeded in so putting him in fear of the law that he was heard of no more and the shopkeepers of Cambridge were able to go back to sleeping in peace thanks to the robust Christianity of their often maligned vicar. Looking back later on this period in his life Simeon confessed that he found these college responsibilities a considerable strain. 'Power is a troublesome matter to have,' he said at one of his conversation parties; 'When I was Vice-Provost, thirty years ago, although I hope I acted a faithful and approved part, I was very glad to lay down the office.'

In his official capacity he was never really at home in King's College. For twenty years from 1805 he held no post, and when he was appointed Dean for the last time in 1827 he only accepted the result of the election because it was the happy climax of a tussle amongst the dons to oppose him.[6] Perhaps he remembered the time forty years earlier when, as he said, 'if I went into the Senate House I was stared at as a monster'. He was just never popular with his fellow academics. On one occasion when a don was actually prepared to be seen walking on the lawns with him he was quite taken aback. Even when he was over sixty he still sometimes received such treatment from one of his colleagues which 'if practised by me', he said, 'would set the whole town and university aflame.' Winstanley tells us that 'the manners of the Fellows of the eighteenth century were probably more deplorable than their morals. Often of the very humblest origin, and frequently unacquainted with any other society, they were apt to remain almost as boorish and uncouth as they had been on first coming to Cambridge.'[7] Most of them had nothing to do. Walking was their chief recreation and drinking their chief relaxation. Simeon, with his fondness for riding and his strict personal attitude to drink was greatly interested in neither. His refusal to live by the standards of his fellow men, and his natural tendency to be unsociable except in a circle of committed or enquiring Christians, made things very awkward for him. 'He was among us – not of us' remembers W. H. Tucker who, speaking as a Christian undergraduate also recalls that he was 'singularly gentle, and invariably received the greatest respect from us.'[8]

One don in particular, who lived on the same staircase as Simeon, was quite unbearable. He was the Reverend 'Billy' Moore, 'one of the most extravagant and dissipated men in the university', as Gunning remembers him. He had the nasty habit of waylaying Simeon's visitors from the parish or villages around when they came to bring him presents of one kind or another, and peering into their baskets. Armed with the information thus acquired, and 'a fertile imagination, he contrived to amuse his companions in the combination room at his neighbour's expense'.[9] Moore, when not riding to hounds, singing ballads or drinking to excess, was wont to frequent places of amusement 'where none would have supposed either from his dress or address that he was in holy orders.' He spent his time writing a book called *A Ramble through Italy* for which a publisher paid him three hundred guineas even though he had never in his life set foot in that country. He was not Simeon's sort.

Nor were some others. Simeon used to have his college meals in a parlour just outside the entrance to the dining hall with a few other senior colleagues. One of these, Peter Hinde, a parson who never got priested and who detested Simeon's so-called 'Methodism', was never on speaking terms with him.[10] Nor did he have anything in common with the Reverend Edward Pote who was chiefly remembered by Tucker for the black coat and white ducks in which he used to go shooting, and for the memorable occasion when, in the middle of such an expedition, he approached a village church, asked his friend to hold his gun and his dog, and slipped inside to take a funeral, and then came out and carried on with his shooting.[11] All very unprofessional and unSimeonlike. No wonder Simeon felt lonely at times.

Though he has been described as the most notable Fellow of his time, Simeon's influence in the university at large cannot be measured by his status in King's. It was when he was on his own ground, expounding what the Bible has to say on the fundamental issues of life for which there is no purely academic answer, that his significance can chiefly be seen.

This was particularly marked when he was chosen to be select preacher. To preach before the university is regarded in academic circles as one of the greatest honours the Vice-Chancellor can confer, and in the ecclesiastical world as marking the favoured preacher as 'having arrived.' It is a privilege much valued and not often repeated. Yet Charles Simeon, in spite of the fact of the initial unpopularity of his appointment to Trinity church and the perennial unpopularity of the gospel as he declaimed it, was chosen as select preacher on no less than ten occasions, several of these, as the custom then was, involving a series of four separate sermons. The first such time was only four years after his ordination.

Dr Glynn, for many years the leading physician in Cambridge, who as we have seen later shared disciplinary duties in King's with Simeon, seems to have been one of the few dons who recognised and appreciated the new young Fellow as a man of some potential. When it came to his preaching in the university church for the first time he invited him to read his sermon through to him on the day before.[12] Encouraged by his kindly criticism and support, and with the manuscript improved by the good doctor's helpful comments, Simeon faced the ordeal of climbing up that invisible staircase and emerging, as they used to say of their preacher, 'like a slow jack-in-the-box', in the great oak three-decker pulpit which stood in those days at the west end of Great St Mary's. Here he spread out his eight pages of carefully written sermon on the pink cushion with tasselled corners, and looked out on the galleries all round him, the box pews below, and the backless benches in the centre provided for late-comers. He could see rank on rank of dons, MAs, and undergraduates drawn together by their wish to hear for themselves what this young man with the growing reputation of a powerful preacher might have to say. Some of the congregation had come to scorn, and some to 'scrape', the tiresome undergraduate custom of showing disapproval or boredom by shuffling their feet on the floor, a practice with which we are told even Hugh Latimer was acquainted some two centuries earlier. But in fact, right from the first, as Oliver Goldsmith wrote of his faithful parson, so Simeon himself discovered,

> Truth from his lips prevail'd with double sway,
> And fools, who came to scoff, remain'd to pray.

Simeon's total command of his subject and the earnestness of his manner gripped the attention of one and all. When they came to disperse afterwards one of the leading objectors was heard to say to his friend, 'Well, Simeon is no fool,' to which his companion replied, 'Fool! did you ever hear such a sermon before?' Charles Jerram, who as we have seen was not blind to Simeon's shortcomings, was enormously impressed by the ability he showed on these important occasions: 'His manner was dignified and, if I may be allowed the expression, peculiarly academic.'[14] The *Christian Observer* commented that 'Even strangers in the university have been struck with the softened and solemn air which reigns throughout his lettered congregation when he is called to address them.'[15]

It had not always been so. Gilbert Wakefield records that between 1778 and 1788 the attendance at university sermons had been so deplorable that it was proposed, and supported by the Provost of King's himself, that either undergraduates should be compelled to attend or that these addresses should be abolished.[16] The proposition however was not accepted, and it fell to Simeon to rescue this ancient university tradition from obloquy. He built up such a reputation for himself as select preacher that Great St Mary's church, seating over a thousand, in 1811 was 'overflowing', in 1814 had 'scarcely room to move', in 1815 its 'audiences were immense', and in 1823 many had to be turned from the door.[17] Of course by this time the number of undergraduates in Cambridge had greatly increased compared with the nadir of the 1780s.

Simeon has often been disparaged for holding an important academic post without being a first-class scholar. But what he possessed was something far more valuable than academic distinction. This was a clear thinking mind and deep spiritual insight which enabled him to grasp the true meaning of wisdom, and to impart this to the highly intelligent congregations that gathered for these university sermons. 'Much as we revere human knowledge,' he would tell them, 'we must declare that, in comparison of that which we have been considering, the wisdom of philosophers is of no account, for this knowledge is at once the *most sublime*, the *most certain*, the *most attainable* and the *most useful* . . . Your learning must not be set in competition with the word of God, but be made subservient to it.' 'Reason, in those things that are *within* its sphere, is a useful, though not an infallible guide. And, in the things that are *beyond* its sphere, it has its office: it ceases to be a guide indeed; but it becomes a companion . . . The only use of reason, as applied to revelation, is to ascertain whether the revelation, purporting to be from heaven, be indeed of divine authority; and what is the true import of that revelation.'[18]

On Founder's Day in 1828 Simeon preached in King's College chapel when the completion of Wilkins' new hall and the screen along King's Parade was being celebrated. His subject was *The Use and Excellency of True Wisdom*. 'Let me not be thought to undervalue science', he said. 'It has in the world a just pre-eminence above rank or wealth . . . We have long been, through the munificence of our founder, and are now become in a more especial manner, elevated to a very high degree of celebrity through the splendour of our outward appointments. Why then should we not be alike distinguished for our eminence in those moral excellencies which he wished us to aspire after?'[19]

Simeon perhaps rose to his greatest heights in his series of four discourses preached in 1815 under the title *Appeal to Men of Wisdom and Candour*. He began with the clear statement that 'though revealed religion is neither founded on human reason, nor makes its appeal to it, yet it is perfectly consistent with reason.'[20] He goes on to concede that, 'We should consider ourselves as liable to err no less than others. To imagine that we are in possession of all truth, and to take for granted that all who differ from us must of necessity be wrong, is not consistent with Christian modesty.' Having thus disarmed his audience and encouraged them to give him a rational hearing, he proceeded to expound the depravity of man, the power of the new birth, and justification by faith. He carefully distinguished between baptism which provides a Christian with a change of *state* and the work of the Spirit in the heart which leads to a change of *nature*. The whole series discloses the clear thinking of a trained mind taking the New Testament as it stands and deriving his theology directly from its source.

From time to time Simeon was challenged about his sermons and found himself against his will in argument. 'I have neither taste nor talent for controversy,' he wrote to a friend. By nature he was a man of peace, but when the subject concerned was the truth of God as he understood it, he was more than prepared to engage in a war of words with anyone whatever his distinction. By the time his various contentions had come to an end, as a battered protagonist of the word of God he would have been very ready to agree with the equally battered politician Edmund Burke's reflection that 'the church is a place where one day's truce ought to be allowed to the dissensions and animosities of mankind.'[21] Simeon had no intention of himself stirring up controversy, but such was the challenge of his powerful addresses to the accepted theological views in which the divinity faculty in Cambridge was entrenched, that their spokesmen in the persons particularly of Dr Pearson and Professor Herbert Marsh were goaded into entering the fray. The result was the writing of a series of open letters and pamphlets which went backwards and forwards trying, not entirely successfully, to silence the opposition. The reading of such publications, which fall with deadly boredom on modern ears, was a highly popular exercise in those days when reading matter was limited and verbal combat had considerable entertainment value.

The first of these disputes was sparked off by a sermon based on the General Confession of the Anglican Prayer Book which Simeon preached before the university on December 1st, 1805. It gathered the eventual title of *The Churchman's Confession* and was printed in full several times.[22] The chief objector here was Dr Pearson, master of Sidney Sussex, who addressed a letter on the subject to the *Orthodox Churchman's Magazine*. His main objection was to the doctrine of the depravity of human nature and the idea that the salvation provided by Christ is in response to faith rather than as a reward for obedience. In this matter Simeon was very sure of where he stood. 'The ground I feel is tenable against the whole world.' He was happy to let things rest there.

The second time Dr Pearson took up his pen was in November 1809 after a university sermon on *Evangelical and Pharisaic Righteousness Compared* based on Matthew 5:20. In his critical pamphlet Pearson acknowledged 'a great personal regard for Mr Simeon and for his zealous exertions', and their dispute was conducted in a most gentlemanly fashion. It ended with two personal letters from Simeon in which he said 'I know and feel within myself (as most probably you do also) that controversy is hurtful to the spirit . . . it gratifies some of the worst passions of the heart. Happy shall I be, Sir, to have no occasion ever to resume it . . . it is my earnest wish that the only strife we may ever know in future may be that which the Apostles recommend, of "contending earnestly for the faith once delivered to the saints", and of "provoking one another to love and to good works".' In the course of this dispute Simeon had been wise enough to consult a like-minded and wise friend before rushing into print in the manner of so many pamphleteers. His adviser was William Farish of Magdalene College, vicar of St Giles' and Professor of Chemistry. He was to prove a staunch supporter of Simeon on many occasions. One of his best pieces of advice was the necessary reminder, in that age of satirical pamphleteering, that irony does not pay and that 'ridicule, as the test of truth, is a very powerful weapon' and quite unfit for a Christian to use.

Simeon's second opponent was not quite so easily countered. This was Doctor Marsh, Lady Margaret Professor of Divinity, who later became Bishop of Peterborough. It was of him that Thomas Babington Macaulay, while at Matthew Preston's private school at Little Shelford, wrote to his father at the age of fourteen to say that after 'looking at him for about ten minutes' he had come to think that he was 'a very ill-favoured gentleman as far as outward appearance is concerned.'[23] Again the dispute arose from Simeon's use of the university pulpit in Great St Mary's. This time the subject was *The Excellency of the Liturgy* of the Church of England, presented in a series of four addresses in November 1811.[24] The background to this controversy was the widespread interest being aroused throughout the country by the formation of the British and Foreign Bible Society. Dr Marsh had launched the affair by publishing a very widely read pamphlet in which he maintained that the Bible should not be distributed by itself without the Prayer Book being available at the same time to give it balance, or one might say, an Anglican slant. He also accused the clergy who supported it of being Calvinists.

This was all too much for Charles Simeon who decided to answer Marsh in these sermons by defending the liturgy of his church which he believed 'has been brought to such a state of perfection as no human composition of equal size and variety can pretend to.' He wanted to make it quite clear that he was as loyal as anyone to his church and to the Prayer Book. His support of the Bible Society's policy, which was to include dissenters in its government from the start, in no way meant he was indifferent to the attitude of the Church of England. Indeed, he took a very poor view of the free and easy approach to divine worship which was associated with the nonconforming denominations. In the third of his four sermons, with perhaps scant thought for the devout chapel worshippers around, he expatiated on the subject: 'Take the prayers that are offered on any sabbath in all places out of the establishment; have them all written down . . . then compare them with the prayers that have been offered in all the churches of the kingdom; and see what comparison the extemporaneous effusions will bear with our pre-composed forms . . . proceed to do it for a year; and . . . methinks there is scarcely a man in the kingdom that would not fall down on his knees and bless God for the liturgy of the established church.' Dr Marsh was never won round, and even after becoming a bishop he could not resist the temptation to go for the evangelicals. He tried to exclude them from the diocese of Peterborough by requiring every candidate for ordination to answer an examination consisting of eighty-seven subtle questions designed to trap so-called Calvinists, an act of prejudice for which he was severely taken to task by Sydney Smith in the *Edinburgh Review*, and which gained no support from any other diocesan bishop.[25]

Simeon was only obliquely concerned in a third controversy which shook the university to an extent it is hard to understand today. It was again concerned with the Bible Society which in 1811 was establishing auxiliary branches throughout the country. In Cambridge a group of some two hundred keen Christian undergraduates, the forerunners of the Christian Union of a later day, decided that they should try to form a branch with university support and began to make arrangements for a public meeting to launch it.[26] They had reckoned without two inhibiting factors. One was the violent objection of Marsh, who thundered out an anathema from the pulpit of St Paul's Cathedral that 'without the liturgy the Bible may be made to lead them into doctrine and discipline most discordant with our own',[27] and therefore in the name of true orthodoxy the scheme must be resisted at all costs.

The other difficulty was the almost paranoid fear on the part of the authorities, born of panic about revolutionary ideas from France taking root in impressionable young minds, that if religious undergraduates were allowed to organise meetings on their own it would not be long before subversive organisations would start springing up. Isaac Milner, the redoubtable Christian President of Queens' who had been the means of leading William Wilberforce to faith in Christ, became involved in the issue on this occasion. He greatly sympathised with the ideals of these young Christians and the principles of the Bible Society, but he was quite obsessed with the view that undergraduates could and should never be trusted with getting up meetings of any kind. Their duty was just to attend those organised for them by their seniors. A deputation of four of the instigators attended on Milner and Professor Farish to canvass their support. Milner was immediately attacked by a spell of cold feet and told them they should 'retire from conduct of the affair and place it entirely under the control of their superiors in the university.' He urged that the matter be dropped for a term. Farish, on the other hand, who very much sympathised with the proposal, disappointed its supporters because he 'sat with his head on his hand and said very little.'

The undergraduates took all this very badly and eventually Simeon was called in as one who well understood their youthful enthusiasm and yet was a great stickler for propriety. He told them that it was a Christian duty to obey those placed in authority and advised them to leave matters in his hands for the moment. Although many of their number were getting fanatically impatient with the hesitation of their seniors and more keen to act on their own, Simeon's calming influence had the desired effect. He proceeded to visit his good friend Farish who told him that he had decided that he himself would certainly attend such a meeting 'even if I stand on the platform alone.' To which Charles immediately replied 'You shall not stand alone, my brother, I will go with you.'[28] In due course, after William Wilberforce had become involved and successfully persuaded the new Chancellor, the Duke of Gloucester, to express his support, and Isaac Milner at the last minute had withdrawn his objections, on December 12th the Town Hall was the scene of a memorable meeting which raised £900 for the Society on the spot. Charles Simeon, always sensitive to the workings of providence when they seemed to coincide with the way he was praying, recorded, 'Truly God showed that He reigns in the earth!'

When Simeon felt that he was contending on the side of the truth, though it was not really his nature, he did undoubtedly take a certain relish in fighting for his faith. Unfortunately, the opposition to his ministry was not confined to academic arguments, nor could he always deal with it by giving as good as he got, though he did his best. We have already seen how his arrival at Trinity church was greeted with abuse. When it was discovered that he was not only an unwanted interloper, but a 'Methodist' type of preacher as well, the opposition increased still further and he was frequently attacked by town and gown alike simply for that. It is a melancholy story cheered only by the remarkable spirit of the man who cared nothing for his own popularity, but would never stand by if insults were cast at the house of God or the truth of the gospel. In the early days he was so ostracised by the townspeople that 'no one with a decent coat on his back would venture to speak to or notice him in the street.'[29] When on one occasion a poor man in passing actually took his hat off to him, Simeon was so touched that he had to hurry back to his rooms where he broke down in tears of gratitude.

One day he who had always prided himself on his appearance was seen returning from church to King's with his face and clothes covered in dirt and smeared with rotten eggs. Humiliating though such experiences were to him, Simeon never resisted any attack on his own person. William Cowper might well have been writing of Simeon when he described George Whitefield as one who

> loved the world that hated him: the tear
> That dropped upon his Bible was sincere;
> Assailed by scandal and the tongue of strife,
> His only answer was a blameless life;
> And he that forged, and he that threw the dart,
> Had each a brother's interest in his heart.

When the honour of God and not just his personal popularity was involved it was quite another matter, and then Simeon would by no means let an offence pass. In 1810 for example he got one John Quince, a carpenter, imprisoned for disturbing the congregation while at worship, though when he agreed to apologise Simeon took it no further.[30] In November the same year he had to send for a constable during the service to deal with an offender, and on another occasion it was a banker, a captain in the local Home Guard of the time, who spent two nights in the town jail for similar conduct. None of such offenders were released until they had agreed to make a public apology in the local press, and to give Simeon a sum of money to spend on bread for the poor of the parish.

When it came to dealing with troublesome undergraduates Simeon realised he would have to be equally strict for he held a university post and was expected to maintain discipline. He arranged for people armed with white wands to patrol the church during a service. Things were sometimes so bad that he had to make a public statement: 'We have seen persons come into this place in a state of intoxication; we have seen them walking about the aisles . . . without the slightest reverence or decorum . . . the devotions of the congregation have been disturbed by almost every species of ill conduct.' He would himself march down to the porch at the end of a service to help prevent the gownsmen offending church members as they left. 'I endeavoured,' he said, 'always to act with mildness, but yet with firmness; and, through the goodness of God, was enabled to keep in awe every opposer.' His noble colleague, William Farish, popular university don though he was, was also prepared to stand by Simeon and help keep order at the door. One memorable day in 1794 an undergraduate of Pembroke College, Charles Randall, broke one of the church windows and then entered and boasted of his vandalism. For this he was duly reported to the Vice-Chancellor who insisted on him reading out a public apology in church. Simeon wrote it out for him, and because he did not raise his voice enough the vicar himself repeated it word for word from the pulpit so that all the congregation, who by now were standing on the pews out of curiosity, could hear every detail. When the service was over, harbouring no ill feelings now that amends had been made, Simeon took the young man into the vestry and there, with many tears we are told, urged him to turn to God. He then knelt down and prayed for him 'with so much affection as to melt the stubborn heart of that hitherto unfeeling offender.' Subsequently he became Simeon's staunch ally trying to the best of his powers to protect him from further trouble.[31]

Even as late as 1820 James Scholefield, Fellow of Trinity and later Professor of Greek, when his curate, used to take students to 'dear old Simeon's church' and often en route 'heard the coarse abuse he met with from the idle undergraduates who rejoiced in nothing more than hooting at Simeon or his curate'.[32] An incident with a happy ending concerned two young men who began behaving in a disorderly fashion, one of them actually having the audacity to stare Simeon in the face when reproved. He was told never to enter the church again unless he had a change of heart. He was there however the next Sunday and continued coming throughout the term during which time he became soundly converted. This was John Sargent, one of the few members of Simeon's own college who made any overt Christian profession. He was eventually ordained and became one of Simeon's most respected friends to whom in 1830 he gave his precious Greek Testament. In 1828, in writing to Lady Grey after the death of her husband, Simeon said how thankful he was that they had John Sargent as their minister: 'In my opinion the world contains none superior to him as a sympathising counsellor, and few, if any, that are equal . . . the person of all others in the world whom one would wish to see in a sick chamber.'[33]

The kind of reception that Simeon received would have been enough to crush the spirit of any ordinary clergyman, and he was certainly at times brought very near to despair. But he knew where to turn when in trouble. Of one particular experience he recorded:

> When I was an object of much contempt and derision in the university, I strolled forth one day, buffeted and afflicted with my little Testament in my hand. I prayed earnestly to my God that he would comfort me with some cordial from his Word, and that on opening the book I might find some text which would sustain me . . . The first text which caught my eye was this:
>
> 'They found a man of Cyrene, Simon by name; him they compelled to bear his Cross.' You know Simon is the same name as Simeon. What a word of instruction was here – what a blessed hint for my encouragement! To have the Cross laid upon me, that I might bear it after Jesus – what a privilege! It was enough. Now I could leap and sing for joy as one whom Jesus was honouring with a participation in his sufferings . . . I henceforth bound persecution as a wreath of glory round my brow!

CHAPTER SIX

With Men for The Ministry

Joseph Milner of Hull, brother of Isaac, deeply concerned about the state of the parishes of the Church of England in 1789, wrote 'It is an affecting consideration to reflect what a number of clergymen there are whose lives demonstrate them to be totally void of any religious sensibility whatever, with whom "to pray and to sermonize" is the same thing as to till the ground or to navigate the seas, a mere secular trade, and unconnected with any concern for their own salvation or that of the flocks committed to their charge.'[1] A few years later he had the opportunity of visiting Cambridge and judging for himself to what extent the ministry at Holy Trinity was an exception to the dismal rule. He was glad to be able to send a friend of his this report: 'This place has obtained more evangelical means since I was here last. There is now Simeon; and it is to be regretted that his congregation is not so large as were to be wished. Of those, however, who do attend, there are a number of solid Christians; and whether God may please again to make this place a nursery for the gospel, as doubtless it was in a very high degree at the time of the Reformation, we know not. But times are different.'[2]

After seven years' devoted work the attendance at Simeon's church was not yet impressive. It had been and always was to be a hard slog, with the opposition doing all they could to make things more difficult for him than they need have been. A weaker man than he would have given up long ago and looked for a sphere where his gifts and message would be more appreciated. But Simeon was of stern stuff, and on top of his natural obstinacy, he was a committed man. He had asked God for this church. He had offered himself to him for this special ministry. He had knelt at his ordination and prayed for grace to fulfil his vocation there. He was, above all things, 'in earnest.' That was how, in his diary for 9th November, 1797, William Wilberforce summed up his friend Simeon on the occasion of their dining together to discuss the beginning of missionary work overseas. James Bean, the author of *Zeal without Innovation*, a valuable critique of the place of evangelicalism in the Church of England written in Simeon's day, was emphatic that whatever other qualities he might require, a minister who was not in earnest was of little value to church or nation:

> It may be lamented that there is something in our national character that is not favourable to great earnestness in ecclesiastical affairs . . . The temperature of the times is not that of a religious fervour . . . We may therefore consider an earnest piety as a quality . . . which needs cherishing in those who have it; as a quality, moreover, which when accompanied with other fitnesses, the state of our country now so much demands in those to whom parochial instruction is committed that it ought to be diligently sought for.[3]

Being earnest, or 'serious' as it was often expressed, was the distinct feature in the lives of truly converted men which marked them out as different from others. Those who did not share the experience of conversion tended to resent this quality in their neighbours. Yet to be serious in this way did not mean being unbearably solemn. Indeed, it was perfectly possible for an earnest man like Simeon to be at the same time full of a joyful vitality which could be quite infectious. Certainly it bore him up throughout the long rough passage which he embarked upon at his conversion. He knew that he was engaged in a lifelong spiritual struggle in which there could be no half measures. Charles Kingsley portrayed just this spirit in his saga of Saint Elisabeth's total commitment to the service of God:

> God! Fight we not within a cursèd world,
> Whose very air teams thick with leaguèd fiends –
> Each word we speak has infinite effects –
> Each soul we pass must go to heaven or hell –
> And this our one chance through eternity
> To drop and die, like dead leaves in the brake . . .
> Be earnest, earnest, earnest; mad, if thou wilt:
> Do what thou dost as if the stake were heaven,
> And that thy last deed ere the judgement day.

Armed with this God-given enthusiasm, Charles Simeon devoted himself to working as assiduously amongst the undergraduates around him as he did with his parishioners. By the year 1811 he reckoned that two-thirds of his time and energy were expended on them. In due course his labours were rewarded and by 1829 he was able to tell one of the crowded conversation parties where he got to know these men so well, 'Thirty years ago five hundred pounds could not have collected such a party as now surrounds me in this room. It was a university crime to speak to me, and was reported to parents; and now my views are received with respect and even esteem by men of rank, by Archbishops and Bishops.' He modestly attributed the change not to his own perseverance but to the new outlook brought about by the work of the Bible Society in distributing copies of the Scriptures so that men and women of all walks of life could see for themselves what Biblical truth was. In fact the work of this Society and of the Clapham Sect was so effective that the evangelical viewpoint gradually became tolerated. But nothing should detract from the significance of Simeon's personal and prolonged efforts to evangelise the gownsmen.

His greatest contribution to the life, and indeed to the revival, of the Church of England in the course of his long ministry was undoubtedly his work amongst ordination candidates. In the university world as a whole we have seen that Simeon became respected rather than followed, and his academic contribution to Cambridge life was non-existent. But when it came to the many young men, about half the total undergraduate number, whose only purpose in coming to college was to qualify for holy orders, he discovered a field of operations where his not inconsiderable talents could be used to the full. He turned to it with unrestrained zeal and before very long he had a following such as any don could be proud of. One needs to bear in mind that most of such young men had really no idea of what the calling of a parson is meant to be. They thought in terms of qualifying for a family living perhaps, as a reasonable way of spending their lives, and in reasonable comfort if the living was a good one. Or maybe they came of humble parentage and ordination for them would mean a climb of several rungs in the social ladder. In any case a clergyman's was generally regarded as a respectable if not very rewarding profession. As for the spiritual side of the work, this was seldom commented upon. Few aspiring to ordination would have seen anything out of the ordinary in Fielding's Parson Adams carrying a copy of Aeschylus in his pocket rather than a New Testament.

Such an attitude was to Simeon a total betrayal of the calling of a clergyman as he understood it. He could not bear to see year after year men going out to be in charge of churches all over the land who had no message to deliver and no idea of what is meant by 'the cure of souls'. His own sense of vocation could not have been higher. When his friend John Venn was about to be ordained he wrote to him, 'I most sincerely congratulate you not on permission to receive £40 or £50 a year, nor on the title of Reverend, but on your accession to the most valuable, most honourable, most important and most glorious office in the world – to that of an ambassador of the Lord Jesus Christ.' There is an echo here of the teaching of the veteran Henry Venn, John's father, to whom Charles owed so much when he was an undergraduate. He had spoken of a parson's life as 'the best service that men or angels can be called to work in.'[4]

When Simeon was asked how a man could be sure that he was truly called to the ministry he answered in words that every theological student could note with profit: 'He must have a deep feeling of the value of his own soul, and of the souls of others; must have a deep love of Christ, readiness to give up all for him and for his work, and for the good of souls.' He felt it was wrong of parents to press their sons to take up this profession for the very practical reason that many of them are not really cut out for it. He had enough disappointments amongst some of his young men to make him specially cautious of encouraging them to be ordained indiscriminately. 'Even devoted men ought not to think of themselves "called of God" unless they feel an adaptation to the work, ability to speak or to do the duties of the office. Many mistake their calling and with devoted hearts are nevertheless out of their sphere when they enter the ministry.'

However, as soon as he was convinced that a young ordinand had true potential and was fully committed to Christ, there was nothing he would not do for him. He longed to provide in his own person what he himself had so grievously missed when he was in their position, a wise, experienced and kindly person to whom to turn for advice and encouragement. So he made himself as accessible to them as he possibly could. Because there was no special theological training of any kind provided by either the church or the university, he in fact became their unofficial tutor in the things of God. It is hard to envisage a situation such as prevailed then when the ordination examination consisted merely of the construing of a passage from the Greek Testament, and was taken on the day of ordination itself so that any thought of anyone's name being withdrawn as unprepared or unsuitable was out of the question.

At first Simeon seems to have wanted to act the don and provide an informal and almost academic series of lectures, without of course any official recognition by the divinity faculty of the university. His subject when Thomas Thomason attended in 1792, *Natural and Revealed Religion*, was certainly a topical one, and an evangelical slant upon it would have been welcome to many aspiring young theologians. Thomason at least tremendously appreciated these Sunday evening lectures which, he said, Simeon 'studies and puts together with much pains and attention. He reads the fruit of his labours to us and explains it.' Later Simeon took to giving more specific sermon instruction in classes held in his rooms after church on Sundays. Then some years later still he began holding open house once a week to answer students' questions on any topic relevant to their calling.

Simeon saw himself as supplying his beloved Church of England with generation after generation of young clergy instructed in their faith and trained to express it clearly. Through them he believed an effective and evangelical ministry would spread throughout the country for 'many of those who hear me are legions in themselves because they are going forth to preach, or else to fill stations of influence in society. In that view, I look on my position here as the highest and most important in the kingdom, nor would I exchange it for any other.' We may forgive him the arrogance of the last sentence. The fact is that certainly by 1817 gownsmen comprised about half of his congregation. Over the fifty-four years which he devoted to this work, hundreds of young ordinands were like George Eliot's Amos Barton of Shepperton 'whose Christian experience had been consolidated at Cambridge under the influence of Mr Simeon.' When they left to minister in their churches they were able to do so with marked conviction. There is no doubt that the whole Church of England thus received an injection of fresh vitality which could be traced back to a revered apostle of Christ whose rooms in King's College and whose church near the market place in Cambridge were remembered by many with the deepest gratitude and affection.

One of the principal sources whereby young men of evangelical views were enabled to go to Cambridge to study for the ministry was a society which still exists today for the same purpose. It was brought into being by Henry Venn and others as far back as 1767. Ten years later when he moved from Huddersfield to Yelling it carried on at Elland in Yorkshire, whence it got its name. Its declared purpose was to raise 'a fund for the purpose of educating poor pious men for the ministry.'[5] Wilberforce was a generous supporter in its earlier days, and described the work of the society in a somewhat atypical manner as 'catching the colts running wild on Halifax Moor, and cutting their manes and tails, and sending them to college.'[6] Simeon himself over the years gave no less than £3700 to its ordination fund.[7] He became the society's supervisor in Cambridge where many of the young men whose names will come before us in these pages were among its grantees.

Before being accepted as an Elland sponsored candidate for orders, each man had to undergo a severe scrutiny and would only be passed if he could convince his examiners of his 'sound and unaffected Christian piety; sound and inquiring mind; conviction of the necessity of order and union in the Church of Christ,' and of his personal loyalty to the doctrine and liturgy of the Church of England.[8] This was followed up by the society's insistence that none of their men should accept a curacy without their permission; that they were to attend only Anglican churches; and as a guarantee that they were truly deserving of financial help it was ruled that 'they shall not employ a barber, supposing they do not wear a wig, or hairdresser except during sickness or when their hair requires cutting... Their dress shall be plain and modest... They shall not purchase books, apparel or furniture without approbation of their guardian,'[9] who would be senior members of their college.

If it be thought that the discipline involved in these terms is on the harsh side, let it be noted that the members of this clerical society applied similar standards to themselves instructing each one to 'endeavour to keep himself and others from all evil divisions and animosities both in heart and voice, in temper and conduct, that Christian love and unity may be kept up and promoted.'[10] The success of the Elland Society in the north, and of a similar group based on Bristol, encouraged Simeon to take steps to establish a society in London on the same lines. In 1816 he managed to get his London Clergy Education Society off the ground with the help, need one say it, of Wilberforce and his friends such as Charles Grant, Chairman of the East India Company. As a result Simeon was able to welcome among his band of brothers in Cambridge many a young Londoner who would otherwise have been lost to the church.

Simeon's sermon classes, which he started in 1792 and continued regularly for forty years, used to attract some fifteen to twenty undergraduates at a time. They were essentially practical, dealing with the techniques of preaching and sermon construction. For example, 'Never weary your hearers by long preaching,' says the minister who normally occupied his pulpit for a full fifty minutes.[11] 'Endeavour to rivet their attention on your message for a reasonable time; but remember,' the wise old man pointed out, 'that the mind, and especially among the generality of persons or the uneducated, will only bear a certain amount of tension.' He was very insistent on a good and clear presentation. 'It is the want of a good and impressive delivery that destroys the usefulness of a great proportion of pious ministers.' He suggested that they might try rehearsing their sermons to a piece of furniture imagining the wooden object to be a listening parishioner, a task most parsons would not find very difficult. No sermon that is inaudible is worth delivering, so he encouraged his men to speak in a natural, relaxed and unaffected way. Perhaps he was aware that many people, certainly at the beginning of his ministry, had thought him affected in the pulpit. Referring to his own practice in the matter of acoustics he said, with that touch of quaint humour which always appeals to the student mentality, 'I preach usually to the small door in the west gallery of Trinity church. It is a good central spot for me to direct my countenance to; it is a fair average of the more distant parts of the congregation. When I perceive that the door distinctly hears me, then I know all the congregation may.'

Simeon, who no doubt never forgot his panic in the pulpit when he once found three or four pages of his written sermon missing, had some wise things to say about not reading one's sermons. He thought that a young minister should not attempt extempore preaching until he had had three or four years' practice delivering written sermons, but he encouraged them to try managing with notes at informal weekly meetings. After a few years he reckoned they would have the confidence to use only notes in the pulpit. But he warned them that in order to accomplish this degree of fluency much hard work was required. When it came to choosing suitable passages from which to preach, he said he believed that 'evangelical preachers too often take routine texts, which they may easily prate about, but comparatively seldom choose texts which require study and thinking over.' He was a great one for putting real industry into sermon preparation.

Simeon's advice about the conduct of church services was as practical as that on preaching. He believed that God was as near to him in the prayer-desk as in the pulpit, and urged his young friends to seek a real spirit of worship throughout the whole of a service and not put everything into the sermon. 'Make all the services of worship spiritual,' he urged them. 'Let there be a spiritual unction, a reality, throughout all you do or say in God's house, and as his official servant. Make each funeral, each baptism, each marriage, a time of blessing, and expect God's blessing on them. Make the words which you then read or pray really exponents of your own feelings, and, if possible, of the feelings of the parties more immediately concerned. Such occasions should be viewed as seasons for the presence of God the Holy Spirit. Do your best to make them so, not in mouthiness but in reality of heart-feeling.' This repeated word 'reality' was Simeon's interpretation of our Lord's emphasis on worshipping God 'in spirit and in truth.'

In addition to the regular Sunday after-church sermon classes, Simeon devoted Friday evenings to what he called his Conversation Parties, which he began in 1813. A later age would have thought of them more in terms of a 'one-man Brains Trust', and a somewhat unsympathetic historian has described them as 'the consulting room of the ghostly physician turned into an operating theatre thronged with admiring students.'[12] But to Simeon they were almost the best part of the day. It was not admiration he sought but fellowship. 'I love these little conversation meetings. They diffuse a spirit of love amongst us. I would I could have them oftener . . . These little meetings seem to me somewhat of a foretaste of heaven.' By nature warm-hearted, by occupation isolated, he longed to find in these informal gatherings the loving friendship of like-minded men – and women – that he could get nowhere else. 'I love to view all my Christian friends as fuel,' he told them. 'Having gathered you all together on my hearth, I warm myself at your fire, and find my Christian love burn and glow.' Thus a real fellowship grew up in those rooms in King's round the Word of God, for he always kept his 'little old quarto Bible within his reach' as the touchstone of all his opinions.

There was a certain old-fashioned and gentlemanly mystique about the way these occasions were conducted. Several vivid records of such meetings have survived. The proceedings began at six o'clock with tea being served from the precious black Wedgewood teapot which is now preserved in the vestry of his church. Two servants were present to hand round as the company assembled, sometimes as many as eighty squeezing themselves into his spacious but limited accommodation, sitting on benches and in the window recesses and no doubt on the floor as well. The more there were the happier the host would be just so long as they all remembered to wipe their shoes on the many mats provided, and took special care not to lean on the set of marble topped tables with slender gilded legs which he valued so highly.

An eye-witness has left us this graphic picture of the proceedings:

> At the entry of each gownsman Mr Simeon would advance towards the opening door with all that suavity and politeness which you know he possessed in a remarkable degree, and would cordially tender his

hand, smiling and bowing with the accomplished manners of a courtier; and I assure you we deemed it no small honour to have had a hearty shake of the hand and a kind expression of the looks from that good old man. If any stranger was introduced to him at these meetings, he would forthwith produce his little pocket memorandum-book and enter, with due ceremony, the name of his new acquaintance . . . As soon as the ceremony of introduction was concluded Mr Simeon would take possession of his accustomed elevated seat and would commence the business of the evening. I see him even now, with his hands folded upon his knees, his head turned a little to one side, his visage solemn and composed, and his whole deportment such as to command attention and respect. After a pause he would encourage us to propose our doubts, addressing us in slow and soft and measured accents: 'Now – if you have any question to ask – I shall be happy to hear it – and to give what assistance I can.'

In this way the acknowledged leader of the evangelical wing of the established church would prepare his young friends to go out into the world better equipped than they could possibly have been had they been left to flounder on their own as Simeon had found himself doing when he was their age.

It is not surprising that over the years evangelical parents began to send their sons to Cambridge simply because Charles Simeon was there to help them. Josiah Pratt, who later became Secretary of the Church Missionary Society, was one of these. Although himself an Oxford man he was happy to see his boys attending Trinity church where they were told to take special note of the sermon each Sunday.[13] Spencer Thornton in 1832 wrote home to tell his mother that he was going to Simeon's church at 10.45 as well as college chapel at 8.0, the university sermon at 2.0 and chapel again at 6.15. He went on to describe how he had taken a friend along to meet Simeon privately. He was engaged when they got there so 'we were shown into another room, and he received us with the greatest possible warmness; and upon our apologising for disturbing him, he said "Oh no! What! are we to sleep? Why, if I were to call upon you in your rooms I should not find you asleep, should I? No, we must work while it is called today". '[14] Every little word of the great man would be treasured and remembered for years afterwards.

Samuel Settle, whose chief memory of Holy Trinity seems to have been a violent disturbance in the church on December 6th 1795,[15] which Romaine Hervey also noted in his dairy, never forgot the day when he 'took a skeleton to Simeon for the first time', and had his initial attempt at sermon writing scrutinised by the kindly eye of the expert. Thomas Thomason, later to become his much loved colleague, was another who wrote home to fond parents about what it meant to them to have Simeon to turn to: 'Mr Simeon has invited me to his Sunday evening lectures. This I consider one of the greatest advantages I ever received,' and to a friend he said 'Mr Simeon watched over us as a shepherd over his sheep. He takes delight in instructing us, and has us continually at his rooms.' Henry Elliott told his mother in October 1810 that as soon as he went up to Cambridge 'Mr Simeon has been exceedingly kind. Almost his first words to me were, "Now, Mr Elliott, remember that these rooms are always open to you. I owe much more to your dear grandfather (Henry Venn) than I shall ever be able to repay by attention to his grandchildren". ' Simeon himself, calling on Mrs Elliott some years later, brought tears to her eyes when he said 'Your sons are my joy.'[16]

It was to men such as these that Simeon often turned for help in his work. He was sometimes consulted by bishops who wanted an assessment of a candidate for holy orders. If he did not know the man well himself he would ask one of his closer friends amongst them for an opinion. Or it might be a case of asking someone to find out the name and college and call on a freshman whom he had spotted in church and wished to get to know. It meant a great deal to Simeon to have the backing of such committed Christian men who shared his hopes and readily worked with him in turning them into achievements. Several of the pick of them he chose to be his curates. Their contribution to the work of the church at large was so important that they deserve a chapter to themselves. They played no small part in commending the evangelical outlook to the outside world for they were men of such distinction that it could no longer be said that it was not academically respectable to be a member of Simeon's church.

There was a time when Simeon tells us he had six senior wranglers, all devout Christians, dining with him at the same time. He always laid great stress on the importance of Christian undergraduates putting everything they had got into their studies, and he rejoiced when so many of them came out at the top. According to John Williamson there had been a time in the 1790s when evangelical fervour so ran away with itself that Christian students were beginning to think that earthly learning was useless and only heavenly teaching worth listening to. Simeon would have none of this. 'We declare unequivocally,' he said in a sermon, 'that it is the duty, the indispensable duty, of all students, whatever be the sphere in which they are afterwards to move, to cultivate human wisdom, and with all diligence to prosecute the work assigned them . . . They would be culpable in the highest degree if they should make religion a pretext for neglecting their academical studies.'[17] 'Your Bible reading (beyond what is needful for daily devotional duties) must be confined to the leisure which you have after spending the proper hours in University study and necessary exercise,' he told one young enthusiast.

This last point was another thing he frequently emphasised. He used to use a quaint way of combining the importance of Christians working hard with the other virtue of their taking regular exercise about which he felt so strongly: 'I always say to my young friends, Your success in the Senate House depends much on the care you take of the three-mile stone out of Cambridge. If you go everyday and see that nobody has taken it away, and go quite round it to watch lest anyone has damaged its farthest side, you will be best able to read steadily all the time you are at Cambridge. If you neglect it, woe betide your degree. Yes, – Exercise, constant and regular and ample, is absolutely essential to a reading man's success.'

The fruit of Simeon's constant labours amongst these men eventually began to show itself. By 1818 Holy Trinity church which then held some nine hundred people was becoming so crowded by gownsmen that he said 'I am forced to let them go up into the galleries (where there were few free seats) which I never suffered before; and notwithstanding that, multitudes of them are forced to stand in the aisles for want of a place to sit down. What thanks can I render to the Lord for a sight of these things?' Numbers continued to increase, so much so that seven years later, in the heat of summer, the vicar proposed to the vestry that the windows be made to open to admit some fresh air into the church.[18] This degree of response, for which Simeon had been working and praying for so many years, was a fitting reward for one who had never spared himself in their interests and who bore them on his heart continually.

As soon as Simeon's followers began multiplying in the university they became popularly known as 'Simeonites' or 'Sims'. Their other-worldliness and professed devotion soon made them the butt of undergraduate humour as, for example, in 1822 when the wits of the day divided society into

> Some given carnally to women and wine,
> Some apostles of Simeon all pure and divine.[19]

A year later, when a celebration was being held to mark the building of the new 'King's Court' at Trinity College, we are told

There was a feast, a mighty feast,
For Science and the Gown;
The College buildings were increased,
The Speaker was come down;
And men of war and men of prayer
And men of every sort were there,
Peer and Professor, Monk and Mayor,
And Simeonite and sinner.[20]

In the rowing world where evangelical undergraduates have so often distinguished themselves, the first boat that Magdalene put on the river, in 1828, was called 'The Tea Kettle'[21] owing to the preference that the Simeonites who abounded in that college had for tea over ale; so much so that it was alleged that 'the Cam which licks the very walls of the college is said to have been rendered unnavigable by tea-leaves.' The Second Trinity Boat Club, now extinct, became known as the 'Hallelujahs'[22] because it was largely composed of 'Sims' who, true to their father-in-God's encouragement of muscular Christianity, would don their traditional straw hats, blue jackets and striped trousers as they set about coping with the four foot wide oak cutters which were the precursors of the modern racing eights. It was in much the same vein that a hundred years later the Emmanuel boat which had a high proportion of Christian Union members was rumoured to have 'easied' during a violent thunderstorm because they believed it signalled the end of the world.

Magdalene College had more evangelical men in residence than other colleges largely because Samuel Hey, the Acting Master, William Farish and Henry Jowett, tutors, were all of that persuasion. They became known as 'sober Maudlins' but according to Romaine Hervey's entertaining diary of 1796 they seem to have shared the high spirits which have been a feature of young evangelicals from time to time ever since. He remembers violent fireworks being let off in their rooms on Guy Fawkes night and colleagues making the night hideous with a cacophony of posthorns. One party ended up with the Reverend William Farish in his capacity of tutor chasing the offenders round a room by the light of a piece of burning paper.[23] Hervey does also record the more sober memory of the day when he 'went to Simeon's for the first time to read Claude.' Describing an occasion when there was a campaign in the college to guard the freshmen from the influence of the evangelical contingent, he wrote with indignation, 'The President had the impudence to ask who attended Simeon's church.'[24]

It is somewhat reassuring to those who find contemporary biographies and obituaries painfully fulsome and sentimental to know that there was a human side to these very devout men's lives, and that the exuberance usually associated with students was shared by Simeon's disciples. But it cannot be denied that although he himself gained enormous respect as the years went on, his clientele did not as a rule have the same reception among their fellow undergraduates who found, for instance, their readiness to preach the gospel in hall both tiresome and out of place, not to say totally lacking in sensitivity.[25] An anonymous letter by a member of Trinity College, referring to Simeon's 'unspotted name', went on 'It would be desirable if some of his nominal disciples would imbibe something of their great master's good sense. The shaking head and uplifted hand are not always indications of sincerity.' Censoriousness has ever been the most unpleasant of all evangelical weaknesses.

A vivid illustration of this failing is provided by the author of that book of light-hearted and intriguing reminiscences of 1827, *Alma Mater*, from which we have already quoted. He records what purports to have been a *sotto voce* conversation during evensong in chapel. The perpetrators were summoned afterwards to see the Dean, but the record remains. It throws considerable light both on the vigorous health of the ageing minister then approaching his fifty-eighth birthday, and on the behaviour of the earnest young men who could not quite keep up with him in more ways than one. It would perhaps be wise to point out before we get too deep into the incident, that in university jargon of that time the verb 'to bitch' for some obscure reason was the technical term for taking tea with someone. The whispered dialogue runs as follows:

P. Riding to the Gogmagogs today I fell foul of old Simeon. The gay old cushion-thumper was amusing himself with leaping over the ditches. He's as good a horseman as a preacher, and that's saying much for his jockeyship; for much as he's sneered at for his works of supererogation – for his evangelisation, he's the most powerful expositor and advocate I have ever heard. But, as I was saying, he was leaping and making his servant follow him. One, however, which he took, the servant dared not attempt, at which the fine old fellow roared out 'You cowardly dog, why don't you follow?' This scene took place in the 'Senior Wranglers' Walk' even at the time when it was crowded by Simeonites.

M. I don't believe Simeon himself is half the hypocrite that nine out of ten of his proselytes are.

P. All his actions – his liberal and highminded generosity to his reduced brother, the baronet – his benefactions, public and private of every kind, most nobly illustrate the doctrines which he promulgates. His words and deeds harmonise well together, and on this account, if ever I go to church (and I go oftener than you think, Tommy), I go to Simeon's.

M. It's such a d——d humbug system altogether that, whether or no Simeon be sincere, I'll not mix myself up with them . . . I fancy I see myself at old Simeon's Bitch Levée. I should cut a pretty figure, with my lingo, amongst these saints.

P. You would indeed! They would not think of making a missionary of you, depend upon it. If you spoke but a dozen words, you would convince them, my boy Tommy, there was enough to be done at home . . . Much as I like old Simeon, the Simeonites I hate indiscriminately, as I do all serpents.

Whereupon he explains why. On one occasion when a couple of local inhabitants were making love under his window in Trinity Lane, two Simeonites who happened to be 'bitching' with him at the time collected all the slops they could find and poured the lot out of the window on to the unwise couple below. They got such a kick out of doing this that they developed a somewhat unhealthy taste for it, visiting him frequently in order to give the shower-bath treatment to any others who might be using the lane as a lover's walk. This struck him as unworthy behaviour for professing Christians, and he received them no longer.[26]

The liability of earnest young Christians to fail in this way to harmonise what they professed with what they practised, is something which Simeon himself seems to have overlooked. He may simply never have heard of such goings on. He himself was so free of anything approaching humbug or insincerity, and so ready to believe the best of his followers, that we do not find him taking them to task for inconsistency as one might have expected. At least, he is not recorded to have done so, though we know he was always anxious that they should all commend their Master by the way they lived.

J. H. Overton, a historian of the more orthodox school, writing in 1893 but referring in particular to the years 1808–10, rightly points out a danger not confined to Simeon's day:

It is not an unmixed advantage to gather, at a place like Cambridge, young men into cliques, which from the nature of the case keep them

> more or less aloof from the general life of the university; still less so, when they come to fancy that the reason why they hold aloof is because *they* are the pious ones, while all the world around them lieth in wickedness. It is no use denying the fact that outside their own circle the 'Simeonites' or 'Sims' were looked down upon; and the mischievous result was that many who regarded piety and Simeonism as synonymous terms were repelled from religion altogether.[27]

This has been true many times since the early nineteenth century, and is a matter about which Christian undergraduates today are often reminded. Whenever evangelicalism becomes popular there will be a fringe group of superficially committed believers climbing on the bandwagon because they feel it meets their needs without probing too far. Men who do this are too often blind to the effect it has on those whom they should be winning who regard it as plain humbug. This kind of thing happened in Simeon's day and has happened often since. But to judge a movement fairly one looks at the best and not the worst exponents of it.

One of the fields in which some of Simeon's young men found an outlet for their zeal was in Sunday School work. The beginning of the nineteenth century saw the development throughout the land of the Sunday School movement, and Cambridge was affected in a special way. Simeon had had some kind of parish school going for quite a time, but according to John Adeney of St John's there were 'no respectable and hardly any suitable teachers in it.'[28] This was in 1822. A rather different and more successful enterprise came into existence five years later. It originated amongst a group mostly of Queensmen who used to talk together in their rooms and discuss Mr Simeon's sermons, read the Bible, sing a hymn and pray. One day, inspired by a particular sermon, a Mr Wright in whose rooms they happened to be meeting, said that he thought it was time they stopped talking and did something. Their attention was drawn to the village of Barnwell on the outskirts of Cambridge, and now in the middle of it, which at that time had been sadly neglected by the church. Three of these men, including Abner Brown whose reminiscences of Simeon have been frequently quoted in these pages, set out to visit Barnwell. They wanted to see if the children from that area for whom nothing was being done would be willing to come into Cambridge itself if classes were arranged for them.

The effort was an immediate success. After canvassing from house to house no fewer than two hundred and twenty children arrived on the doorstep of the Friends Meeting House in Jesus Lane on the opening day.

Twenty gownsmen and a few older men's wives set about welcoming the dirty, ragged and lovable mob. They divided them into twenty-six classes, and began a course of instruction which was both popular and effective. One of the children grew up to be a missionary in Canada and another went out to India. The school flourished from the start encouraged by Farish, Scholefield who became curate at Holy Trinity, Carus who followed him in the same post, and of course Charles Simeon himself. When the organisers wanted to expand and open up other branches in the town, the one whose sermon had triggered off the whole scheme said to them, 'Put your hand in my pocket when you want anything.'[29] He and his colleagues had sown the seed and were now happy to leave the school entirely in gownsmen's hands thankful for their vision and enthusiasm. It was an ideal field of practical training for would-be clergy, and remained so for over a century. In calling it the most famous of all Sunday Schools in the country, Eugene Stock in his history of the Church Missionary Society enumerates no less than sixty of its former teachers who went out as missionaries with the CMS.[30]

CHAPTER SEVEN

A Band of Brothers

In the saga of Simeon there is a long roll of honour of really remarkable Christian men who owed their conversion and progress in the Christian faith to the life and witness of the Old Apostle of King's and Holy Trinity church. It is time we had a good look at them. Their contribution to the work of the church near and far is now part of history. There seems to be some competition in evangelical annals for the honour, if such we may term it, of being Charles Simeon's first convert. Mr Ian Rennie, in an unpublished thesis entitled *Evangelicalism and English Public Life*, states that W. Carus Wilson who went up to Trinity the same year as Simeon took over Holy Trinity church was 'the first gownsman converted under Simeon's ministry at Cambridge.'[1] He was one of the few Simeonites who did not proceed to ordination. Owning considerable property in the north-west he was a man of means, eventually becoming Member of Parliament for Cockermouth in 1821. It was his son who followed him to Cambridge and became better known. He had been at first refused ordination by the Bishop of Ely on the ground that he was too extreme a Calvinist. On consulting the oracle as to what he should do about this, Simeon advised him not to provoke his Lordship by argument but to explain that his views were not as rigid as he thought them to be. The advice was followed and the young man was duly ordained. He went on to become the headmaster of Cowan's Bridge School whose spiritual pride, love of power and ignorance of human nature, according to Mrs Gaskell, made him the Brontë girls' bugbear for two fateful years.

Simeon himself used to call Robert Housman of St John's College his eldest son in the belief that he was the first undergraduate whom he had led to Christ. Housman was ordained priest with Simeon in 1783. He went on to Lancaster where he was the means of getting St Anne's church built. He became its minister for forty-two years, finding himself at first suffering from the same kind of prejudice and opposition that plagued Simeon's early years. During part of his time at Cambridge he had shared rooms for three months with Simeon and they became very close friends. It was of these days that he once wrote: 'Never did I see such consistency and reality of devotion, such warmth of piety, such zeal, such love. Never did I see one who abounded so much in prayer. I owe that great and holy man a debt which can never be cancelled.' Which is more or less exactly what Devey Fearon, friend of Henry Martyn, also said. Writing to Simeon after his ordination he enthused: 'To you I owe the joy, the peace, the tranquillity I possess amidst a thousand cares . . . I trust I shall ever remember that you were the blessed instrument in the hands of my merciful God, in calling me to the knowledge of Jesus Christ my Lord. O! may I never give you cause to be ashamed of me. I entreat your prayers that I may . . . live and die Christ's faithful soldier and servant . . . Believe me, your affectionate son in the gospel of our Lord Jesus.'

Thomas Lloyd of King's was also regarded by Simeon as 'a son in the faith', but it seems that his conversion was a gradual process. He was a real academic. He won the Norrisian essay prize and became a brother Fellow to Simeon from 1785 until 1807 when he moved to an obscure living in Northamptonshire. While at the university he gave lectures in classics and philosophy which became very highly thought of. In due course he came to share Simeon's views, and when the latter became Dean of Divinity he encouraged him all he could: 'Lay yourself out for usefulness no less in the university than in the town. Your influence in your own college is evidently increasing; nay, further, the provost is inclined to co-operate with you in reforming the college . . . Give the present state of our college and of the university at large its proper proportion of your attention and your prayers.'[2] In 1790 when Simeon was made Vice-Provost and Lloyd himself the Dean of Divinity, he prayed that together they might set themselves 'faithfully to the very arduous work of reforming the college, and not be afraid of reproaches!'

Simeon greatly valued his help to 'raise the college from its present low estate of sloth, ignorance, immorality and irreligion'.[3] But at the same time, Lloyd, though he was five years his junior at college, reserved to himself the right to be honest with Simeon and to point out to him some of his failings, the sure sign of a really good friend. With typical modesty the vicar of Holy Trinity, still only twenty-seven years old, writes to thank him 'most sincerely for your kind observations respecting misguided zeal.' He goes on to share his profound belief in the possibility of victory in these matters. He says that he believes that what is a man's 'besetting sin in a state of nature will most generally remain so when he is in a state of grace; with this difference only, that in the former case it has the entire ascendant over him – in the latter it meets with continual checks and is not suffered to have dominion.'

John Sargent was another King's man who owed his conversion to Simeon. We have seen in a previous chapter the episode when he did his best to break up one of the services in Holy Trinity, only to find himself being gradually brought round to see the error of his ways, and join in happily with those he had expected to scorn. He was a Fellow of King's for three years from 1802 and on being married went, like so many of these young evangelicals, to an out of the way parish in Sussex described by Samuel Wilberforce as being 'amongst the ignorant and unpolished,'[4] where he remained for the rest of his life. In his biography of Thomas Thomason, Sargent recalls how impossible it was in the 1790s to find any clergyman willing to associate himself with Simeon and his church, leaving the vicar single-handed for fourteen years: 'Those who worshipped there were supposed to have left common-sense, discretion, sobriety, attachment to the establishment, a love for the liturgy, and almost whatever else is true and of good report, in the vestibule.'[5]

George Hodson, who when Archdeacon of Stafford was invited to preach at Trinity church on the Sunday after Simeon's funeral, was another of his converts. On this occasion he told the Old Apostle's now most affectionate congregation: 'I must say, if ever I loved or honoured any human being, your revered pastor was that man. Never can I forget the day when first, in a remote province of the kingdom, I heard him – and I was then a boy at school – I heard him teach the blessedness of the saints. Never shall I forget when a few years afterwards he exhorted me, with parental tenderness and many tears, to give myself wholly to the Lord.' Samuel Marsden, likewise, was befriended by Simeon when he first went up to Magdalene in 1790 and 'earned his undying affection' in those early days of struggle.[6] Marsden's later exploits in Australia and New Zealand are now part of the history of the growing British Empire. He had been granted an audience with George III who gave him five of his own Spanish sheep to take out with him. They became the progenitors of Australia's superb wool bearing flocks.[7] The religious side of this versatile Christian pioneer is reflected in his student memory of once finding Simeon at his devotions. He never forgot the absorption with which his senior was contemplating God oblivious to everything around him till he finally burst out with the words 'Glory! Glory! Glory!'

We have already seen in passing something of the attachment that Charles Simeon had to members of the remarkable Venn family. We must take a closer look at this association and what it meant to the young vicar in Cambridge with so many problems before him and so many weaknesses within. His first contact with the family is clearly stated in John Venn's diary: '1782, June 1. Drank tea at Atkinson's with Simeon, an undergraduate Fellow of King's, a religious man.'[8] John's home was at Yelling not far from Cambridge, a small village to which his father Henry, who had worn himself out in years of service at Huddersfield, had moved in 1771. Here, by way of contrast, his congregation consisted of a handful of shepherds and village rustics who made little demands on Henry's very considerable preaching and teaching ability.

However, this plump and jolly country parson, as he described himself, who sadly recorded that 'none of the clergy of the neighbourhood nor of the gentry come near us'[9] because of his views, began to find fulfilment in a ministry to Christian undergraduates from Cambridge who immensely valued the sixty-year-old veteran's understanding, guidance and wise advice. Charles Simeon, deprived as he was at that time of any like-minded colleagues, needed no encouragement, when he had a few hours to spare, to leap on his horse and ride the twelve miles there over the open countryside. What these visits meant to him he expressed forty years later in a letter to Henry Venn's grandson: 'Though in the efforts of a thousand years I never can repay my obligation to him for all his labours of love.' He reminded his son John of a lesson learned at father Henry's feet when only once, in all the twenty-four years he knew him, did the old man speak unkindly of someone, and on that occasion 'I was particularly struck with the humiliation he expressed for it in his prayer the next day.'[10] It was the kind of object lesson that the hot-tempered and impetuous young Charles was not likely to forget in a hurry.

Simeon, when he first made the acquaintance of the Venns, was still immature and needed a great many awkward corners knocked off his somewhat affected personality. This was so much the case that Henry's daughter Eling, who was twenty-four at the time, never forgot her first impressions: 'It is impossible to conceive anything more ridiculous than his look and manner were. His grimaces were beyond anything you can imagine. So, as soon as we were gone, we all got together into the study and set up an amazing laugh.'[11] For this she and her two sisters were duly reprimanded. They were taken by their father into the garden and told to bring him a peach. But as it was still early summer they had to make do with an unripe one. 'Well, it's green now,' said the kindly old man, 'and we must wait; but a little more sun and a few more showers, and the peach will be ripe and sweet. So it is with Mr Simeon.'[12]

Henry Venn was as excited about Simeon's appointment to Trinity church as he was himself. He exchanged pulpits with him from time to time and in 1786 wrote and told his friend Rowland Hill all about it. 'You will be agreeably surprised when I tell you I preached in exchange for dear Simeon at Trinity to many of the gown . . . Indeed there is a pleasant prospect at Cambridge. Mr Simeon's character shines brightly. He grows in humility, is fervent in spirit, and very bountiful and loving.'[13] The reference to his increase in humility is an important and welcome one for a letter to John Venn during his time at St Edward's church four years before shows a rather shocking turn of conceit in the popular young preacher. He tells John how when he was expecting the incumbent, Atkinson, to return from his summer vacation he so arranged things that he, Charles, would be sure to be the scheduled preacher for his first Sunday back at his church. He says that then 'If A. should come he may hear how I think he ought to speak . . .'[14] But those were early days. After four years' hard slog in Holy Trinity with Henry Venn breathing over his shoulder with kindly Christian advice, a second letter goes to Rowland Hill from a greatly cheered Henry: 'I have now been twice at Cambridge, and both times have had my heart much warmed with what I have seen and heard. How delightful the prospect, that when we old and worn out servants and soldiers shall be called out of the field, others are entering in who will do valiantly under the banner of our dear general who has died for us.'[15]

Venn was beginning to feel his age. One of the things which specially used to cheer him up was a visit from 'my affectionate friend Simeon.' They would often sit together in Henry's dark book-lined study, and share their experiences. 'Oh! how refreshing were his prayers! How profitable his conversation! We were all revived; he left a blessing behind him,' Henry happily recalled. And again, 'He calls me his father; he pours out his prayer for me, as an instrument from whose counsel he has profited.' The old man loved these calls, and still from time to time could summon up the energy to repay the compliment and ride over to Cambridge. On one such occasion the servant who accompanied him was given such a warm Christian welcome by Simeon's 'merciful, loving and righteous' followers that he said 'he wished to live amongst them and thought he would then grow in grace fast.'[16]

John Venn, Henry's only son, was three years senior to Charles, going up as a poor student or sizar to Sidney Sussex in 1776, it being the only

College which would accept the son of so outspokenly evangelical a parson as the rector of Yelling. Charles never forgot that John was 'the first spiritual acquaintance that I had in the world.' We have seen how they met, only a few months before John was to leave Cambridge to become rector of Little Dunham, a small parish in Norfolk of some hundred and seventy souls, which he held for the next nine years. John Venn, 'a very gracious youth' and 'a polished shaft' as John Berridge told his friend John Newton[17], and Charles Simeon became friends as soon as they met. They had much in common including a view of Cambridge society as 'breathing the spirit of anti-Christ.' But their friendship in later years was more on Charles' side than on John's. Meeting only just before he went down, they never really had long enough in each other's company to get used to their different ways of expressing themselves. The result was that painful misunderstandings arose from time to time in their correspondence which put some strain on their relationship.

Simeon at that time was desperate for friends. He was lonely and isolated in King's College and his warm heart tried to cling to Venn too much for his liking. He had recently been married, had his own like-minded family not too far away, and so felt the need for a close friendship much less. He seems in fact to have preferred the company of Edward Edwards, another convert of Simeon's, with whom he used to fraternise a good deal, rather more than Simeon appreciated. It is not possible here to follow out all the ramifications of these somewhat intense associations which occupy a good deal of Simeon's correspondence. In 1783, for example, we find him writing almost in panic and apologising for having said something to upset John, admitting himself as 'very highly deserving of censure.' In 1792 he even writes 'If ever you should want a friend to stand in God's place as a father to a child of yours, you may find one I hope in your old and loving friend C.S.'[18] Although he had eight children, John does not seem to have taken up Charles' offer of being godfather. Three years later he writes again quite desperate lest 'any expression or gesture of mine should give offence, and I should grieve one whom my soul most ardently desires to please.'

After Venn's move to Norfolk he and Simeon and William Farish and others used sometimes to ride to an inn at Thetford as a half-way house where their friendship was expressed 'in consultation and prayer.' Once Venn entertained them to a New Year's Day turkey dinner which would have been specially relished by the gourmet from King's who knew well enough how guests should be entertained.[19] One day in 1785 Simeon conducted an evangelistic service in John Venn's rectory where as many as seventy people crowded into the main room and down the passage, 'all hearing with attention, and many with apparent emotion and an understanding heart'. The rector of Little Dunham was greatly cheered by this for he had become depressed by the limitations imposed on his parish work in so small and remote a spot. Simeon's friendship meant a good deal to him at times like these. But he seems to have been very easily hurt, for when Simeon did not accept an invitation to visit the parish a second time, he somewhat unreasonably assumed that it was because there would not have been a sufficiently large or important congregation for him to address. He might have given Simeon credit for concentrating upon his own people for he had not yet won his way to their hearts, and could hardly spare time for distant visits.

However, there is no doubt that Charles Simeon was his own worst enemy when it came to establishing close friendships. His angular and sometimes arrogant personality, against which he battled all his life long, more than anything else stood in the way. Though highly sensitive himself, it was a long time before he learned sensitivity to the feelings of others. For this reason he lost much of Venn's affection, though his other colleagues who knew Simeon better and considered themselves less, had no undue difficulty in making a lasting friendship with him. John Venn did his best to help Simeon to see how upsetting his prickliness could be. Referring to the dangers that lie in the path of 'a man of warm temper' he writes to him in April 1783: 'I hope it will be an unnecessary caution in me to remind you that Satan will make his attack on you' in this matter. 'Excuse me, my dear friend, in presuming to give advice to one so much my superior. But as I know you are in so critical a situation, I cannot help adding my whisper to the constant advice you have had from my father and the rest of your Christian friends.' By 1794 we find Simeon becoming much more conscious of his failings and writing to John: 'I covet, exceedingly covet, a closer intimacy with you than ever. We are indeed cast somewhat in a different mould; and I am sensible that my complexion necessarily induces a conduct sometimes which needs forebearance, particularly from those whose natural dispositions do not altogether accord with mine . . . I now assure my dear friend that (d.v.) I will never more misconstrue his natural shyness into any declension of love towards me; I heartily beg his pardon that in his last visit to Cambridge I was in some measure guilty of it.'[20]

John Venn did not answer this letter, and Simeon hung on to his hopes and prayers that the attenuated friendship might not be severed. He gives us a glimpse of how deeply he felt it when telling John of what happened as he was riding to Everton to preach for John Berridge. When he passed Yelling church his praises went up to God for his loved Henry Venn, and 'I then proceeded to offer up my poor thanksgivings for you; for the graces and gifts with which he has mercifully endowed you; for the little family with which he has blessed you; for the use he has made of your ministry . . . I then endeavoured to remember your dear children, and to implore all needful blessings upon their heads . . . The ground whenever I pass over it, appears to me to be consecrated ground; the spire, as soon as ever it comes in sight, says to me *Sursum Corda:* and as long as it continues in sight, I consider it as my duty to spend my whole time in remembering those by whom I trust I am also sometimes remembered; and in interceding for those whom I ever think of with unfeigned affection, yourself and family.'

Simeon never gave up caring for John Venn. In 1792 when the South London parish of Clapham became vacant he took the most extraordinary action. The living was on offer to Henry Foster, but knowing the virtues and abilities of his special friend, and longing to see him in a sphere where these could be more fully employed, Simeon stepped in. Where could John's talents be better used, he thought to himself, than in the parish of Wilberforce and the Thorntons and those who were gathering round them. Although he was not the patron of the church, he had the nerve to write to Henry Foster, a gracious man whom he knew slightly, and tell him that he did not think he was really suitable for that particular post and would be wise to decline it. He advised him that if it was income that was the consideration, he himself would make it up out of his pocket. Foster very nobly accepted Simeon's assessment of his inferiority and very honourably turned down the proffered compensation.[21] John Venn, blissfully ignorant of what lay behind Foster's withdrawal, then accepted the living and went on to make that church a hub of lay Christian activity. Henry Foster remained in London where he continued in his capacity of private chaplain to Henry Thornton and lecturer at a number of different churches before eventually becoming vicar of Clerkenwell where he died in office at the age of ninety-nine. This bluff Yorkshireman seems to have held no grudge against the man preferred before him with whom he worked happily in harness in many evangelical enterprises. Nor apparently did he show any resentment against the one whose high-handed interference had deprived him of a good living, even though it was done in the name of the Lord. These devout men certainly had their saintly moments.

Amongst the family for whom the Cambridge vicar on horseback so earnestly prayed were John Venn's two sons, Henry and John, both destined to go up to Queens' and sit at Simeon's feet. Henry became Fellow, Dean and lecturer of his college, rector of Drypool, Hull, vicar of St John's, Holloway and finally for thirty-one years, in true Simeon tradition, Secretary of the Church Missionary Society. While at college his chief recorded connection with Simeon seems to have centred in his anxiety about his young brother John who was thinking of going out to India with the East India Company, but whose health was not too good.[22] This John went up to Cambridge in 1823 at a time when 'Simeon had then nearly, but not quite, got past the stage of obloquy and insult.' He particularly remembered an episode in Trinity church when at a solemn pause in the service one Sunday evening an undergraduate threw open the door and shouted out 'Charley' to a startled congregation.[23]

That was the kind of atmosphere that William Farish of Magdalene was accustomed to as we have seen. Born the same year as Simeon, Senior Wrangler at the early age of nineteen, Fellow and Tutor, Professor of Chemistry and then Jacksonian Professor of Natural Philosophy, he must certainly be ranked amongst Simeon's real friends. Never ashamed of his Christian faith, ready to stand by the vicar of Holy Trinity in rough times as in smooth, he was in many ways a second Simeon. He was too withdrawn a character ever to enter into the warm kind of male friendship which came so naturally and innocently to Charles Simeon. But he very much deserves his place amongst that 'band of men whose hearts God had touched', for he was in on almost everything that Charles got so excited about – visits to the Venns, meetings of the Bible Society, getting the Church Missionary Society going, and so on. For forty years he combined being vicar of St Giles church in Cambridge with his many academic duties, and while not the fluent speaker that Simeon was, he equally devotedly gave himself over to a student ministry. Indeed, when Simeon was away ill in 1807 it was to Farish's services that the undergraduates gladly turned instead.[24]

Farish was a remarkable man. He combined practical ability of the highest order with the professor's inherent right to be eccentric and, or, absent-minded from time to time. Two stories are particularly associated with him. In the one it was said that en route to take a service somewhere he mounted his horse on one side and then dismounted again on the other under the impression that his task had been accomplished.[25] The other tale is of how he is reputed to have boiled his watch for supper while timing it with the egg in his hand. In the early days of the railway Farish's advice was professionally required by a Parliamentary Committee.

However, when he stated that he believed trains might one day travel at sixty miles an hour, they asked him no more questions. He heard later that they all thought he must be of 'unsound mind'.[26] He is also said to have told his students that 'in time men would very probably voyage through the air by yet undiscovered agencies of impulsive powers'.[27] What his students thought of this brave forecast is not recorded. But we know that his lectures drew large and fascinated audiences, largely because of the intricate working models of all kinds which he made himself to illustrate his points. He also is reputed to have the distinction of having 'devised and introduced the startling innovation of assessing the merits of examination candidates in terms of marks.'[28]

At first Simeon found William Farish too slow moving for his fervent spirit, but as time went on he noticed how enthusiastic he was growing about evangelical enterprises such as the opening up of missionary work in Asia. He commented on this with a touch of his usual heavy wit in a letter to Thomason in 1824: 'Dear Professor Farish has become an itinerant advocate for the Church Missionary Society. A few years ago I should have as soon expected that he would be historical painter to his Majesty, or Envoy Extraordinary to the Court of China. His soul is surprisingly quickened, and his powers are increased.' Charles Simeon, John Venn and William Farish made a formidable force for the spreading of the gospel where it mattered so much – at the place where half the country's ordained clergy took their degrees. As true Christian friends they kept each other up to scratch, rejoiced in each other's successes, forgave each other's mistakes and tempered each other's zeal, setting an example to their many young admirers of what Christian brotherhood can really mean.

For the first fourteen years of his ministry, apart from these like-minded friends of his own age, Charles Simeon was single-handed in the parish. Here he had considerable pastoral responsibilities with some twelve to fifteen marriages and more than thirty baptisms and funerals each year. He was greatly relieved when in 1796 he was able to appoint a full-time assistant curate. From then on there were always two and sometimes three on the staff of Holy Trinity. Curates in the modern sense of the term were a rare species in the early nineteenth century. Oliver Goldsmith, no doubt recalling the limited means of his parson father in Ireland, immortalised a curate as an underpaid surrogate 'passing rich with forty pounds a year.' Many such men though fully responsible for a church whose true incumbent was an absentee, had large families and were often receiving as little as £15 or £30 a year.[29] Simeon's friend, Thomas Jones of Creaton, who had his coat turned inside out to save the cost of a new one, was paid £25 and had to live in the local inn, Highgate House, as he could not afford a housekeeper.[30] With this kind of penury threatening a parson's future, perhaps it is not entirely surprising to read in a daily paper an advertisement (certainly no Simeonite appeal) which ran 'Wanted – a curacy in a sporting country where the duty is light and the neighbourhood convivial.'[31]

The unhappy lot of such men as these was often the theme of poets and cartoonists. The caricatures of clergy by Gillray, Rowlandson and Bunbury, while no doubt well deserved, did nothing to add to the respect in which the clerical profession was held by the public at large who in the eighteenth century found cartoons and ribald pamphlets one of life's greatest diversions. Isaac Cruickshank's drawing, published in 1807, of two mounted clergymen titled *Clerical Prosperity* and *Clerical Adversity* summed up the popular understanding of the word curate. The one, perhaps Cowper's 'cassocked huntsman,' 'Riding with the wind', is a fat, bewigged, very comfortable looking rector on a prancing horse with a dog at heel and a manservant following on his own hack. The other, 'Riding against the wind', portrays a drooping bony horse, fetlock-deep in mud, carrying a scraggy, sagging curate in shabby clothes, all by himself and not exactly on top of the world.

There were no such contrasts as these when Simeon came to appoint an assistant. For one thing, he never shared the popular view that curates were a lower form of life. For another, he was not looking for someone to do his work for him but for someone who would be happy to work with him. However, having for many years had to undertake every parochial chore himself, he was very ready to hand over to his assistant such tasks as would set himself more free to concentrate on his preaching, and on the field provided by undergraduates and ordinands. Thus we find that after he had acquired a colleague, out of five hundred and seventy weddings at his church, Simeon himself took just eleven, and of over a thousand baptisms between 1813 and 1830 he took precisely fifteen, three of them being students. No doubt all this was splendid training for the ordained men who joined him, but one or two of them found it a little tedious. Simeon chose men of such outstanding intellectual ability that they were inclined to be more at home at their reading than in the daily round of pastoral visitation and attendance at parish functions. Two of his men were Senior Wranglers, than which one can go no higher in the examination scene, five others were Wranglers and another was to become a professor. With the arrival of all this talent Holy Trinity gradually became if not respectable, at least respected in the eyes of the university. The authorities could not but be impressed by the way highly intelligent men could also be men of faith and devotion and even 'enthusiasm'.[32] Simeon was very well aware of the importance of the church being served by a learned clergy and the team he gathered round him, far excelling his own academic ability, was a visible demonstration of the importance of younger men not neglecting their studies, a theme he reverted to again and again as we have seen.

What Simeon looked for in a prospective curate, apart from intelligence, was someone in tune with himself, who was prepared to ignore the abuse that came the vicar's way, and become a real personal friend. 'Not my curate, my brother,' – was how he liked to speak of them.[33] When Lord Nelson, at just about the same time, was summing up his indebtedness to his fellow-officers it might have been Charles Simeon himself enthusing about his colleagues: 'Such a gallant set of fellows! Such a band of brothers! My heart swells at the thought of them.' He achieved this happy relationship with almost all of his appointments, and was able to tell his students from his own experience 'to bear in mind how much the comfort of a minister depends upon the good conduct of his curate'. He was, as can be imagined, a demanding man to work for, but he never asked of them more than they were capable of. Indeed, he was ready to reprove any incumbent if he thought he was being too hard on one of the young men he sent him. He warns Samuel Carr of St Peter's, Colchester, a man in whom he had great faith, 'It will be well for you to consider whether you do not require too much of your curates. You may easily get a bad name in this and reduce yourself to great difficulties.'[34]

There was a time in 1812 when Simeon seriously wondered whether he and a new curate would quite hit it off. He shared his anxiety with Thomas Thomason with whom such problems had never arisen. Looking within himself for the cause of the strained relations he wrote 'I should be sorry indeed if after moving in such sweet harmony and love with you and dear Mr Martyn, I had undergone such a change as to render it difficult to move in concert with me . . . I know how blind we are to our own failings and how partial a monitor conscience is.' But the problem in this case really lay in the young man's tendency to depression and melancholy, and eventually he had to give up. Simeon cannot have been an easy person to work with. One might either be smothered by his demonstrative affection or kept at a distance by his awkward manner. But those who got close enough to him to appreciate and love the real

Christian that existed within the unusual exterior, found his friendship the inspiration of their lives.

They particularly valued the Sunday evenings when they all had supper together in King's, talked over the day's activities, and ended by praying for one another. It was on one such occasion that Simeon is remembered as saying 'I am an eight-day clock. Now I am wound up for another week.'[35] His younger friends were often amazed at his constant energy. They would remember their own student days when they used to stimulate each other in small groups such as the one Charles Jerram wrote about: 'Now and then when we could do it without the risk of drawing upon us invidious notice, we heightened our social pleasures by singing our favourite psalms and hymns. Mr Thomason was but a bad singer, but delighted exceedingly in the performance.'[36] This was the gentleman that Charles Simeon, who was totally indifferent to people's musical talent, chose as his first curate. He stayed no less than twelve years before embarking on a remarkable career in India. We know a good deal about him because most of Simeon's recorded correspondence was addressed to him, and also because his biographer was John Sargent, who, as we have seen, made up for disturbing one of Simeon's services by becoming converted and going on to write Henry Martyn's memoirs as well as those of Thomason.

Housing and income for the new curate and his wife were provided by Simeon making himself responsible for the curacy of Stapleford, a village a sharp half-hour's canter from Cambridge. There went with it a charming residence in Little Shelford nearby with the river Granta flowing along the bottom of the garden, the Manor House. Here the Thomasons set aside a prophet's chamber opening on to a walled garden where their honoured friend loved to come and meditate undisturbed. He would frequently spend a few days in their home enjoying the domestic change from the monastic unsociableness of the dons at King's, and in the long vacations he would live with them for two or three months on end. He used to comment how, on his coach journeys from London, after the beauties of Hertfordshire, the landscape around Royston was too dull for words, but when Shelford came in sight he was more than ready to agree with Thomason's verdict that it was indeed 'the garden of Cambridgeshire'. It was in these blissful surroundings that the warm affection of Simeon towards Thomas and his wife developed. 'His friendship I must name amongst my chief blessings,' Thomas wrote to his mother who herself became very closely attached to Simeon in later years. 'He is more and more dear to us, as indeed he ought to be; his kindness to us is wonderful. It quite overpowers me when I think of it.'[37] Simeon in a similar vein enthused about this 'friend with whom I live in daily habits of communion, the friend that is as my own soul'.

At first most of Thomason's time was devoted to the church at Stapleford though on occasion he also took services in Holy Trinity. Simeon used often to go visiting the cottages with him and while doing so discovered how extremely poor most of the villagers were. Finding so many of them unable to obtain employment, and being just as concerned for their physical welfare as for their souls, he established at his own expense a small factory for the plaiting of straw. This became quite successful and was stated to be still going strong several years after Simeon's death. When in 1808 Simeon's health broke down and he had to spend some eight months recuperating in the Isle of Wight, it fell to Thomason to step into the gap and preach as many as five times on a Sunday in Trinity church and Stapleford. He surprised himself and everyone else by developing a preaching ability almost equal to his vicar's, at which Simeon, totally free from any suggestion of professional jealousy, greatly rejoiced. He quoted the scripture, 'He must increase; I must decrease,' and told a friend 'Now I see *why* I have been laid aside. I bless God for it.'

No one, as we shall see later, could be in the company of Simeon long without having his attention drawn to India. Thomason was no exception. The time came when the call from that country broke up the close partnership between these two men of God that had been nurtured at King's, Holy Trinity and Little Shelford. Looking out on the fashion of ambitious and worldly-minded men to make a quick fortune in the service of the East India Company, Thomason said, 'I consider that what others expose themselves to for lucre and worldly honours, ministers ought to endure for nobler ends.' So, following the example of David Brown and Henry Martyn who got there before him, he offered for service as chaplain in John Company and was accepted. When he came to sail, there was his fifty-year-old vicar, after a long coach trip from Cambridge via London, ready to see them off from the Isle of Wight. He even travelled with them on board as far as he could before catching the pilot boat back. They held a moving prayer meeting in their cabin, and Simeon continued with his prayers for them till the boat was out of sight some fifteen miles away. It was with a sad heart that he went to communion the next day where he told Thomas in the first of a quantity of affectionate letters, 'I had about half an hour to remember you and your children.'

His prayers were not misplaced for the journey to India took them five months ending in the early hours of November 7th 1808 with a spectacular shipwreck within sight of Calcutta. All was well in the end but the young couple lost everything they possessed. Charles Simeon was never given to weakening anyone with soft sympathy. When he heard the news he was greatly concerned, but mostly as to whether or not it had weakened Thomason's resolve. It had not. They were men of like mind. In one of his many letters home from on board ship Thomason describes the effect on them both of unpacking a picture of their loved friend, displaying that facility for tears which marked devout souls in those days, including Simeon himself. 'We have looked and wept', he wrote, 'wept and looked. These are not tears of worldly sorrow but spiritual joy; we weep for more of his spirit. We thank God for the love and union that subsists between us which we humbly hope will keep us one for ever and ever.'[38] They did indeed keep in touch with each other throughout Thomason's twenty years service in India. In Simeon's memory he was always one, as he told one of his classes, whose 'brokenness of spirit and lowliness before God, and humility before men,' marked him out as different from so many young and zealous Christians. 'I lived two years with Mr Thomason,' he reminded them one evening, 'and never saw one cross look or word or altered countenance, towards wife, child or servant. The test of a man's religion is not what he is abroad, but what he is at home.'

In all fairness to the many other good and faithful Christian men who worked with Simeon over the years, the roll of honour should be completed but space does not allow it. Henry Martyn is rather special and will appear in a later chapter. But there are other curates and close friends without whose glimpses of Charles Simeon his portrait cannot take proper shape. One of these was the brilliant young poet Henry Kirke White, much admired by Byron and Robert Southey who edited his works. The son of a poor butcher he was only enabled to get a place at Cambridge through Simeon's personal generosity. He had first begun to think seriously after reading Thomas Scott's *Force of Truth*, a book of great influence in the early days of evangelical awakening in the Church of England. He was thus very ready to sit at Simeon's feet where he drank in the teaching which he hoped would set him on his way to ordination. He is best known today as the author of the hymn, 'Oft in danger, oft in woe', a composition which has suffered at the hands of editors some of whom preferred the present opening line to the poet's own 'Much in sorrow, oft in woe'. After winning the highest honours in his year at St John's, Kirke White died of consumption after only one year at college. Byron affectionately remembered him, if not as a Christian, at least as a promising poet:

> Unhappy White! while life was in its spring,
> And thy young muse just waved her joyous wing,
> The spoiler swept that soaring lyre away,
> Which else had sounded an immortal lay.
> Oh! what a noble heart was here undone,
> When Science' self destroy'd her favourite son!

Rather similarly, Thomas Sowerby, who succeeded Henry Martyn as second curate with Thomason in 1805, was only destined to live a few years. He was Senior Wrangler and Tutor of Trinity and later of Queens' College, who right up to the time of taking his degree was violently opposed to Simeon and all that he stood for. But one day he ventured to visit Holy Trinity church out of sheer curiosity. The sermon so struck him that he felt he must there and then discuss it with someone. Finding a Christian friend willing to talk, they paced the college court together oblivious of the time and thereby missed hall and all chance of supper. The involuntary fast did them no harm, and after continuing the discussion over the next few days, Sowerby's doubts gradually dispersed until during a long vacation holiday in Cumberland the light finally dawned on his soul. It was not long before he found himself enrolled as an assistant in the very church which he had so despised throughout his undergraduate days. In this happiest possible way he spent the last three years of his life.

Sowerby was followed by Matthew Preston who with his wife, so Simeon reassured Thomason, 'are holy and happy and exemplary, and a great joy to all around them'. They also lived at Little Shelford and carried on Thomason's good work. In addition to his pastoral duties Preston ran a little school for twelve boys one of whom was his most promising pupil of all, Thomas Babington Macaulay, who went there in 1813. The next year Preston and his wife moved the school to 'a most noble house' near Buntingford with "such magnificent rooms I have rarely seen,' all carpeted. This was the school which so impressed Simeon that he chose it for his godson from India, Thomason's son James. He knew he would then be in good hands even if, with a room all to himself, he was not in danger of being spoilt. In May 1807 whem Simeon was having a rest in the home of a friend, William Marsh, he commented on how well Matthew Preston was doing in his absence: 'The Lord deals with me in the greatest mercy. He has been doing some little good by me;

now he has laid me by . . . My curate, who took an under part when I was in health, is now exceedingly growing in grace and is wonderfully acceptable to my dear people. I am not wanted at all . . .'[39] His curates must have loved to know how much their work was valued by their vicar.

Patrick Brontë was another who became an enlightened and convinced Christian under Simeon's ministry. In September 1802, with £7 saved up from his very short teaching career, this twenty-five year old farm-hand's son from Ulster entered St John's College as a sizar. Henry Martyn took him under his wing and wrote to William Wilberforce asking him for some financial help towards his expenses: 'There is reason to hope that he will be an instrument of good in the church, as a desire of usefulness in the ministry seems to have influenced him hitherto in no small degree.' Wilberforce responded, and in April 1806 the future father of three illustrious daughters took his degree, owing a great deal to the example of Charles Simeon who would, however, have strongly disapproved of his somewhat free and easy way with sermons. But clear traces of Simeon influence can be seen in Patrick Brontë's statement in his novelette *The Maid of Killarney*: 'I do believe that no preaching is good or calculated to profit except that which is truly apostolical . . . Let the minister hold up Christ and he will draw all men after him. Let him preach the doctrines of the gospel faithfully and plainly, and his church will be crowded.'[40] This certainly became true of Holy Trinity, Cambridge and also of Haworth. The unfairly maligned rector was in fact a worthy son of Simeon, and his daughters owed a great deal indirectly to the ideals of Christian family life and worship which were so faithfully being taught to young ordinands like Patrick Brontë.

Thinking of such men as these it really is remarkable how eminent many of the undergraduates who worshipped at Holy Trinity in Simeon's time later became. Samuel Lee is a case in point. Son of poor parents from a small Shropshire village, he became 'one of the greatest linguists of the nineteenth century.'[41] He taught himself Latin, Greek and Hebrew before going up to Queens' in 1814, and then went on to acquire Malay (during a two-month holiday), Chaldee, Syriac, Samaritan, Persian, Arabic, Ethiopic and Hindustani. Not surprisingly he ended up as the University Professor of Arabic and then of Hebrew. He co-operated with Henry Martyn in translation work, and with it all remained throughout his life a simple Christian believer whose memory was treasured because of 'the faithfulness with which he adhered to "the truth as it is in Jesus".'[42]

Charles Perry was another intellectual who, like Thomas Sowerby, completely changed his attitude after attending Holy Trinity, which he did for a while incognito. He was distinguished as having been a foundation member of Trinity Boat Club and a member of the first eight-oared boat that the college put on the river. He obtained a first-class degree in classics, became Senior Wrangler and Fellow of his college, and then vicar of the new church of St Paul's, Cambridge, for the building of which he himself had found the funds. In 1847 he was made first Bishop of Melbourne, a diocese which at that time boasted just three clergy and one church building.[43]

Two other eminent colleagues of Simeon's, one of his mature years and the other of his old age, complete our roll-call. James Scholefield joined Simeon when Preston left in 1813 and stayed with him ten years. In fact he remained in Cambridge all his life combining the post of Regius Professor of Greek with being vicar of St Michael's church until his death thirty years later. As an undergraduate Scholefield had occasionally attended Holy Trinity, always looking left and right before entering the gate in case any of his friends should see him. Simeon testified that while he was on his staff he was 'most laborious and wholly given up to his work . . . a man of great talent.' The work was indeed pretty hard as the vicar was away sick sometimes for months on end, and his curate then had three services on Sunday and one on Thursday to cope with in addition to his own work. But when Simeon was fit, Scholefield found it somewhat frustrating that he was so reluctant to share the pulpit. One memorable occasion when he was actually allowed to preach his aged father was present and electrified the congregation by following his son up the pulpit steps, ear-trumpet in hand, and leaning on the pulpit door so as not to miss a word of James' sermon.[44]

On the whole these two worked well together though it was not unknown for the future professor of Greek to find his vicar's exegesis faulty. 'I wish that dear man would not attempt to improve our translation, for he has made a sad blunder today,' he was once heard to say to a pupil. However, these things did not worry him very much for his hands were full with visiting, taking in pupils, and arranging for a weekly 'lecture' at the Old Workhouse in King Street on Friday evenings. This gave a chance to the aged and infirm who could not get out to church to have a service of their own to go to. There were many too poor, who could not afford churchgoing clothes, but who found in this highly intelligent curate a man who did not grudge time spent with the underprivileged. It was this Professor Scholefield who was invited to preach Simeon's obituary sermon in Great St Mary's. In it he commented upon the remarkable revival of spiritual enthusiasm of the right sort that had taken place during his long ministry. 'Being deeply convinced that our church is more in danger from the want than the excess of it, I joyfully and thankfully hail the symptoms of its increase among the clergy.'

Simeon's last curate, who eventually edited his memoirs, was William Carus. He went up to Trinity in 1821, got his Fellowship in 1829, became Dean from 1832 and at the time of Simeon's death in 1836 held the lectureship of Holy Trinity. In a letter to his friend Samuel Carr, Simeon once more has compliments to shower upon one of his colleagues. He was particularly glad that, while he himself was unavoidably absent for a while, the rebuilding of the east end of the church was in Carus' capable hands. 'To tell you all that is going forward here through the instrumentality of Mr Carus would be almost impossible . . . What a joy it is to me to see it before I go to a better world!'[45] As we have seen more than once, his ready appreciation of the good work of his colleagues was one of Charles Simeon's most endearing features. His joy knew no bounds when he heard on his death-bed that the bishop had agreed to William Carus succeeding him as incumbent. He did indeed carry on where Simeon finished at Trinity church, and in addition had responsibility for the university church of Great St Mary's settled upon him. Evangelicalism was by then deeply entrenched at the heart of Cambridge.

CHAPTER EIGHT

Reaching Beyond Cambridge

It was quite impossible for a character as ebullient as Charles Simeon to be confined to the important but limited sphere represented by his parish and his college. Out of the power-house of his rooms in King's the influence of his enthusiasm in the cause of vital Christianity spread far and wide. He had still eight years of reasonably active life left to him when, in 1828, John Keble on a visit to the south-west with his future wife and mother-in-law commented on 'The amazing rate at which Puritanism seems to be getting on all over the kingdom,' referring, so his biographer rather grudgingly says, to 'The party in the church which was then fighting its way upwards to what I suppose it must be admitted that it has now attained, a more than equal share in numbers and influence.'[1] The Oxford Movement, which had not yet got going, was of course far more than merely a reaction to the successful advance of evangelical religion. But the element of spiritual rivalry cannot be entirely eliminated from the story of the post-Simeon era. He himself would have been pained to know that the spread of that movement had called out invectives amongst his successors such as Francis Close of Cheltenham who wrote the Tractarians off with some scorn as 'Idle men who had nothing to do but deluge the country with their opinions.'

The rampant 'Puritanism' which so worried Keble was in fact very largely the overflow from Charles Simeon's fifty-year spell in Cambridge, though Puritanism was as unfair a description of Simeon's outlook as 'Romaniser' was of Keble's. Simeon's teaching was positive, gracious and utterly sincere. And it met the needs of the church of the day to an extent that was not so true of the movement that emanated from the sister university, for it appealed to the man in the pew, and it provided for needy congregations a ministry which understood their longing to be taught the gospel and urged to respond to it. It was in this way that

Simeon's reach was so far extended throughout the land that Lord Macaulay, looking back on his Cambridge days in the twenties and commenting on Sir James Stephen's essay on the Clapham Sect, was able to write to one of his sisters in 1844: 'As to Simeon, if you knew what his authority and influence were, and how they extended from Cambridge to the most remote corners of England, you would allow that his real sway in the church was far greater than that of any primate.'[2]

Simeon himself had urged his congregation to pray that, like Elisha pouring salt into the stagnant waters, God would grant that the fountain where his ministry was centred, 'from whence so many streams are issuing, being rendered salubrious may fertilise this whole land, and be the means of diffusing life and salvation to the remotest corners of the globe.'[3] Great minds thinking alike, Thomas Chalmers of Glasgow, who first came across Simeon in 1815 ('one of the most remarkable men I have met'), and whose district visiting scheme established in 1820 showed many signs of having been copied from Simeon's,[4] wrote to him at Cambridge commending a young student to his care. In his letter his thoughts also ran to the prophet Elisha: 'It is my earnest prayer . . . that salt through your means may long continue to be thrown into such a copious and emanating fountain as your university, and that days of glory and of holiness may speedily come upon the Church of England.'[5]

The prayers of Scottish divine and Trinity church people were abundantly answered as we shall see. The indefatigable Old Apostle when not composing or delivering sermons, or lecturing to and advising young ordinands, or ministering to the needs of his parishioners, organised and attended endless meetings, addressing most of them, supported societies of many kinds, wrote a phenomenal number of letters, and travelled frequently to London and the south, twice toured Scotland, paid Ireland a visit, and went to the continent several times. The record leaves one almost breathless. His restless efforts to buy up every opportunity that came his way to share his concern for souls, for the church, and, as we shall see later, for the spread of God's kingdom overseas, absorbed most of his energies as he became better known in the Christian scene, and hardly diminished at all with advancing years. In a day when travel was slow, hazardous, and exhausting, when letters had to be written by hand and often by candlelight, and meetings dragged on for hour after hour, it is quite remarkable how Simeon's constitution stood up to the strain. But by the grace of God, as he would be the first to admit, Simeon was able to write only two months before he died, in his usual humble and grateful manner, to Daniel Wilson, Bishop of Calcutta, 'that God can and does work by the meanest instruments, I am a living witness; but my sphere has been small, a mere nothing in the comparison of others. Yet I have lived to see the triumph of my own principles throughout the land.'

Amongst the more novel aspects of Christian experience which in due course Simeon was able to export from Cambridge to churches far and near was the fellowship in Christ which like-minded and thoroughly converted men and women could share. The church at large knew nothing of it. Attendance at cold and unfeeling services in church was so far removed from real Christian fellowship that the term 'novel', at least as far as the Church of England was concerned, is a fair one. John Wesley had encouraged such fellowship with his class meetings but though he himself remained within the national church all his life, he was never personally able to get anything of this sort established within its framework. But to Charles Simeon it was so valuable a part of his own experience that he was determined to devise ways and means of making sure that his evangelical colleagues could benefit from it. His first step in 1796 was to arrange annual summer house-parties for clergy and their wives. Some twenty or thirty would come together for two days at a time and meet in a suitably large house such as the Thomasons' Manor House in Shelford, where the garden and river were an added attraction, or, as later, in Matthew Preston's prestigious school building, Aspenden Hall in Hertfordshire.

The mornings were spent in conference, Simeon presiding, when their discussions would centre as often as not round the study of *A System of Revealed Religion* by John Warden. This substantial tome of seven hundred pages, first published in 1769, consisted of a collection of texts and short passages of Scripture, almost without comment, systematically arranged by subjects to cover the Nature of God, the Nature of Man, the Redeeming Love of God, the Person of Jesus Christ and of the Holy Spirit, Christian Duties and Virtues, the Nature of the Church and so on. It thus provided a good concentrated post-breakfast meal for the hungry minds of those earnest but isolated evangelical clergy who attended. Evangelicals, as we have seen, had the greatest difficulty in getting a parish. When they did it was as likely as not to be somewhere like Creaton, the hamlet of forty-six cottages in Northamptonshire where Thomas Jones carried on such a remarkable ministry for forty-three years,[6] or Long Stanton near Cambridge, the scene of William Cecil's fifty-nine faithful years as rector. In many such places there might be hardly a single other Christian man of the social and academic standard of the minister, and so they were often starved of solid Bible study such as Simeon provided for them at these house-parties.

The ladies were also catered for. They joined their menfolk for meals, but had their own morning session together, upon which it would have been entertaining to eavesdrop. One cannot help wondering what it was like to be married to one of these potent evangelical clergymen, however saintly. Simeon was well ahead of his time in his great regard for clergy wives whom he would refer to playfully as 'Ministresses, half-Ministers, often the most important half in your husband's parishes.' He encouraged them to enter fully into the proceedings and to take an active part in the more informal mixed gathering in the evenings. Clergy and their wives were thus enabled to pick each other's brains and share each other's experiences. Charles Simeon seldom enjoyed himself more than on these occasions though he expressed it to a friend in terms which seem today to suggest a more rarefied spiritual atmosphere than probably was the case: they were 'precious times', full of 'solemnity, tenderness, spirituality and love'. His comments on the fellowship they all enjoyed together sound quaint to modern ears, but those who have attended such house-parties themselves, though they would express it so differently, will know what he meant when he said 'O for more of that divine composure, that tender love, that heavenly ardour which animated the whole company! Less mixture of the animal I never expect to see in this world. Humility, meekness, gentleness, love, stillness, the full eye, the tender look, the slow unimposing voice . . .'

Simeon's house-parties were unique in including the womenfolk. He also took a full part in the more exclusively clerical societies which such men as Samuel Walker of Truro, Henry Venn when he was at Huddersfield, and his son John at Little Dunham in Norfolk had organised. Other similar clerical gatherings were held at Creaton, at Rauceby in Lincolnshire and at Hotham in Yorkshire. At the inauguration of all of these bodies the records tell us Charles Simeon's name appears.[7] Of the members of a society formed in 1816 at Matlock Bath to cover the north Midlands, most of those who attended were Simeon's men from Cambridge days.[8] He fully realised how much such clergy hungered for each other's company and fellowship. Many of them remembered nostalgically their university experiences when, for example, Thomas Thomason and Charles Jerram in Magdalene used to rise at five in the morning to have their quiet times with God together.[9] So these occasional gatherings with their fellow evangelicals from as far as thirty or forty miles around were a spiritual bonanza not to be missed.

The most interesting and influential of all these bodies was the Eclectic

Society. It was founded in 1783 by John Newton when he was rector of St Mary Woolnoth in the city of London. At first it limited its membership to thirteen who had to be evangelical clergy or laity working in the metropolis. In 1798 it extended its bounds to include thirteen country members in addition, and Charles Simeon, as one might expect, was one of the first of these to enrol. They began by meeting in a tavern in Aldersgate Street, the 'Castle and Falcon', but a few years later moved to the vestry of St John's, Bedford Row, where Richard Cecil was the minister. They met once a month, absentee members being fined two shillings and sixpence. Tea was served to them during the proceedings from a silver tea pot which is still in the possession of the Church Missionary Society which, as we shall see, sprang from one of these meetings. The matters which the Eclectic Society dealt with covered ground which many of the more extreme evangelicals would hesitate to embark upon such as the implications of the French Revolution, the attitude of members to war, the Slave Trade, Roman Catholic Emancipation, and other social and political themes.[10]

Simeon himself seems to have taken no part in discussions when such subjects as these were on the agenda. He was not really at ease unless the theme was clearly related to the exposition of Scripture or the spread of the gospel. But between 1798 and 1811 he made a ready contribution on thirteen occasions, and some of these are worth noting for the light they throw on his personal religious views. In studying the book of Job, for instance, he maintained interestingly that 'This book is a poem. Part of it may be allegorical, as Satan's appearance before God,' a point which was objected to by the more conservative Richard Cecil. In a discussion on defects of character, Simeon bared his soul to his colleagues by mentioning how Miles Atkinson, renowned evangelical vicar of Leeds, had advised him in trying to overcome his temperamental weaknesses to 'lean on the side opposite to your constitutional bias.' During a session on special temptations of ministers he was more than ready to take part, making mention of the sins of neglecting one's children or servants, or failing the laity by not 'endeavouring to bring into action the faculties of our people.' He reminded them that there was always the danger 'while cultivating the vineyard of the Lord, of not sufficiently attending to our own vineyard.'[11]

Charles Simeon never minded differing from other evangelical clergy so long as he was convinced that his view derived from a fair and open reading of the Bible. Nor did he ever try to hide from his brothers his own weaknesses, nor yield to the temptation to present himself as the perfect parish parson, though there were times when, flattered perhaps by the rapt attention given to him by the young men of Cambridge, he gave the impression that he thought he had all, or at least most, of the answers. Certainly he had a great many, and people were always wanting to hear them. He spent hours of his time carefully and prayerfully composing letters which conveyed the benefits of his clear, original and profound approach in the application of Biblical principles to the personal affairs of those who wrote to him from near and far for advice and guidance. Simeon is portrayed in Jackson's portrait as seated with quill in hand beside his candle and inkstand, an outline of his beloved Trinity church in the background, showing a kindly smile on his face. It is as if, before writing a word, he was trying to conjure up in his mind the image of the one he was about to write to, and thus greet him or her as if there in person. His last curate, William Carus, remembered how he would sit in his drawing room facing the west windows that overlooked the lawn below, on a leather sofa writing on his knee with his legs crossed.[12]

The sheer quantity of Simeon's letters is borne out by the fact that on his own confession by 1829 he had copies of no less than seven thousand filed away on his sideboard. He says that for nearly fifty years he had been in the habit of keeping duplicates of his more important letters, which suggests that he wrote not less than three of these a week, many of them running to half a dozen quarto pages, quite apart from those that required no copy retained. A modern letter-writer would quail at the thought of such a task over so long a period without the aid of secretary, typewriter or carbon paper. But in the early nineteenth century letter-writing was not considered a tedious burden. It was indeed at best something of an art, and at worst a form of occupational therapy for the leisured classes for whom the world provided few ideas for the spending of time apart from gaming, theatricals and somewhat boisterous sports. Jane Austen, in her last and unfinished novel *Sanditon*, describes how girls set aside a portion of each day simply for letter-writing. Fanny Burney, Horace Walpole, the Wordsworths, William Cowper, Lord Chesterfield, Lord Byron and many others were at this time raising correspondence to the level of true literature for which historians and students of the English language will ever be grateful.

In Charles Simeon's day letters to and from London were reasonably prompt. In 1796 the mail coach from Cambridge, 'The Fly', left the 'Rose' in the market place daily at seven in the morning, offering four passengers seats at eighteen shillings a head, and travelling via Epping arrived all being well at the 'George' in Holborn about five o'clock in the evening. Local letters being conveyed 'post haste', which meant at walking pace on horse-back, were less regular being very dependent on road and weather conditions. It was when letters were sent to and from correspondents overseas that the slowness of the mails became a cause of frequent anxiety. Henry Martyn in India suffered agonies of apprehension over the letters to his ill-fated but adored Lydia which so often crossed with those of hers to him. News of Martyn's death which took place on October 16th, 1812 did not reach Simeon until February 12th the next year.

With all the delays and uncertainties of travel in the eighteenth and early nineteenth centuries, it is not surprising that the careful Simeon kept copies of so many of his letters. But he did it not only as a safeguard against loss or delay, but also to avoid the dangers of misunderstandings from which he had suffered so much in his younger days, and was never really free. In his position of religious leadership he was a marked man, and as he never hesitated to express his views forcibly there were many only too ready to twist his meaning and distort his opinions. He could not care less about his own reputation, but was determined at all costs to defend the truth of the gospel. 'It may be that in many things I have acted unwisely, but I hope no man shall ever have it in his power to say that I have acted wickedly,' was as far as he was prepared to go in self-defence. But for the sake of God's truth, so that no one should be able to trip him up by accusing him falsely, he was careful to keep duplicates of much of his voluminous correspondence. But how did he do it? For the first twenty or thirty years of his active ministry it appears that if he wanted a copy of any letter it had to be done by hand. But in November 1811 he wrote with great delight to Thomas Thomason to tell him that his mother, Mrs Dornford, had given him a present of a 'copying-machine' by which 'I am enabled to write two letters at once.' If this was the newly invented Hawkins' patent 'polygraph', a most complicated machine, it would be interesting to know for how long Charles had the patience to manipulate it.[13] He was fond of new things, and a gadget of this sort clearly appealed to him at first but it must have been something of an obtrusion on his normal writing methods.

Although he wrote so many letters Simeon was very well aware how much better it was, if possible, to talk rather than write, especially when a 'delicate or much-controverted point' arose. With his usual sensitivity to the feelings of others, he said 'If I *speak* with a man, I can stop when I see it is doing harm; I can soften off the truth so as not to fly in the face of his cherished views ... Written words convey ideas, convey sentiments, but they cannot really convey exact feelings.' Simeon was a thinker who also 'felt' a great deal. He wrote when there was no other way of communicating with a person, but realised all the time the many limitations of letters, particularly in expressing emotions: 'You cannot *hesitate* upon paper; you cannot *weep* upon paper; you cannot give upon paper the tone of love; you cannot *look* kindness upon paper,' though he tried his hardest to do so. At any rate, the difficulties and drawbacks in communication in those days do not seem to have deterred him from putting his pen to paper almost every day.

When one comes to study those many letters from Simeon which have survived and been treasured for a century and a half, there are certain things we need to bear in mind. For one thing, verbosity was very much the order of the day. As everyone tended to be long-winded nobody in the least minded a writer taking his time to reach the point. The holy terminology in which it was all wrapped up, which strikes a modern reader as sanctimonious, did not appear so to the recipients for the ordinary conversation of believers was heavily larded with what later was to become an evangelical jargon. However, Simeon's letters, laborious though they often were, were markedly free from pious clichés. He hated any kind of sham, and particularly disliked pious writing:

> As for sitting down to write a religious letter, it is what I cannot do myself; and what I do not very much admire, unless there be some particular occasion that calls for it. I love rather that a letter be a free and easy communication of such things as are upon the mind, and such as we imagine will interest the person with whom we correspond ... Doubtless when the mind can soar, and we can dip our pen in angel's ink, it is most delightful to prosecute the heavenly theme: but to sit down in cold blood and say, I must now write a religious letter, is to me an irksome task; or rather, a task which I leave to those who have talents for it. In a word, religious communications are then most delightful when they proceed from the abundance of the heart; but all the sweetness of them is taken away when they are constrained and formal.

Fortunately for the hundreds of believers and others who received letters from Simeon, his heart was more or less permanently 'abundant'. He proved himself a spiritual director with a deep pastoral sense and, for his time, an advanced understanding of the interplay of mind, conscience and temperament. This is particularly evident in the considerable correspondence he had with the first Earl of Harrowby about his son, Granville, who went up to Cambridge in 1823. Lord Harrowby was very worried about him because he was suffering from religious depression, morbid spells of self-denigration, and exaggerated guilt-feelings. It will help us to appreciate the depth of Simeon's insight of such cases if we bear in mind the background relationship of father and son. Lord Harrowby was a very able and very eminent politician rising to become Lord President of the Council from 1812 to 1827. A liberal-hearted evangelical, subscriber to twenty-five societies and good causes,[14] who supported Wilberforce over the slave trade and voted in favour of repealing the discriminatory Test and Corporation acts, he was acknowledged by all as a man of integrity. But with it Lord Grey regarded him as a bore, pretentious and 'snappish'. Charles Greville, a fairer judge of character and free from all malice, while admiring him for his many virtues, said he was at the same time 'peevish, ungracious and unpopular.' After eulogising his friend Lady Harrowby whom he greatly admired, and giving the Earl credit for his freedom from selfishness and ambition, he had to go on 'Lord Harrowby has all the requisites of disagreeableness, a tart, short, provoking manner, with manners at once pert and rigid', all of which 'prevented his being agreeable in society.'[15] In fact, he was a man who shone more in public life than in private, not an easy father for a son to approach or to please.

Our sympathies go out to the youth, the second son of the family easily overshadowed by his brilliant elder brother who got a double first at Oxford and of course was destined to inherit the Earldom. Granville, on the other hand, had been put into the Navy at the age of fourteen coming out as a midshipman nine years later. He then went up to Cambridge armed, no doubt, with a pretty formidable sense of inferiority. He took refuge in religion and plunged himself into the life of Holy Trinity church where there was much to encourage his feelings of guilt. Subconsciously he seems to have succeeded in getting his father's attention, which he had previously lacked, by wallowing in a trough of self-accusation which was far from healthy. It is at this point that we find Charles Simeon called in to help. If his attitude to this unfortunate young man is typical of how he dealt with others tempted to depression, it is no wonder that he gained the reputation that he did for being a pastoral director of remarkable empathy and understanding.

Simeon's first letter, a long one, was written on February 1823 to tell Lord Harrowby that he had just had an hour's conversation with his son and thought he was improving even though 'he does indeed take the same line of self-condemnation as before.' Realising that most of his friends had probably told young Granville to 'cheer up' and 'pull himself together', or the nineteenth century equivalent of such advice, he countered this by accepting the young undergraduate's estimate of himself as a miserable sinner instead of telling him that he was exaggerating. He thus took the wind out of his sails and effectively prevented him from indulging any further in the luxury of thinking himself too specially bad to be forgiven. This is how, as Simeon explained to Lord Harrowby, he was setting about the first stage of his son's mental and spiritual restoration:

> You see yourself guilty of sins which preclude a hope of forgiveness. Your friends have endeavoured to shew you that you judge yourself too hardly. In this they have erred for, if they have succeeded, they have given you a peace founded on your own worthiness, a peace that would last no longer than till the next temptation arose in your mind... if they have not succeeded, they have only confirmed you in your views. I say to you the very reverse. Your views of yourself (your own sinfulness) though they may be erroneous, are not one atom too strong. Your sinfulness far exceeds all that you have stated, or have any conception of. 'Your heart is deceitful above all things and desperately wicked: who can know it?' But I have an effectual remedy for them all – 'The blood of Jesus Christ cleanseth from *all* sin.' I grant that you are lost and utterly undone. So are all mankind – some for gross sins – some for impenitence – some for other sins. You are lost for the very sins you mention, hardness of heart, indifference etc...
>
> Do this then, take a book as large as any that is in the Bank of England. Put down all the sins of which either conscience or a morbid imagination can accuse you. Fear not to add to their number all that Satan himself can suggest.
>
> And this I will do. I will put on the creditor side 'the unsearchable riches of Christ' and will leave you to draw the balance...[16]

Simeon then told the father, when he saw his son next, not to be surprised if the very fact of their meeting again stirs the young man up. He would probably be unwilling to climb down and acknowledge that he no longer held the views about his sinfulness which he had previously made such a song about. Moreover, Simeon was fearful lest Granville's worldly friends should once again take so different an attitude from his own, and urged Lord Harrowby to invite a Christian friend to stay with them as company for his son. A week later he wrote again, having some misgivings in case Granville either turned against him on account of the line he had taken, or quoted him 'as an oracle' without personally accepting his advice.[17] However, the crisis passed though the young man's 'tender conscience' continued to trouble him.

Simeon very much hesitated to advise a father of such distinction about what attitude to adopt towards his own son, and feared lest he be guilty of coming between them. So in June of that year he wrote to Granville's aunt, the Duchess of Beaufort, whom he knew well, asking if she would tactfully approach Lord Harrowby as she could do it more appropriately than he. He hoped that she would drop a hint to his Lordship about taking no notice of his son's self-denigration and not try to correct it each time it was expressed, for it was but a symptom and not a cause of his trouble. He particularly wanted him to avoid getting involved in discussions which would only disturb Granville more. Perhaps the Duchess would also suggest to father that his son be given freedom in the matter of what amusements he should or should not indulge in, and be encouraged to fraternise much more than at present with like-minded Christian friends. 'The whole matter,' he wrote, 'in my judgment turns on the condescension that may be shown to the morbid feelings of his son.'[18] He then brought the correspondence to a close by writing direct to Lord Harrowby who, like many a father anxious to see quick improvement, was liable to be impatient. He reminds him that whatever happens, his son's heart was in the right place: 'If your Lordship's son, through the depression of his animal spirits, should not set off the beauties of religion as we could wish, I feel no doubt but that, in the sight of the Omniscient Judge he is in a state highly to be envied: his heart is upright; his conscience tender; his spirit humble; his conduct uniform and holy.'[19]

We have quoted fairly fully from this correspondence partly because most of it was not included in William Carus' memoir as both parties were still alive at the time of writing. Partly also because of the enormous interest it will be to anyone engaged in counselling a depressed or over scrupulous person of which there are quite as many today as there were in the time of Simeon. It is some proof of the effectiveness of Simeon's therapy that the repressed second son was eventually able to prove himself to his overbearing father and to himself by finding a suitable young lady to marry two years later, Georgiana the daughter of the Duchess of Beaufort, and also by entering politics in 1830, becoming Member of Parliament for Tiverton and later for Hertfordshire.

Simeon's skill and sheer common sense in diagnosing and dealing with cases of depression is shown again in correspondence recorded by his colleague William Carus. In a letter to Thomason about a mutual friend he points out that without seeking for some mysterious or deep-seated inner conflict, there are often cases where a man can become depressed simply through over-work and physical strain, though he does not often recognise it as much. 'From what I have seen in the Christian world,' he writes, 'I should be ready to judge that his morbid state of mind originates in an excess of worldly care. He has felt his spirits oppressed with the business he has undertaken; and having a tender conscience, he has imputed to a want of spiritual life the langour that has proceeded from a defect of animal spirits (a favourite phrase of Simeon's) and of physical strength. This is a process which those who experience it scarcely ever understand; but we who stand by and make our observations in a more dispassionate manner can discern it.' Long before the terms became commonplace psychiatric terminology, Simeon was distinguishing between merely reactive depression, easily accounted for, and the endogenous depression whose cause lies out of immediate reach or recall, and needs more professional attention. We have seen also the deep insight which enabled him to sort out genuine from false guilt feelings in those whom he was counselling.

Simeon told one of his Conversation Parties, 'When persons come to me in deep distress of mind, my first inquiry is as to the state of their bodily health, for I find despondency often proceeding from some physical cause. My next inquiry is whether some social or domestic trial be not preying on their spirits; some unfortunate attachment; some restraint put by parents on their following the pursuits on which their hearts are bent; some unhappiness caused by the conduct of their families or children; some embarrassment in business. These two inquiries dispose of nine-tenths of such applications. Not above a tenth of those who attribute their depressions to religious causes are really under conviction of sin.' He was most anxious that Christian men and women should play their full part in bringing help to people in trouble, and so went out of his way to explain to them something of the workings of a disturbed mind. He often preached on this subject and the following two short extracts show the message he was trying to convey:

> The effect of sympathy is to make the sorrow of another our own; and to produce in our hearts those very feelings of grief and anguish which the afflicted individual himself is called to sustain . . . Be not hasty to offer advice to those who are bowed down with a weight of

trouble. There is a sacredness in grief which demands our reverence; and the very habitation of a mourner must be approached with awe . . .

The composure of the mind, the bringing of it to a state of resignation and submission, and particularly to a state of peace with God, will exceedingly promote the recovery of the body . . . . If the disorder is very intimately connected with the mind, (and how many nervous disorders arise from the pressure of worldly troubles), it is obvious that the spiritual physician may be more useful than a medical attendant.[20]

It takes a great deal of reading between the lines of Simeon's letters and memoirs to discover what books he read other than the Bible, and to trace where some of his ideas came from. We know that he specially valued W. B. Sprague's volume of *Lectures on the Revival of Religion* for he wrote in the copy that the author sent him, 'A most valuable book. I recommend my executor to keep it; as there are few, if any, others in this kingdom. I love the good sense of Dr Sprague.' In the case of his able advice to those suffering from depression and their relatives and friends, there are many echoes from a small booklet by Benjamin Fawcett published in 1780 under the title *Observations on the Nature, Causes and Cure of Melancholy*. Simeon gave a copy of this to his friend Sir John Stirling whose daughter at the time was 'in a very dejected state of mind'.

Drawing heavily on Burton's *Anatomy of Melancholy* and on some of Richard Baxter's sermons on the same subject, it must have been invaluable to Simeon himself. He would learn in its small compass at least three vitally important things: that depression is a disease rather than a state of guilt ('What these sufferers imagine to be their guilt is only their affliction')[21]; that no mere argument can make the slightest difference to a disturbed patient; and that there are times when even religion cannot cure but only help the sufferer to hold on. Fawcett quotes a Doctor Clarke saying 'The principal sign by which we may judge when the indisposition is chiefly or wholly in the body is this: that the person accuses himself highly *in general*, without being able to give any instance *in particular*; that he is very apprehensive of he does not know what; and fearful, yet can give no reason why.' He goes on himself to comment: 'Though his case be the same with many others, yet he is prone to look upon it as singular . . . and to say that no one was ever afflicted as he is. He loves to be alone and is afraid and weary of company . . . His thoughts are most of all about himself in unprofitable or rather mischievous anxiety . . . He is seldom better for any advice.' The author then so wisely tells those who try to help such cases not to make light of the depressive state nor try to cajole the sufferer into laughing it off. He cannot. It is too real. 'Avoid charging them with fancy, imagination or whim, for their disease is real, their misery is great, and a distempered fancy is often very tormenting . . . Let us demonstrate to them that we make their case our own, feel for them, yearn over them and are afflicted in all their afflictions.'[22] This is exactly what we find Charles Simeon doing.

He had clearly studied this modest publication to some purpose. Towards the end of his life he summed up much of his accumulated insight into the workings of the human heart in a particularly helpful letter written to a woman who complained of feeling depressed. He begins by wishing it were possible to speak with her rather than write for 'words on paper are as a painted sun in comparison of words uttered from the inmost soul and breathed out with a divine unction'. He reminds her that depression is quite common and therefore she must not think, as so many do, that no one else has been so low as she feels herself to be. He then says how he longs to be able to get alongside in spirit and feel with her. What better description of our modern term 'empathy' than his words, 'Could our souls be tuned by the same divine hand, I should understand and feel every note you strike'? He goes on to sum up her problem: 'Your case in few words is this: I was once in earnest about my soul: I have since declined: I feel but cold at this moment and unhumbled, whilst confessing what ought to humble me in the dust. What must I do to get myself quickened in the divine life, and stimulated to run the race set before me?'

The 'correct' answers to this, such as more Bible reading, prayer and faith, which she already knows to be of first importance, he freely admits are not, and cannot at present be, making any difference to her. She is too ill. He proceeds from there: 'There are two errors which are common to persons in your state; first, the using of means, as though by the use of them they could prevail; and secondly, the not using them, because they have so long been used in vain. The error consists in putting the means too much in the place of Christ, and in expecting for *exertions* what is only gained by *affiance*,' by which he means a state of simply accepting the situation and trusting God in blind faith whatever the circumstances or feelings. He then takes his patient and urges her to try to sound the depths of our Lord's own sufferings and to assess her real position accordingly. 'There is a passive state of mind – a lying like clay in the hands of the potter – and a casting yourself on the Lord Jesus Christ, content to sink if he will let you sink, and to be marred if he choose to mar you.

This willingness to be saved by him altogether from first to last, and in his own time and way, and this determination to trust him though he slay you, and to praise him though he condemn you, is what you particularly want.' Then, anticipating that his correspondent is also certain to be indulging in a measure of self-pity, he adds, 'There is another thing which I would suggest . . . namely that you are too much occupied in looking at yourself, and too little in beholding the Lord Jesus Christ. It is by the former you are to be *humbled*; but it is by the latter that you are to be *changed into the divine image* . . . You are nothing, and it discourages you; but you must be content to be nothing that Christ may be "all in all".'

A great many of Simeon's letters were naturally addressed to his old boys engaged in the everyday problems of a clergyman. He realised well enough that it was one thing to be a keen member of the fellowship they enjoyed at Holy Trinity, but quite another thing when in the exalted position of sole incumbent or curate a young man finds himself alone and vulnerable. Quite early on in his own ministry he sent this encouraging letter to a young friend who was trying to establish a ministry on spiritual lines in his first parish where previously it had been very different:

> Your difficulties are only such as might be expected at your first coming to a town where you have been so long known. It is natural to suppose that they who remembered you gay would still wish you to participate in their pleasures; nor will their hopes of keeping you in their shackles be diminished by anything you say from the pulpit; they have been so used to see an opposition between the precepts and practices of ministers, that they do not even consider a worldly pleasure-able life as inconsistent with our profession. But blessed be God that you have been enabled in some good measure to withstand their solicitations; your taking of a decided part at first will keep you from a multitude of snares . . . Well, my dear brother, go on; faint not, neither be weary, for in due season thou shalt reap if thou faint not. Christ has promised us grace sufficient for us; let us therefore wait upon Him and we shall renew our strength, and mount up with wings as eagles, we shall run and not be weary, we shall march onward and not faint.

In April 1830 Simeon had cause to write to one of his young friends who was in danger of overdoing things in his zeal for the Lord:

> I am grieved to hear that you are ill. But I am not surprised. I know it

> must be so, if you will not take more care not to exceed your strength. God has given you a zeal for his glory; and to check it would seem on my part a sinful intrusion, & on your part a sinful compliance. You must from experience learn the extent of your physical powers and the measure of exertion which you can bear . . . Nobody *will* speak to you as I do; nobody *can* speak to you as I do; because no one has suffered so much by over exertion, or retained his renewed strength so much by a resolute adherence to self-denying moderation. Greatly as I love you, I have not yet dared to say half that I would say, if I were not afraid lest I might grieve you. You cannot understand me yet awhile: you must have a little more of personal & painful experience: *that* will give both *import* and weight to my admonitions . . . One thing I will venture to say, namely, that it is wise to proceed only at the rate at which you may reasonably hope to continue your labours . . .

Anxious as always to retain his friendships and yet never be guilty of keeping back advice for fear of causing offence, he ends this letter 'When you return, tell me, my beloved Brother, that I have not grieved you; and that you will receive my suggestions with all the love with which they are offered you by Your most tenderly affectionate Father, Brother, Friend, – C. Simeon.'[23]

Simeon could be as outspoken in his letters as in his sermons, and did not hesitate to state his mind if he thought his correspondent was in need of reproof or correction. For example, he wrote quite mercilessly to an undergraduate follower of his who had been guilty of writing flippant remarks in the margin of books in his college library. He told him, in effect, that he had no wish to see him again until he had confessed his misconduct to his tutor and got the matter put right. On another occasion, one of his younger clergy seems to have run into trouble with his bishop in the matter of introducing hymns into his services which so upset the congregation that they complained to his Lordship. The old apostle who had had tricky bishops as well as people to deal with, and had had to learn patience the hard way, advises his zealous young friend to go slow and to take the long view.

> Circumstanced as you are, I feel no hesitation in saying that you should avoid everything that can give offence, except the faithful preaching of 'Christ crucified'. Why should you stand out about the hymns? You are very injudicious in this. You should consider that when a storm is raised you are not the only sufferer. Pray study to

> maintain peace, though you make some sacrifices for it . . . You have evidently some very injudicious advisers about you. Be content to let your conduct be misinterpreted for a season. Be as regular as possible in everything; and in a year or two your enemies will be put to silence.[24]

In a frank letter to an older man Simeon discloses as much of himself as he does of the one to whom he is writing:

> I seem to feel that I can say anything to you without offence and without suspicion: without offence because of the ardent love I bear you; and without suspicion because you well know that I am, and ever have been, as far from a timid, temporising character as a man can be. I have heard with deep concern that, whilst all unite in loving and honouring your general character, a great number of persons are grievously offended with the style of your preaching . . . which I am told is unnecessarily harsh and offensive: and that on this being suggested to you by Mr – you gave him notice to quit the curacy. Will you forgive me, my dear Friend, if I say that in both these respects you have erred. It is not by coarseness of expression or severity of manner that we are to win souls, but by 'speaking the truth in love'.

Suspecting that he was probably too old and set in his ways to change, he then advises him, if he cannot produce the tact and affection which such an important and 'delicate' position demanded, he should resign and seek a less demanding sphere. It was a very real temptation to evangelical preachers in those intense days to overdo their evangelistic approach.

Simeon had always urged moderation on his zealous hearers. 'Young Ministers,' he told one of his groups, 'should inquire, not what can I teach my people, but what can they receive. Jesus did not tell his disciples that which they could not bear, but spake to them as they were able to bear it.' In another letter he was equally candid. His enthusiastic correspondent had been urged by the more fanatical members of his flock to 'preach very strongly.' But it was having disastrous results. 'What is your object?' he asks. 'Is it to win souls? If it be, how are you to set about it? By exciting all manner of prejudices and driving people from the church? How did our Lord act? He spake the word in parable *as men were able to hear it.* How did St Paul act? He fed the babes with milk and not with strong meat.' And so he advised him not to be afraid of 'the religious world' who often could not care less if the ungodly were offended so long as they themselves got their way. Without 'unfeeling harshness, only speak from *love* to man and not from the *fear* of man, and God will both accept and prosper you.'

These few excerpts from Simeon's many letters show him to have been a man of remarkable understanding and a very warm heart. Having himself for so long been the butt of unkind criticism by so-called earnest Christians he was very well aware of how easily religious people can turn censorious. We can end this chapter most happily by hearing him speak over the years to us today as he did in a letter written in July 1817 on how to cope with evil-speaking:

> The longer I live, the more I feel the importance of adhering to the rules which I have laid down for myself in relation to such matters.
> 1st To hear as little as possible what is to the prejudice of others.
> 2nd To believe nothing of the kind till I am absolutely forced to it.
> 3rd Never to drink into the spirit of one who circulates an ill report.
> 4th Always to moderate, as far as I can, the unkindness which is expressed towards others.
> 5th Always to believe, that if the other side were heard, a very different account would be given of the matter.
>
> I consider love as wealth; and as I would resist a man who should come to rob my house, so would I a man who would weaken my regard for any human being. I consider, too, that persons are cast into different moulds; and that to ask myself, what should *I* do in that person's situation, is not a just mode of judging. I must not expect a man that is naturally cold and reserved to act as one that is naturally warm and affectionate; and I think it a great evil that people do not make more allowances for each other in this particular. I think religious people are too little attentive to these considerations; and that it is not in reference to the ungodly world only that that passage is true, 'He that departeth from evil maketh himself a prey'; but even in reference to professors also, amongst whom there is a sad proneness to listen to evil reports, and to believe the representations they hear, without giving the injured person any opportunity of rectifying their views and of defending his own character.
>
> The more prominent any person's character is, the more likely he is to suffer in this way; there being in the heart of every man, unless greatly subdued by grace, a pleasure in hearing anything which may sink others to his level, or lower them in the estimation of the world. We seem to ourselves elevated in proportion as others are depressed.

Under such circumstances I derive consolation from the following reflections:

1 My enemy, whatever evil he says of me, does not reduce me so low as he would if he knew all concerning me that God knows.
2 In drawing the balance, as between Debtor and Creditor, I find that if I have been robbed of pence, there are pounds and talents placed to my account to which I have no just title.
3 If man has his day, God will have His. See 1 Cor. 4:3, the Greek.

So Simeon ends this candid commentary on how to deal with calumny by looking back to St Paul who, like all true ministers of the gospel, had had his share also. The opening words of the sermon on the text quoted above, born of painful personal experience, are: 'The ministers of Christ are generally either unduly exalted or undeservedly depreciated, by those around them: but they should discharge their duties with fidelity, without any regard to the opinions of men, and approve themselves to him who will judge them righteously in the last day.'[25]

CHAPTER NINE

With the Wider Church

Charles Simeon did not work in isolation. He liked to keep in touch with other movements that he heard about which were concerned in the spread of the gospel. He also valued any opportunity of sharing in the life of the wider church whether it was in Scotland, Ireland, the continent or far away India. His visits north of the border at a time when travel was slow and hazardous were so eventful that they must not be overlooked. By the end of the eighteenth century coaches practically covered the country. Their running days were advertised in the local press. In Scotland one firm claimed that its coach would run six times a week 'God willing', but twice a week 'whether or no'.[1] Presbyterian faith in public conveyances led to some theological confusion at times.

Simeon made his travel plans more on the basis of whether or not his precious church and parish could be left in safe hands. He had no sooner got his curate Thomas Thomason into the saddle than he felt free to take what was in fact the first long break after fourteen years of continuous and solitary ministry at Holy Trinity. When he returned ten weeks later he 'found all things as I had left them', as he had expected. For Simeon a holiday meant a number of chances of further preaching. He would hardly have known what to do with himself if there had not been pulpits open to welcome him. Sightseeing made little appeal and his interest in history or nature was distinctly limited, though he did let himself go at times. For instance he thought the view from the top of Ben Lomond was 'inexpressibly majestic', Glencoe 'wonderfully grand' and Tayside 'exquisitely beautiful'. But these were rather incidental matters.

His journey north took a very roundabout route. He started in May, 1796, by travelling to London to pick up his companion, Doctor Walter Buchanan, a minister from Edinburgh 'whom I think it was one of the greatest blessings of my life ever to have known.' They first visited

Windsor where he took great pleasure in showing his friend Eton and attending the 'Montem' celebrations at which the king was present that year. They arrived at Henley, he notes, 'not without tears of joy' though quite why they felt so much on top of the world at that point he does not say. It did not take a great deal to bring tears to Charles' eyes. He was in many ways an emotional man, and lived before the days when our public school system had introduced the stiff upper lip as the ideal reaction of a true gentleman to painful or moving circumstances. Perhaps on this occasion he had never before realised what a relief it can be to leave one's responsibilities behind for a while and be free of the pressure of continuous parochial demands.

They soon moved on to Oxford, Bath and Bristol, and visited Cowslip Green in the Mendips where they were able to hear at first hand of how that 'remarkably vicious and abandoned place has become sober and industrious' under the evangelising influence of Hannah More and her sisters. Thence they travelled to Gloucester, Birmingham, Buxton and finally, a fortnight after setting off, they reached Edinburgh. There, at the somewhat uninviting hour of eight a.m. on their first day, Simeon says 'I was fortunate enough to hear a sermon annually preached' on the king's birthday. Three days later he went to hear a famous preacher but instead found himself sitting at the feet of 'one of the most drawling and uninteresting teachers I ever heard.' However, he took himself to task for not accepting this poor performance as 'the word of God to my soul.'

After a week's stay in the capital where he left Dr Buchanan, Sir John Stirling, to whom he had recently been introduced, offered him his own mare for his intended journey further north. From the excited comments in his diary we can assume it was a good horse. But in the event, he had to fall back on buying a horse which, on account of its colour, he christened Duns Scotus. For once Simeon seems to have failed in judgment for it proved a bad buy. One day when admiring the view at Killiecrankie he was suddenly thrown almost on the edge of a precipice, an accident he took with calm acceptance of providential protection.[2] It was not the first nor the last time that this competent rider had a fall from his horse. Bishop McIlvaine recalls a time when he saw him rise from the ground and, finding no bones broken, 'stretching out one limb after another and redevoting it to God', mount again at once.[3] Simeon wrote and told Thomason about this incident, 'I could not help saying in the words of David that all my bones should praise him.'[4]

He may have been disappointed with his Scottish horse, but he was thrilled with his chosen companion, a man of like mind ten years his junior, James Haldane of Airthrey. He was the younger of two brothers, men of wealth, who had turned their backs on the world of fashion and society, and set their hearts on spreading the gospel. This they did with a zeal which sometimes surpassed the bounds of discretion. In James, however, Charles found one with whom quite happily and naturally he could pray on top of a mountain or distribute tracts in the lanes through which they rode. This last activity was one which as far as we can tell Charles did not practise in his parish or in his travels in the south, but he seems to have taken the lead in it when out with Haldane. Included in their ammunition was one tract specially written by Charles himself with the somewhat enigmatic title *An Advice to all whom it may Concern.*[5] When these two came to part after three weeks in each other's company, Simeon records, 'We were mutually affected with fervent love to each other, and with thankfulness that we had been permitted so to meet together.'

Simeon was always ready to plunge into any religious activity that was going. But he was a little taken aback when, on his second Saturday evening in Edinburgh, being the day before their quarterly Sacrament Sunday, he was expected to attend a four-hour service at which two sermons were delivered in succession, each over an hour long. 'The length of the service wearied me exceedingly. Nor was I singular; the whole congregation were much like myself; many were asleep, and all the rest had a stupid unmeaning stare.' However, by next day he had recovered and at the Holy Communion was once more in tears as, 'I made a free, full and unreserved surrender of myself to God. O that I may ever bear in mind his kindness to me, and my obligations to him!'

It was a week after this that Simeon and Haldane came to Moulin near Pitlochry, not far from the scene of the memorable Highland victory of Killiecrankie just over a hundred years before. Their visit had not been planned, was indeed fortuitous, or as they would say, providential. It arose from Simeon being overtired after a long walk which they had had to make, his fractious horse having gone lame. When they reached the village the minister, Dr Alexander Stewart, offered them beds for the night in the manse, hoping Simeon would be good enough to preach for him next day. Physically weary and spiritually 'barren and dull', he found that Sunday duty difficult and unrewarding. But he was soon to learn that God often blesses his servants in their weaker moments and all unknown to them uses their infirmity to inspire and help someone in need. That evening the minister of the kirk and the Church of England clergyman were led into a deep heart-to-heart conversation. Dr Stewart, a brilliant Gaelic scholar, confided in Simeon that he felt dispirited and had no real personal faith. The result of their subsequent talk together is best described in the minister's words: 'Their visit has been blessed to me more than any outward dispensation of Providence that I have met with . . . Ever since the blessed period of Mr Simeon's visit, my thoughts have continued more steadily fixed on divine things; and my communion with God has been much more lively, by many degrees, than I remember to have experienced before.'[6]

In fact, it was the beginning of a revival not only in the minister's heart, but in his church and the district round. One outcome of it all, quite unforeseen at the time, was the fifty-year ministry in India of the great Alexander Duff whose father we are told was converted through 'the remarkable ministry' of the revived Dr Stewart who himself traced his renewal to 'the Prince of Evangelicals of the Church of England', who 'happened' to be staying in his manse that night. Forty years later, by a strange providence, young Alexander Duff visited Cambridge where he was able to meet the aged Simeon a few months before he died.[7] He was happy to tell the one to whom his parents owed so much about his own work in India, a country which we shall see was never far from the old apostle's thoughts and prayers.

But that is anticipating. Simeon had not long been back in Cambridge after his Scottish tour when he received a letter from the minister of the kirk in Moulin which included these words: 'I wish I knew how to express my filial regard and attachment to one whom I have every reason to consider as my spiritual father . . . O my dear Sir, praise the Lord on my behalf, who hath given me to perceive something of his glory and his grace as displayed in Christ Jesus, though I have a great deal yet to see and to learn.' He went on to say how his preaching had been revived and he was now using skeleton outlines in Simeon fashion, and his sermons as a result had become 'more energetic'. To this Simeon replied: 'Among the many rich mercies which God vouchsafed to me in my late excursion, I cannot but consider the sweet interview which I enjoyed with you as one of the greatest . . . O how desirable is it for all, but especially for ministers, to have their souls deeply and devoutly impressed! What is religion without this? What are duties without this? Alas! a dry, insipid, unsatisfying, unproductive form. Surely this is happiness, to taste the love of God, to find delight in his service and to see that we are in a measure instrumental to the imparting of this happiness to others – this, I say, is a felicity which nothing but heaven can exceed.' Simeon had certainly enjoyed his holiday.

Two years later he was prevailed upon to make a second visit to Scotland where many hundreds of people had taken to their hearts the great preacher who spoke with such warmth and vitality, and whose thoughts were so clearly and forcefully expressed. This kind of thing had been all rather new to them and they wanted more. Simeon was ready to go but he could not hide the fact that he found the length of their services a great trial. He said of one particular occasion that 'those who could stay there from the beginning to the end with any profit to their souls, must be made of different materials from me.' In talking of it later he likened it to eating turtle and venison after a good meal of roast beef and plum pudding.[8] However, undeterred by prospects of spiritual indigestion, Charles Simeon set off again in May 1798, punctuating his coach journey northwards with visits to evangelical churches en route where his rare appearances were welcomed with congregations of over a thousand at times. His progress slowed somewhat when he got off the beaten track and had to travel on foot or horseback. He often never knew quite when he would reach his destination or, roads and weather being so unpredictable, when he might return from such trips. Once he managed to hitch a lift from a lady admirer in her carriage over a road which 'had I taken a hack I might very probably have broken my neck; at all events I must have been wet through twice.'

Dr Buchanan was again Simeon's companion on this journey which included an eventful rowing cum sailing episode between Oban and Staffa during which he tells us that his mind, wandering off matters of strong wind and impressive scenery, 'was somewhat occupied about my dear brother Thomason and my people.' But his programme was too full to allow him time to worry unduly about how things were going on in Cambridge. After he eventually got back, in his usual meticulous way, he sat down to work out how many places he had visited, how many sermons he had delivered and to how many people. Between May 18th and August 19th he calculated that he had given seventy-five addresses to a total of 87,310 people,[9] a substantial achievement for a holiday tour, but then in 1798 Simeon was still on the right side of forty, and was never so happy as when he was in demand as a preacher.

After this strenuous effort which had taken him through the Highlands to the Hebrides and then down to Glasgow, Simeon returned to Edinburgh to find trouble. A number of stout Presbyterians, unaffected by the wave of spiritual interest that had accompanied Simeon's travels, began to object to an Anglican preaching in their pulpits. Simeon himself had justified his accepting the ministers' invitations to take part in their services, including their occasional communions, and preach, on the grounds that Presbyterianism being the established religion in Scotland, as a member of the English establishment he had a right to do this. 'If the king, who is the head of the establishment in both countries, were in Scotland, he would of necessity attend at a Presbyterian church there as he does at an Episcopalian church here; and I look upon it as an incontrovertible position that where the king must attend, there a clergyman may preach.' It was an argument that convinced no one but Simeon himself.

The situation had not been made any easier by him somewhat indiscreetly praying at a service in the Tolbooth church that the General Assembly of the Church of Scotland 'might do no evil.'[10] It had never occurred to the divines of that church that such a possibility existed and they did not take kindly to the suggestion that their Synod might be in error. In 1799 the Synod closed the door by ruling that 'no preacher... and no minister who has not been ordained by some Presbytery of this church, shall ever be employed in any of our pulpits under severe penalties.' These restrictions naturally discouraged any further preaching tours in Scotland, and Simeon's friends in Edinburgh and elsewhere had to wait many years before seeing him again. However, in 1815 he paid a short holiday visit taking with him Thomason's mother and his son James. This was the occasion when on his return to Cambridge he found trouble brewing in his parish through some of his laymen having got the bit between their teeth and refused to acknowledge Simeon's authority. His last journey north was four years later when he undertook to promote the causes of the Jews and the Bible Societies. His colleague this time was a much valued friend, William Marsh, 'the loveliest of men'. Together they had a most successful time returning with five hundred guineas contributed to the funds.

It was in the same two causes that Simeon paid his one visit to Ireland. He had already been in correspondence with and been consulted by members of the Irish Protestant church about ways and means of better evangelism. His suggestion of sending out lay readers or catechists to different areas who would settle for a month, visit the sick and catechise the children, had been quite widely adopted with encouraging results. But his journey in 1822 was somewhat hindered by the strong prejudice that existed against 'Calvinism, by which term they designate all vital religion', not realising that Simeon was far from being a true Calvinist. However, with the stimulating companionship once more of William Marsh, he enjoyed a generally warm welcome. Indeed, at one point he was quite taken aback to find himself called upon by 'Earls and Viscounts, Deans and Dignatories, Judges and Bishops desirous to see me.' He secured the blessing of the Archbishop and held forth freely and vigorously about the evangelisation of the Jews and the needs of the heathen. 'God seemed to be manifestly with us,' he said. After all this excitement, his voyage home was just one more memorable episode. A furious storm broke out as they were approaching Holyhead leading to the loss of ten vessels including a naval ship of eighteen guns and several packet boats similar to the one in which they were sailing. Simeon, who does not ever seem to have been troubled by seasickness, weathered the storm kept, as he expressed it, 'through the tender mercy of God . . . from any apprehensions, having my mind sweetly employed in travelling between heaven and earth, with all my friends successively in my head.'

Simeon's vision of the wider church was by no means limited to the British Isles. We must now turn to see how deep was his concern for the work of God overseas, particularly in India. It all started when he was only twenty-nine and still had enough parish problems to absorb his full attention. These were days when the churches of Britain looked little further afield than the bounds of each parish or the member lists of each church. When in 1786 William Carey approached his fellow ministers on the subject, and was told by the chairman of the meeting 'Sit down, young man. When it pleases the Lord to convert the heathen, He will do it without your help or mine,'[11] the speaker was not expressing just the views of hardened Calvinists. Similarly, and almost unbelievably, in 1796 the General Assembly of the Church of Scotland carried a resolution affirming that 'to spread abroad among barbarians and heathen natives the knowledge of the gospel seems to be highly preposterous, in so far as it anticipates, nay even reverses, the order of Nature.'[12]

Warren Hastings in 1774 had made it a fundamental rule of policy 'to discourage missionary effort', and as traders the East India Company were adamant about keeping missionaries away lest they disturb the natives. The ardent Carey who pioneered his own way to India in spite of the discouragement of his church officials, had as a consequence to take refuge under the Danish flag at Serampore as his own countrymen would not receive the 'consecrated cobbler' when he landed in Bengal. Wilberforce did all he could in 1793 to persuade the Company to relax its attitude but it was another twenty years before they did so.

Difficulties and opposition of this sort deterred Charles Simeon no more than William Carey and William Wilberforce. They soon came to learn patience in such matters. If missionaries could not be sent abroad there could at least be no objection to the appointment of chaplains to minister to their many countrymen who had gone overseas in the armed forces or as servants of the East India Company. So they concentrated on this. The first such appointment was David Brown who entered Magdalene college in 1782 and ended up in Calcutta in 1786. Simeon remembered his having become a Christian while attending Holy Trinity, how 'his religious faith had not darted suddenly into his mind as the ray of heavenly light which otherthrew an opposing Saul; but rather, as the least of all seeds, had grown with his growth and strengthened with his strength.' He was a man of like spirit to Simeon. A member of his church described him, as Simeon himself and others were also described, as 'so much in earnest.' When his horse died suddenly at the door of the Old Mission church in Calcutta, his comment was that he hoped he would stick to his work till he 'dropped like a horse in harness and not like one in a stable.' This was the man who, if he had had the chance would have gladly been 'dear Mr Simeon's curate' as so many of his future colleagues were, the first man picked on by Simeon to consider India as a future sphere of service.[13]

In his journal he records with grateful affection how, when his time came to sail in November 1785, his father-in-God went to the trouble of travelling to London to see him off from Tower Bridge, and on the next day amazed him by appearing on board at Gravesend whence he had ridden in order to give his adventurous young friend a second farewell. Like almost everything that he did, Simeon said goodbye in a big way. David Brown was not a disappointment. His ministry in Calcutta was much appreciated by the Governor-General, Lord Wellesley, and by his illustrious brother Arthur, future Duke of Wellington. For seven years he held the post of Provost of Fort William College, the predecessor of Haileybury as a training establishment for sixteen-year-old cadets from England. In all David Brown spent twenty-five years labouring in the heat, the stench and the pressure of Calcutta. But it was in the very year after landing that, in collusion with his Christian administrator friend, Charles Grant, he drew up 'A Proposal for establishing a Protestant Mission in Bengal and Bahar'.

As Christian men they were concerned that Britain should make some substantial return to India for all the economic benefits that trade through the East India Company was bringing, and could think of nothing more valuable for a Christian country to export to a heathen one than their religion. So with great hopes that the powers that be would agree, they wrote:

> Among all advantages accruing to Great Britain from the acquisition of Asiatic Territories, the power of introducing the Light of Truth among them, of making known to them the way of Everlasting life, and the true source of temporal happiness, has hardly been mentioned . . . A Government which would withhold the knowledge of the True God and his Laws from the people, or in other words refuse them happiness, must be . . . unjust . . . The people are lamentably destitute of those Principles of Honesty, Truth and Justice which are necessary to the Well-being of Society.

They urged that 'fit men of free minds, disinterested, zealous and patient of labour' be sent out to serve as full time missionaries in the hopes that John Company would not be long in changing its attitude.[14]

Charles Simeon was the obvious person to whom this memorandum should be sent for, as their letter ran, 'we understand that such matters lie very near your heart, and that you have a warm zeal to promote their interest. Upon this ground we invite you to become agent on behalf of the intended mission at home.' Simeon was very touched by the confidence shown in him and treated this document with loving care as sacred orders from Above. In 1830 he wrote this note upon his copy: 'It merely shows how early God enabled me to act for India – to provide for which has now for forty-two years been a principal and an incessant object of my care and labour.' Brown and Grant's proposals did not receive a very warm welcome when presented to Lord Cornwallis the Governor-General, but he said he would not oppose the scheme if it ever came to fruition.[15] Meanwhile David Brown wrote and told Simeon what type of man he hoped he would be on the look-out for amongst those who attended his church in Cambridge: 'You will be aware that zeal and grace, though essentials, are not the only requisites on this occasion. They must be men of general knowledge, and possess such a share of science as may make their conversation interesting to the learned Brahmins who will only be communicative in proportion to the returns made them by those with whom they converse.'

The next to sail to India as chaplain, and one of the ablest, was Claudius Buchanan. His was a truly remarkable story. As a love-lorn youth he left his ancestral home in Scotland under a cloud to travel south, with a fiddle as his only means of support. He had grandiose ideas about working his way to the continent, but after one crisis on top of another he ended up destitute on the streets of London. Here in the mercy of providence he found his way to John Newton's church in the City where, in 1791, he made peace with himself and with his God. Eventually by the generous support of Henry Thornton a place was found for him in Queens' College which he entered at the age of twenty-five. Here he at once joined Simeon's Sunday evening groups and, anxious to make up for the wasted hours of his youth, adopted a rigorous personal code, disciplining himself to rise at 4.30 a.m. in order to spend the early hours before breakfast on devotional studies. In no time Simeon had him under his wing, helping him with elocution no doubt to counteract his strong Scottish accent, and vetting trial sermons one of which is said to have consisted of twenty-seven pages.[16]

In 1795 Buchanan was ordained and went to join John Newton as curate in the church where he had found Christ. He sailed for India the next year and soon showed outstanding ability and devotion. His grasp of the implications of applying Christianity to the responsibilities of government was shown by his being the first man to agitate against the Hindu practice of *suttee*, when dutiful widows were expected to burn themselves on the funeral pyres of their late husbands. He was also, with Daniel Corrie, the first to make public the fact that the East India Company was making considerable profits from the Pilgrim Tax which recognised and exploited idolatry to the benefit of its shareholders and members.[17] He proved to be a man of very different character and temperament from Simeon who at times found himself somewhat out of his depth with him. 'He is a little ardent in his views and statements, or rather not a little,' he wrote to Thomason, but went on 'He attracts much attention and will do much good.' In reference to his remarkable and important *Christian Researches in Asia* published in 1812, and his *Brief View of the State of the Colonies of Great Britain in Respect to Religious Instruction*, of 1813, Simeon seemed to have forgotten that his former protégé had been given an honorary DD by his university, and showed some lack of enthusiasm in stating that 'He is quoted everywhere as an authority, and is supposed to be quite correct.' However, when in due course his biography was published Simeon read it with great avidity, and with that generosity of spirit which endeared him to so many, remarked particularly on Buchanan's 'certain dignity of character very uncommon in religious men. His independence and generosity and capacity to adapt himself to all persons of every station, yet accompanied with such a surprising state of mind, cast an air of nobleness and majesty around him that I have never met with in any other man . . . Many equal him in what we should call piety; but there is a luminousness and a grandeur about him that is very uncommon.'

This brings us to the heroic Henry Martyn who has so often caught the Christian imagination to overshadow, perhaps unfairly, his many eminent colleagues in Cambridge and India. His life, however, is such an integral part of the study of Simeon, and, even though often told, so challenging to lethargic stay-at-home Christians, that we must on no account underestimate it. The son of a labourer in a Cornish tin mine, Henry was eventually enabled to go up to St John's College, Cambridge, as a pensioner in October 1797 when still only sixteen. With scarcely a thought of religion in his head, he found his earnest sister's constant appeals to think of his soul both annoying and irksome. During his first three years he does not seem to have come under the influence of Simeon. But after the death of his father in 1800 he started attending Holy Trinity church where 'he gradually acquired more knowledge in divine things.' He then wrote to his still anxious sister and told her that he was being brought 'to a sense of things gradually.'[18] Through John Sargent he was introduced more personally to Charles Simeon and a close and memorable friendship soon grew up between these two men.

Not surprisingly, before very long Henry Martyn, having passed his final examinations with the distinction of Senior Wrangler, began to think seriously about being ordained as so many of Simeon's close friends did. When in 1802 he won the Latin prize and was made a Fellow of his college, Simeon began to look on him as a potential curate. A year later he was made deacon and joined Thomason on the staff of Holy Trinity with special responsibility for the little village of Lolworth, a six-mile ride on the road to Huntingdon. Henry made more heavy weather of his curacy than any of Simeon's other colleagues though this does not seem to have marred the close relationship between them, certainly on the older man's side. Holy Trinity was still the scene of undergraduate mockery and disorder. In his journal for April 22, 1803, Martyn records 'Was ashamed to confess to – that I was to be Mr Simeon's curate, a despicable fear of man from which I vainly thought myself to be free,' thus disclosing a lifelong inclination to disparage himself and bemoan his sinfulness. Simeon's frank manner of training his assistants by not overlooking their faults did little to lessen the introspection of this young man who was so anxious to please his vicar. Simeon grew more gentle as he got older, but at the age of forty-four he expected of others, even those half his age, all that he demanded of himself. We can read between the lines of Henry's journal that it was a considerable strain trying to rise to Simeon's standard: 'Mr Simeon drank tea with me in the evening . . . Told me that concerning the trials and temptations attending the Christian life, I might know just as much as about the distances of the planets . . . I was vexed at finding I was not so forward in religion as my pride suggested.' 'Learnt from Mr Simeon that my views . . . were wrong.' 'Mr Simeon's sermon in the evening on 2 Chron. 32:32 discovered to me my corruption and vileness more than any sermon I ever heard.' 'After evening church Mr S. told me I ought to read with more solemnity and devotion, at which I was not a little grieved and amazed.'

Henry frequently complained of the time it took to prepare his sermons which did not come at all easily to him. He bemoaned his 'shortness of prayer through incessant sermon-making'. The standard of those sermons he listened to was a bit high for him. 'I find that preaching well and living well in humiliation and communion with God have no necessary connection,' he commented somewhat enigmatically. 'Mr Simeon, in his excellent sermon tonight, observed that it was more easy for a minister to preach and study five hours than to pray for his people one half-hour; this I believe.' 'In the morning felt resentment at Mr S. and found it very difficult to regain a right spirit in prayer. But at length I felt patient and forgiving.'[19] 'At dear Mr Simeon's rooms I perceived that I had given him pain by inattention to his kind instructions. Base wretch that I am, that by carelessness and unmortified pride, I should thus ungratefully repay his unexampled kindness.'[20] 'At night was at church when almost for the first time I observed Mr Simeon's manner, and conceived great admiration of him as a preacher; supped with him alone afterwards; he prayed before I went away and my heart was solemnly affected.'[21]

On that note we may leave the young Henry's none too happy reactions to his work and his spiritual director. It is possible here and there to find more cheerful passages in his diary such as when on New Year's Day, 1805, he recalled his slow conversion with gratitude to God for the joy it had brought him: 'I can truly say that in the course of this time every successive year, every successive week, has been happier than the former.'[22] It was well for him that he knew whence he could draw the true happiness he needed to counter his natural diffidence and self-depreciation, for he had two major problems to face in his personal life. The first of these was the call to leave the academic world of Cambridge to which in many ways he was so well suited, and where there were good Christian friends to take him out of himself. It was after a powerful sermon by Simeon about the life and work of William Carey that Henry Martyn first began to consider the possibility of himself serving as a missionary. This was followed up by a memorable ride which the two of them made one day to Shelford to visit Thomason there. During the four-mile trot that summer afternoon of 1804 Simeon discussed with his young friend the work in Bengal, the problems of getting there, and the qualities he would need whether as a chaplain like David Brown and Claudius Buchanan, or as a missionary, of which there were so few from England as yet. The result of all this was that in July, 1805, all obstacles having been overcome, immature and unsure of himself though he still was, Henry Martyn sailed for Asia to serve as yet another of Simeon's chaplains in the East India Company, and to do what missionary work might be possible in the circumstances. Charles Simeon saw him off from Portsmouth, and they were never to meet again.

The other great problem that had haunted Henry Martyn's last months in England was his love for Lydia Grenfell. The sad story of how through her mother's objection and her own diffidence Lydia declined to follow Henry to India in spite of his repeated appeals, has often been told. It is not known when Henry first met or fell in love with Lydia who was nine years older than himself. He visited her during the summer before he left Cambridge, and again during the weeks of delay that occurred before sailing. Nothing he could say or do would overcome her indecision. So he turned to his bachelor father-in-God for advice. Not surprisingly it was to the effect that being single set one more free for God's work, and Henry would be wise to accept the situation as the will of God for them both. On that note he and Lydia parted for ever. From time to time they wrote to each other, Henry desperate in his loneliness, Lydia torn and uncommitted. In April 1806 the situation was such that Simeon felt he owed it to his former colleague to visit Cornwall and see if he could in person do anything to ease the relationship that had developed. Lydia seems to have welcomed his call for she wrote in her diary: 'April 24. The arrival of dear Mr Simeon has been a cordial to my fainting heart. Lord do thou comfort me by him . . . April 29. Almost constantly do I remember my dear absent friend; may I do so with less pain.'[23] When, however, Simeon discovered that Lydia's mother was adamant in refusing to agree to her going overseas, he felt he could do no more. He never would, on principle, recommend anyone to go abroad unless his or her parents gave their full consent, even though as in this case the one concerned was over thirty years of age.

Henry Martyn, having left England in August 1805, was welcomed to Calcutta in May of the following year, after an almost interminable voyage, by none other than the great William Carey whose life-story had been the first thing that turned his thoughts to India. At home

Charles Simeon was to follow in his constant prayers those seven short years of his dear young friend's distinguished service as translator of the New Testament into Urdu and Persian. After he died he was sent a portrait of Henry painted in India which is now preserved in the vestry of Holy Trinity church in Cambridge. Joseph Gurney remembers seeing it hanging over the mantelpiece in Simeon's drawing-room, and his host telling him of its arrival; 'When I went to India House in London and saw the box opened, I started back with mixed emotions of sorrow and delight when I beheld the countenance of my beloved Henry. As I retreated to the other end of the room, I heard the people saying – "That is his father".'[24] It was almost true, for in Charles Simeon the sensitive orphaned student from Cornwall had found someone without whose love and support he could hardly have survived. Years afterwards, looking at that picture, Simeon would say to his guests 'There! See that blessed man! What an expression of countenance! No one looks at me as he does – he never takes his eyes off me; and seems always to be saying, "Be serious – be in earnest – Don't trifle – don't trifle." And I won't trifle – I won't trifle.'

Hot on Henry Martyn's heels there followed another of Simeon's men, Daniel Corrie, who rose thirty years later to become the first Bishop of Madras, an honour Simeon was delighted to hear about just before he died. Corrie used to speak of the vicar of Holy Trinity as 'the candlestick which was the means of guiding me into divine light and peace.'[25] He wrote once to John Sargent saying 'To that "Father in Israel", Mr Simeon, I owe all my comfort on earth and all my hopes respecting eternity; for through his instrumentality the seeds of grace I trust were, during my residence at Cambridge, . . . implanted in my heart, and have influenced, though alas! unsteadily, my after days.'[26] Referring to his first year at Clare in 1799, after which he moved to Trinity Hall, he said, 'I went occasionally to Trinity church, though I was much disgusted with what I heard there.' Two years later it was a different story: 'I now began to feel a growing attachment to Mr Simeon's ministry . . . I now attended Trinity church regularly; but my walk was very uneven.' He went on to ordination testifying in his journal, 'I would bless the Holy and Eternal Spirit who has enlightened my dark understanding, so that I know not the hour, nor the day, nor the month, nor even the year when he graciously wrought savingly upon me, yet I can say "Whereas I was blind, now I see". O Holy, Blessed and glorious Trinity, let thy choicest blessings descend on Mr Simeon who, regardless of the frowns he might incur, faithfully warned me of my danger.'[27]

Corrie, after serving as a curate in Leicestershire, was ordained priest in June, 1804. A year later he visited Cambridge to receive a Bachelor of Law degree, when Simeon approached him about going out to India. The inevitable consequence of this was that within the same year he also joined the band of Bengal chaplains, to be joined a year or two later by Thomas Thomason, a veritable Simeon enclave five thousand miles from Cambridge. By 1829 Simeon was able to say with all honesty, 'almost all the good men who have gone to India these forty years have been recommended by me.' Such was his remarkable judgment of men and his lifelong concern for the Indian continent. Even on his death-bed the old apostle's heart was out in Calcutta for he wrote to another of his chosen men, Daniel Wilson the bishop, 'I view the sphere of India as immense, the load too heavy to be laid on any human mind . . . Be not discouraged if you should not be able to accomplish all you wish . . . With him at your right hand you have none to fear.'

David Brown, it will be remembered, as far back as 1787, had made proposals for the establishing of missionary work in India which he envisaged being sponsored by government. In 1816 Simeon paid him high tribute when he wrote 'Mr Brown, if not actually the founder of all the great missionary institutions which have been established of late years . . . laboured in this field as much as any who have followed him, and strove to the utmost of his power to kindle that very flame which has burned and is now burning in almost every quarter of the globe.'[28] What had taken place in the thirty years between those dates? The Old Apostle had been busily at work. 'We have been dreaming . . . while all England, all Europe has been awake,' was his challenge to the church as the nineteenth century with all its impending political and social change was about to dawn. At the same time as William Wilberforce was embarking on his mission to abolish the slave trade, his respected friend Charles Simeon was taking up the cause of evangelistic missionary enterprise in India, Africa and the East. In 1795 he heard that a sum of £4,000 had been left by a good evangelical clergyman 'to the best advantage to the interests of true religion', and he was alert at once. Soon afterwards he was present at a clerical meeting held at Rauceby where the possibility of spending this money on a college for training missionaries was seriously considered. In his usual clear way, Simeon crystallised the issues by saying, 'There is no good to be done without difficulties, and this is worth a trial,' and, 'We should roll away the reproach of loving ease from the evangelical clergy of the establishment.'

The matter first came before the Eclectic Society in London on February 8th, 1796, at a meeting which Simeon made a point of attending.

It fell to him to propose the question: 'With what propriety and in what mode, can a mission be attempted to the heathen from the established church?' The result was indecisive, one reason being a natural hesitation lest they interfere with the existing bodies such as the Society for Promoting Christian Knowledge which had been formed in 1699, and the Society for the Propagation of the Gospel which was already ninety-five years old. But Simeon would not let the matter drop and made a point of approaching Wilberforce to gain his support. It was at one of these meetings that the great Christian politician made his famous comment about Simeon being 'in earnest'. He certainly was.

The matter next came up three years later at a meeting of the Eclectic Society on March 18th, 1799, at which John Venn, Simeon's old friend from Cambridge days, was in the chair. After a discussion in which Charles Grant, on leave from India, and Josiah Pratt, future secretary of the Society in process of being conceived, took part, Simeon, anxious that decision should not be postponed again, brought matters to a head by proposing three questions: 'What can we do? When shall we do it? How shall we do it?' They decided to take immediate action and summoned a meeting for the 12th April to be held in the Castle and Falcon Inn in Aldersgate Street. It was here that sixteen clergymen and nine laymen took the momentous step of forming 'A Society amongst the members of the established church for sending Missionaries among the heathen.' And so there came into being, very largely at the instigation and through the persistent persuasion of Charles Simeon, 'The Society for Missions to Africa and the East', later to be known far and wide throughout Christendom as The Church Missionary Society.

With the society formed and its committee ready to canvas support from the Christian public, it fell heavily on Simeon's shoulders to look for the men who might volunteer for service overseas. His reputation for being in close touch with keen young Christians of academic ability meant that great hopes rested on him. But everyone, and Simeon as much as any, was disappointed in the initial response. In August 1800 he wrote from Cambridge: 'I have endeavoured (in a prudent way) to sound the dispositions of the serious young men respecting missions, and I am sorry to say not one of them says "Here am I, send me" . . . I feel a little discouraged at my own entire want of success.' When he preached the annual sermon at the Society's Second Anniversary in London on June 8th, 1802, he had to acknowledge that 'after inquiries made in every part of England none have as yet been found by us endued with that union of talents and of zeal which is requisite for the work.'[29] However, he did what he could and the pace of interest stepped up as the years progressed. As far as his own parish was concerned, the first collections ever taken up on behalf of the CMS were at Holy Trinity in 1804 after Simeon had preached on 1 Chronicles 29:17, 18. His closing appeal to his people was, 'If the raising of God's spiritual temple among the heathen be an object worthy of our regard, let us now vie with each other in our endeavours to promote it, and show our sense of its importance by the cheerfulness and extent of our donations.'[30] The offertory that day was £50, and a similar sum was contributed the next year when Henry Martyn preached his farewell sermons.

Meanwhile Simeon continued looking out for men, and after a few years was rewarded and greatly cheered. 'The whole Christian world,' he wrote to Thomason in 1813, 'seems stirred up, almost as you would expect it to be in the Millenium.' Two years later he wrote to him again saying, 'Four pious ministers are just sent out to you in India, and I am in expectation of sending you immediately three more.' The next year it was a case of sending him a dozen more. Support for the CMS had so increased in Cambridge that no less than £387 was raised by town and gown together in 1816, Holy Trinity's share being £117.[31] No wonder that Charles Simeon was soon enrolled as an Honorary Life Governor of the Society, invited to address five anniversary meetings over the years, and honoured to give the valedictory sermon to sixteen missionaries about to sail overseas in 1817. He had found some of them, he was seeing them off, and he was to write to many when they were abroad to encourage them in what they were to find was a far tougher assignment than his own work in the delectable surroundings of Cambridge. But it was there in his rooms and in his church that he so often knelt in prayer for those in the front line abroad. To his own congregation at home he reversed an exhortation into a question in preaching on Philippians 2:5: 'What would have been the state of the whole world if the same mind had been in Christ that is in us? . . . It may be said perhaps, Why are we to waste our strength upon the heathen? Is there not scope for the labours of all at home? I answer, It is well for us that the Apostles did not argue thus.'[32]

CHAPTER TEN

The Man Himself

Taking Charles Simeon at his word when he said, 'I conceive that neither the worst nor the best of any man can be or ought to be known to any but God,' we must all the same try to see what kind of picture emerges from the jumbled jig-saw of glimpses and impressions which we have received so far. 'The scrupulous and gentlemanly fellow of King's, Cambridge,' as he has recently been described, 'who made Trinity church for a time perhaps the most important centre of religious influence in England,'[1] had been for years the hero of the evangelical wing of the Church of England, and by very many is still so regarded. He must have known certainly in the second half of his life, how his name was one to conjure with. Yet he was very reluctant to make any preparations for his colleague, William Carus, to compile his memoirs and only did so under considerable pressure. During his last illness, referring to Dr Dealtry preaching the University sermon in his place, he asked that 'If anything laudatory be mentioned . . . about me or about my sermons, I entreat from my inmost soul that I may not have it repeated to me: let me go to heaven as the vilest sinner in the universe . . . Satan himself could not be a greater curse to me than the person who would dare to breathe a word upon that subject commendatory of me or anything I have done.' It was the last wish of a man who all through his life had struggled with vanity and was determined to win in the end.

It is difficult to know to what extent he was conscious of people noticing his 'affectation of manner, gesture and speech' and what kindly critics such as Charles Jerram called his being 'over-punctilious in his observance of whatever he conceived to belong to the address and manners of a gentleman.'[2] Gladstone remembered meeting Simeon when his father was consulting him about a possible incumbent. He thought him 'a venerable man, and although only a fellow of a college, more ecclesiastically got up than many a dean or even perhaps a bishop.'[3] Sir James Stephen went so far as to say, in his own inimitable fashion, that a casual acquaintance might regard him as 'some truant from the green-room, studying in clerical costume for the part of Mercutio, and doing it scandalously ill. Such adventurous attitudes, such ceaseless play of the facial muscles, so seeming a consciousness of the advantages of his figure, with so seeming an unconsciousness of the disadvantage of his carriage—a seat in the saddle so triumphant, badinage so ponderous, stories so exquisitely unbefitting him about the pedigree of his horses or the vintages of his cellar.'

Stephen's essay piles on the frank assessment of this man whom no one could ignore, but in the end the writer is driven to confess that Simeon did indeed overcome these very considerable disadvantages:

> He was a man beset . . . by inveterate affectations, by the want of learning, by the want of social talents, by the want of general ability of any kind, by the want of interest in the pursuits of his neighbours, by their want of sympathy in his pursuits, by the want of their goodwill, nay, by the want of their decided and hearty animosity. Yet thus unprovided for the contest, he gained a victory which the sternest cynic . . . might have condescended to envy . . . Slowly, painfully, but with unfaltering hopes, he toiled through more than fifty successive years, in the same narrow chamber and among the same humble congregation—requited by no emoluments, stimulated by no animating occurrences, and unrewarded, until the near approach of old age, by the gratitude or the cordial respect of the society amidst which he lived. Love soaring to the Supreme with the lowliest self-abasement, and stooping to the most abject with the meekest self-forgetfulness, bore him onward . . . His whole life was but one long labour of love—a labour often obscure, often misapplied, often unsuccessful, but never intermitted, and at last triumphant.[4]

He who wanted no panegyrics when he died would have accepted this honest summary and true assessment of himself, though he might have been surprised at some of the strictures in it. He was very ready in 1827 to admit to Francis Close of Cheltenham that 'you perhaps see much amiss in me which my own self-love has hidden from my view. But this I can say, I desire to mortify sin so far as I can discover it; though, alas, my desire is miserably thwarted through my own unwatchfulness.'[5] Simeon certainly had some grounds for conceit. He could not be unaware that his personality was so striking that no one could overlook him. People were bound to take sides when he was about, either accepting everything he said as gospel truth, or seeking out inconsistencies and infelicities behind which they could shelter from his challenge. He must have been conscious of the compliments that were paid him by being so much in demand as a public speaker and as an authority on all manner of Biblical and theological issues. His vanity had much to feed on, but he tried to starve it out as soon as he recognised it.

Consulted by so many and looked up to by young and old alike, so sure that he was right and that his right was God's right, Simeon from time to time became uncomfortably high-handed. The strange thing is that people seem to have accepted this without complaint. It was an age when men were often glad to have their minds made up for them. As early as 1785, when Simeon had only been in holy orders for three years, we find him sweeping away any possibility of opposition in an appointment to a church. At a clerical meeting held in Birmingham he approached one of its members whom he hardly knew personally, grasped hold of his hands in both of his, and without any further preliminaries said to him, 'Will you go to Creaton?' 'Where is it?' was the rather natural response of the astonished clergyman. Simeon had preached there the previous Sunday, found the living vacant, guessed the kind of man needed, and without consulting a soul took it upon himself to urge Thomas Jones to accept it, which he did.[6]

Again, in 1814 he wrote to Thomason one of his usual newsy letters and mentioned how St Peter's church, Colchester, was falling vacant. 'My two colleagues and myself shall have to present,' he writes, and all unconsciously then goes on 'or in other words, to which *I* shall have to present: for they will, I have no doubt, move entirely with me.' Most people did, and he expected them to, but it was not always good for his ego, even though he was nearly always right when it came to the matter of choosing men. 'I am no pope,' he once wrote about a decision taken by others of which he disapproved, but there were times when he looked rather like one. He never found it easy to accept a situation which ran counter to his better judgment.

Simeon's readiness to acknowledge when he was in the wrong or when his pride got the better of him, was borne out by his deliberate attempts to humiliate himself in repentance and self-reproof. He used to devote his birthdays, occasions when most people let themselves go a bit, as times of humbling. On September 24th, 1828, he enters in his diary: 'I spent this day as I have for these forty-three last years, as a day of humiliation; having increasing need of such seasons every year I live.' In his private notebook he wrote out twice over in large letters, 'Talk not about myself.' And back in 1788 he had reason to thank his kind elderly adviser, John Thornton, for the reminder of 'the three lessons which a minister has to learn, 1. Humility—2. Humility—3. Humility.' This was at the time when much of his personal vanity was being forcibly crushed by the unpopularity of his appointment. The sense of self-importance associated with being at the helm, consulted on this and that, becoming one whose word was final, was shorn of most of its disfiguring power by what he went through at that time. It was to develop in him what William Dealtry remembered as a 'remarkable humility which disposed him to listen to the observations of any person however inferior to himself in years or in station, and made him willing to learn of all and to be the servant of all.'[7]

But he never allowed himself to wallow in the self-denigration in which some of his colleagues indulged. He could not share Henry Martyn's fascination for the life of David Brainerd whose introspection he said had 'too much gloom and despondency for me.' But he greatly admired in Thomas Thomason his 'brokenness of spirit and lowliness before God, and humility before men . . . Where is the humility, the esteeming others better in honour, the willing to be the worst of all, the servant of all? Yet that was Thomason.' So he exhorted one of his evening conversation parties when the subject came up. Self-humiliation for Simeon consisted not of belittling the gifts that God had given him or pretending that he was a man of no account, or exaggerating the sins of which he was very conscious. He went about it by consciously bringing himself into the presence of God, dwelling thoughtfully on his majesty and glory, magnifying the mercy of his forgiveness and the wonder of his love. These were the things that humbled him—not so much his own sinfulness but God's incredible love. In an important memorandum which he drew up at a time when he was being taken to task for being serious and introspective, he wrote: 'With this sweet hope of ultimate acceptance with God, I have always enjoyed much cheerfulness before men; but I have at the same time laboured incessantly to cultivate the deepest humiliation before God. I have never thought that the circumstance of God's having forgiven me, was any reason why I should forgive myself.' He goes on to liken his sins to the innumerable stars in the heavens which would 'sink me in utter despair if I had not an assured view of the sufficiency and willingness of Christ to save me to the uttermost.'

Simeon writes warmly of the liturgy of the Church of England Communion Service with its tremendous emphasis on the heinousness of sin and the unlimited extent of the divine mercy, as expressing just what he felt. He then goes on in a truly classic passage:

> I do not see, so much as I could wish, an holy reverential awe of God. The confidence that is generally professed does not sufficiently, in my opinion, savour of a creature-like spirit, or of a sinner-like spirit. If ninety-nine out of a hundred, of even good men, were now informed for the first time, that Isaiah in a vision saw the Seraphim before the throne; and that each of the Seraphs had six wings; and then were asked, 'How do you think they employ their wings?' I think their answer would be, 'How? Why they fly with them with all their might; and if they had six hundred wings they would do the same, exerting all their powers in the service of their God.' They would never dream of their employing two to veil their faces, as unworthy to behold their God, and two to veil their feet, as unworthy to serve him; and devoting only the remaining two to what might be deemed their more appropriate use... I confess that this is the religion which I love; I would have a conscious unworthiness to pervade every act and habit of my soul; and whether the woof be more or less brilliant, I would have humility to be the warp.

The kind of discipline required for acts of deliberate self-humiliation was regarded as a very necessary part of godliness in Simeon's day, and he with his early rising and self-examination was a splendid example to others. The artist Farington remembers being told how he would penalise himself when he failed to get up at his appointed hour by putting a guinea into a box set aside for charity.[8] We may hope, for the sake of the underprivileged, that he was human enough to oversleep not infrequently. This form of personal penalty was rather more sensible than the extravagance of his youthful enthusiasm, flinging a gold coin into the river.

At one of his evening parties he was asked by men who cannot have been unaware of his partiality for the pleasures of the table whether his self-discipline extended to fasting. He replied, 'Fasting is of great value, too much thought of among Papists, too little among us . . . In former years I derived much personal benefit from fasting; but now I cannot (he was then sixty-eight), for I should disable myself from my needful duties, as it would impair my little strength.' In his early days he himself ate only one modest meal a day throughout Holy Week, and would carefully watch his own eating habits. But he was widely known for his fulfilment of the Biblical precept about using 'hospitality without grudging.' When he entertained, which he simply loved doing, he would spare no trouble or expense to make the occasion one that everybody could enjoy.

In a review of William Carus' Memoir of Simeon, the London *Guardian* of June 9th 1847 stated 'Nor should it be overlooked that with all his zeal for the good of others, he had some regard for his own comfort. His servants and carriage and rooms would have astonished the pious King whose charitable foundation contributed to his maintenance; and his character would be acquitted of the remotest tendency to asceticism by those who were his daily companions in the College Hall.' This was not an altogether fair judgment, and gives Simeon little credit for his personal self-denial. He admitted freely that he was 'by nature and habit of an extravagant disposition' and kept his 'establishment on rather a high scale in comparison of others.' Yet he claimed in all sincerity, and we hope modestly, 'I never throw away my money in foolish indulgencies, nor spend more of my income upon myself than I believe God himself approves.' When others were involved he saw no reason why he should treat them with frugality. The good things of life were there to be enjoyed and shared, and Simeon delighted in giving his guests the best.

All the same, he seems to have been glad that his own constitution stood up well to his entertaining for at the age of seventy-five he wrote to his 'friend and brother' Samuel Carr of Colchester: 'I invited a party last night to sup on your oysters, and we had a delicious feast. I beg to return you my best thanks for them. I ate of them with a zest such as I should have felt 40 or 50 years ago; and found not the slightest inconvenience from them . . . They shall make a feast of themselves, said I; and so they did.'[9] One such occasion was long remembered by those who heard about it. Simeon had just given directions to the college cook about the specially fatty loin of veal which he wanted for a large dinner party. It had to be the best, so on the way back from the kitchen he was seen suddenly to retrace his steps and was heard saying 'Be sure, Mr Lawrence, that it is a female.'[10] Of course he could not always live down this sort of thing. Long after his death, in King's College Combination Room stories about Simeon's little ways used to be passed round with the port. One in particular concerned his weakness for woodcocks. Apparently a certain Sir Francis Chantrey one day achieved great notoriety by shooting two woodcocks with one barrel. Some college wag celebrated the event by publishing this verse,

> Let Chantrey boast his wondrous skill,
> Who at one shot two cocks did kill;
> This feat our Simeon's fairly beaten,
> Who at one meal two cocks has eaten.[11]

Those were days before teetotalism was looked on as an essential part of evangelical holiness. Soft drinks and mineral waters as we understand them had not yet reached the table, and the domestic water supply of the eighteenth and early nineteenth century was neither plentiful nor pure. G. W. Russell, sympathetic author of *A Short History of the Evangelical Movement,* once wrote 'I cannot remember that at my father's house I ever saw a water-drinker. Debarred from worldliness, the Evangelicals went in for comfort; and the pleasures of the table were among the few which everyone could enjoy with a good conscience.'[12] In answer to a direct question on this thorny subject Simeon summarised his views in this way: 'When I first came up as an undergraduate, with very scanty means, I made my resolution (and have been enabled to keep it ever since) to show economy to myself, liberality to my friends, generosity to the poor. I never allow myself any indulgence, as such. Fruit and little luxuries I do not allow myself. When an undergraduate, I drank small beer, and gave my ale to the Lord, and this day I did the same feeling that I did not need ale today, and so saved a penny for the Lord. In putting tea into my teapot I have by habit learned to guess the value of even a half-penny, and when I can, to save it for God. But do not mistake me: this only regards myself personally. I never count pence when my friends are near me. I love to make them all comfortable.' Then, as if he realised this sounded rather too pious, he went on with a smile, 'And even as to myself, when sick I put myself at the head of my own poor's list. The Lord understands me.'

Charles Simeon's self-discipline extended to his means as well as his menu. When his friend Arthur Young in July 1804 recorded his stay in his diary, he reckoned that with the perquisites associated with his living in college 'his Fellowship is as good as 400 guineas a year to him',[13] which would be quite four times the average income of most parish clergymen of the time. Simeon himself told Francis Close that one reason why he retained his fellowship at King's (when many expected him to give it up after he came into his brother's legacy) was because it enabled him to live more economically and devote more money to God's work.[14] He kept his accounts with such meticulous and conscientious care that he once, in a rare burst of uncalculated bounty, gave an accountant £20 to discover how an error of one penny had crept in and upset his balance at the end of the year. Such was Simeon's integrity in financial matters that when his beloved Henry Martyn in 1812 was making abortive plans to come home on leave, he told Charles Grant that he would himself underwrite the expense. Having made this promise, he then took steps to alter his will so that in the event of his death Grant would be paid back in full for anything he had spent on Martyn's behalf.[15]

It was Simeon's usual practice to allocate a share of his income to various causes at the beginning of each year. While he never stated as much himself, a perusal of his account books shows that this was, certainly in the early part of his ministry, as much as one third. Having made this allocation, he would argue, he would not be tempted to boast when giving it away as it was already bespoken and, as it were, no longer belonged to him. He adopted an extremely common-sense attitude in this matter of Christian giving. He stated quite definitely that God would not expect a man with a small income and a family to give in the same proportion as a wealthier man with fewer commitments. He was very conscious of the poverty of so many of his fellow clergy, and would often, after listening to their tale of parochial problems, slip a small parcel into their hands on saying Goodbye. He liked to think of their happiness on opening it to find a windfall of two, five or even ten gold sovereigns.

Simeon's generosity was extended to many of the religious societies which in the early eighteen hundreds were springing up like mushrooms in the wake of the revival. He contributed to the African Institution and the Society for the Suppression of Vice,[16] but was equally ready to contribute 50 guineas towards the cost of raising a local Home Guard in 1803,[17] or a substantial sum to a fund for relieving starving German refugees after the French army successes in 1806.[18] But the kind of thing he liked doing best was helping a young man find the means of getting to college, or helping an older one out of financial difficulty. An example of this was the great Thomas Scott, author of *The Force of Truth,* a better Bible exponent than accountant. In 1803 he got into the hands of an unscrupulous publisher and before long was £1200 in debt. In spite of the fact that this Christian brother was known to break every rule in Simeon's book by trusting to 'one hour's peripatetic musing' for the preparation of his sermons, and in the pulpit so scolded his congregation that they were dwindling away, no sooner had Simeon heard of the straits he was in than he sent him a letter enclosing £590 and a considerable sum also for books, contributed by himself and some of his people.[19] Thomas Scott was thus enabled to continue the publication of his great commentary free from further anxiety, making a far greater success of it than of his Sunday sermons.

When Charles' merchant brother Edward suggested leaving him his estate near Ryde in his will he would hear none of it, asking for a limited legacy instead which he could then devote to the work of God more easily. When it eventually came to him as a sum of £15,000, Simeon devoted the whole of the interest each year to charity. In a private memorandum explaining for the benefit of his own executors how he hoped in this way to carry on his brother's charitable work, he wrote: 'Had I wished for money for my own use, I might have had half his fortune; but I wanted nothing for myself, being determined (as far as such a thing could be at any time said to be determined) to live and die in College where the income which I previously enjoyed (though moderate in itself) sufficed not only for all my own wants, but for liberal supplies to the poor also . . . The fact is, I have not increased my own expenditure above £50 a year.'

With all this emphasis on humiliation, frugality and self-denial one is tempted to ask if Simeon had any real sense of humour. We know from at least one of his portraits that he certainly possessed a kindly and winning smile, but did he ever laugh? And if so, at what kind of things? Laughter of course does not preserve well in print and cannot easily be recorded in a diary or memoir. We are dependent on the memories of those who saw a lot of him for an answer. The impression one gets is that he knew he ought, as a Christian, to be cheerful. He realised 'what a gloomy and repellent effect it would have were I a man who dared not smile or laugh.' 'I strive always to be cheerful, and to make religion attractive to the eye of those with whom, in the situation in which God has placed me, I am called into contact. To the ungodly I am a scarecrow, I know, for they avoid the very sight of me; but to other young men I do not find it so.'

He tried hard not to take himself too seriously, but there was always something a little forced and ponderous about his humour. There is no doubt that from time to time a real twinkle came into his eye, specially when he was contriving one of his jokes. Francis Close remembers catching sight of it under 'his great arched eyebrows.'[20] But one cannot help wondering if he really expected his hearers or readers to smile at some of his quaint metaphors and illustrative anecdotes. For example, he described his attitude to controversial issues as 'a man swimming in the middle of the Atlantic, not afraid of striking my feet against sunken rocks and in no danger of running against America or Africa'; difficult passages in Paul's epistles can be looked at, he said, 'as a dog looks at a hedgehog: he knows not what to do with it'; to a young man who asked him whether we should take literally Paul's reference to the 'rock which followed' the Israelites, Simeon's reply was 'Oh yes, of course, with a hop, skip and a jump!'[21] He told Daniel Wilson, apropos of his critics making a great deal of noise, 'I take the moon for my pattern. When she is at the full, the dogs bark at her. But I never yet heard of her stopping to enquire why they barked.'[22] In one of his more intimate letters to John Venn, during their mutual struggles against temptation as young Christians, he might well have caused his friend to smile as he read, 'I am convinced that that sad little impertinent Gentleman called Self, who intrudes himself so much into our thoughts on all occasions, will ever elude my grasp; if I could catch hold of him I think I would throw him where God has cast my sins—into the depths of the sea; I'd drown the Rascal. But I am afraid he would swim like a cork for he is exceedingly light and ever uppermost.'[23]

Towards the end of his life the poor man suffered a good deal from gout. Refusing to be sorry for himself he tried hard to laugh it off, sometimes with tears of pain in his eyes. In a letter to Samuel Carr he said 'The searching for an easy posture for one foot has been ample employment for 7 or 8 hours, whether by night or by day. As my enemy plays hide and seek, and when I had driven him out of one foot ran to the other, I can scarcely say what his conduct may be. For three Sundays he has kept me from the house of God.'[24] Abner Brown remembers him on his sofa, swaying to and fro, holding his painful leg while sweat stood out on his forehead, yet saying to a caller playfully and with a beaming smile, 'My brother, I am trying in vain to find a position in which the gout will let my leg be easy, but it is like the scourged soldier, hit high, hit low, it will not be satisfied.' In commenting to Thomason about his health which was limiting his activity he wrote, 'I compare myself to bottled small beer; being corked up, and only opened twice a week, I make a good report; but if I were opened every day I should soon be as ditch-water.'

Once when kept indoors by wintry weather he apologised for not being at his friend Edwards' clerical meeting in this way: 'I had proposed to be with you tomorrow if I had not been broken in upon by two old friends (unexpected and, I must add, rather unwelcome visitors at this time), Mr Frost and Mr Snow. As they have been with me some days, I was rather in hopes that they would have left before now; but they are not adepts at taking hints; and one cannot well thrust them out of doors against their will . . . When I go out with them, they are apt to take very improper liberties: one spits in my face, and the other pinches me.' Altogether a rather heavy wit. Farington tells how someone, concerned about his affected way of walking, once had the boldness to say to him, 'If he did not learn to turn in, instead of turn out his toes as he does, he would never be able to enter the straight gate.'[25] One cannot help thinking that Simeon was not greatly amused at this. But on the other hand nor was Farington himself when Simeon was showing him round Trinity College. In the colonnade under the Library he asked his friend to watch the knocker on a door at the end. He said he could move it by stamping his foot, which he thereupon did. 'The sound of the knocker striking the door was instantaneous and to my vision the knocker appeared to move. Upon my expressing my surprise at the effect he laughed and told me it was a deception caused by the echo of his stamp.'[26] This was the kind of thing that no doubt caused Arthur Young to eomment after Simeon had stayed a few days with him, 'He is remarkably cheerful and has much wit or something nearly allied to it.'[27] Francis Close, who tended to be pretty ponderous himself, was rather surprisingly intrigued by the older man's brand of humour, saying 'there was a racy wit about him and a natural playfulness perfectly captivating'.[28]

From these and other stories it is quite clear that Charles Simeon was 'a character'. For example, he caused much amusement once when he was sure he understood why a friend's chimney kept smoking, and in his impetuous way tried to cure it by his own devices, but the last state of that room was worse than the first. At one time he thought that he had succeeded in inventing a deaf-aid which he called not very happily 'A Reverberator', 'somewhat of the shape of a cockleshell' and 'capable of being held in the hollow of the hand without being seen', which he hoped would supercede the ear-trumpet. He urged Lord Harrowby to have one made for his son who was hard of hearing, and also for his sister-in-law, the Duchess of Beaufort.[29] History does not relate if anything came of this 'Simeonism'.

From his earliest disturbing impact on the complacency of Cambridge church life to his final triumphant funeral, Simeon must be reckoned as the most talked-about man in town and university alike. He even had a locally born lion-cub named after him when a circus was visiting Cambridge.[30] He seems to have been a source of considerable merriment to the insuppressible Thornton girls who, after a grand dinner party at which he was present, scribbled frivolous remarks against the names of the guests in their host's 'Dinner Book'. Their relevant comment on the preacher from Cambridge was 'Mr Simeon, with his eyes shut (Was this one of his mannerisms?): 'I'm delighted to see you. Peace be with you. May every blessing attend you . . . I can preach in 10 languages.'

One of the things that many people remember finding rather trying was Simeon's fussiness. It is of course the privilege of lonely dons to be pedantic to a degree, but he carried things a bit far. When it came to correcting the proofs of his two thousand printed sermons he did so with the most meticulous care. It was a practical demonstration of his perfectionist principles that he should always 'attend to the dotting of an *i*, or the crossing of a *t*, or the turning the tail of a *y*, if it only made the work more perfect.' A student from Cambridge, enlarging to Joseph Farington on the remarkable attendance of over 150 gownsmen at Simeon's services in 1813, felt he must add that he was 'such a lover of order that if a stick were removed from the place where he had set it he would not be easy till he saw it replaced.'[32] Even in his pocket Bible a footnote of his recalls an apparently unhappy memory . . . 'oil sprinkled (accidentally over my newly papered room)', against the passage Leviticus 8.30. Like many a bachelor don, he was extremely house-proud and very fussy about his carpets. To a careless undergraduate who left a sandy footprint to show he had failed to wipe his feet on the many mats provided, Simeon would as likely as not greet his visitor, 'Sir, is that the way to come into a gentleman's rooms?' and send him out to do what he had left undone. Possibly Matthew Preston had himself erred in some such way for he cannot refrain from stating in his memoir of his former pastor, 'He was courteous and truly kind to all who needed his counsel and assistance, with or without introduction; but no trifler could feel himself easy in his presence.'[33]

But the little storms that arose over his being pernickity did not last long and do not seem to have in any way discouraged the young men from crowding into his rooms in increasing numbers. One of Simeon's greatest attractions was his readiness to apologise when his temper let him down. A particular instance recorded by his biographer, who tended to soft-pedal his deficiencies, concerned an occasion when a servant stirred the fire in a way that Simeon thought particularly stupid, so much so that he leapt to his feet, thumped the poor man on the back and told him to stop. The same evening—it was not Simeon's day—someone put the wrong bridle on one of his precious horses, and at this the Old Apostle completely forgot his high calling and lost his temper. One of his closest friends at the time, Edward Edwards, thought he must reprove him for this and tried doing it by a ruse. He wrote him an anonymous letter signed 'John Softly' purporting to come from the offended servant saying how in the kitchen they could not understand how a gentleman with such a reputation for preaching and praying could not bridle his own tongue. Simeon saw through the hoax and readily admitted that the reproof was 'both just and necessary', signing himself 'Chas. Proud and Irritable'. He also asked his faithful friend and former convert not to flinch from reminding him about this besetting sin of bad temper; he would have done anything to be free of it.

Max Warren, in an admirable summary of both the strength and weakness of Simeon's personality, has written:

> Hot tempered by nature, he found clumsiness and carelessness in others an easy spur to anger. Impetuous in his likes and dislikes, he found it hard to adapt himself to those who moved more slowly. Extravagant in his affections he found the way of friendship often difficult. It is one of the marvels of spiritual history that a man thus tempered should have been able so to subdue his spirit as to face the years of opposition from parishioners, and the contempt and often hostility of the University, and in the end to win from all so great a regard.[34]

Being the honest and humble man of God that he was, Charles Simeon would not expect his limitations and failings to be glossed over. He probably would have agreed wholeheartedly with Charles Jerram that 'he was naturally of a haughty, impatient and impetuous temper', easily upset people, and all in all was one in whom 'the principles of nature and of grace were in direct and constant conflict'.[35] His long battle against that irritability which dogged him right up to his final illness was so much part of his Christian struggle that he would expect it to be recorded. But so also would he hope that his growth in grace and deliverance from falling were also clearly mentioned for then God would receive the glory for what his grace had done in his heart. He liked to think that he was 'the very masterpiece of Divine grace' while at the same time the last and least in the kingdom of heaven.

Much of this battle was fought out on his knees, or walking up and down behind the stone balustrade on the roof of Gibbs' building in King's. He could and did pray anywhere, and sometimes would spend all night in prayer. He also used his daily rides over the fens as 'my season of intercession for all my dear absent friends . . . I ramble all over the world without interruption.' Henry Venn specially remembered the spirit of his praying: 'On Monday my affectionate friend Simeon walked over and slept here. Oh how refreshing were his prayers! We were all revived; he left a blessing behind him.' Mr Simeon did me 'good like medicine; and his prayer with me took off the weight which lay heavy upon me.'[36] J. J. Gurney, a later friend, good Quaker that he was, while appreciating Simeon's free and extempore praying 'poured forth under apparently intense feelings of devotion', went on to emphasise his use of silence in prayer. Simeon had told him that he often encouraged his clerical brethren to wait on God in quietness, and not always to frame their prayer in words. When sharing this kind of silent meditation with him Gurney recalled how 'his countenance, full as it was of strong lines, was marked by such an appearance of devotional feeling as I have seldom seen equalled.' Even so candid a critic as we have seen Sir James Stephen to have been, felt bound in all fairness and a great deal of respect to acknowledge: 'He was indeed one of those on whom the impress of the Divine image was distinct and vivid . . . Neither historian, poet, artist, lawyer, politician, nor philosopher, he was simply a devout and believing man who, in the language of Bunyan, "dwelt far from the damp shadows of Doubting Castle". ' He went on to suggest that the Church of England could do worse than substitute 'St Charles of Cambridge' for some of her less genuine or less inspiring saints.[37]

Perhaps the deepest sign of saintliness in Simeon was his warmheartedness, the love that quickly asked for forgiveness and as quickly offered it, that thought of others before himself and that understood others better than himself. Testimonies on all sides and through his long life tell how Simeon certainly lived out to the full his own repeated principle, 'Love is the universal conqueror.'[38] How often in his notes, diary and letters do we read such expressions as 'Our hearts were full of love to each other,' or 'Love should be the spring of all actions, and especially of a minister's.' Or possibly it is Simeon saying, 'I think that the more intensely I love those who are beloved of him, the more I think I resemble him. The proper model of our love for each other is Christ's love to us.' Or it may be someone else's comment, 'He is full of love towards all who love his Master, and a faithful sympathising friend to those who have the privilege of sharing in his more intimate affections.' Quite early on in his public ministry this was the impression of his Cambridge visitor that William Wilberforce humbly recorded in his journal: 'Simeon with us—his heart glowing with love of Christ. How full he is of love, and of desire to promote the spiritual benefit of others. Oh! that I might copy him as he Christ.'

At the end of his life it was still the same. William Dealtry, for whom Simeon secured the living of Clapham after John Venn's death, spoke in his obituary sermon of the 'love which ever beamed' on Simeon's face. The Duchess of Beaufort, as she told her daughter, never forgot the lesson she had learnt from 'Mr Simeon' when tempted to impatience with and criticism of others' behaviour: 'Let us sit upon the seat of love instead of judgment,' he used to say.[39] He was renowned for 'the candour and kindness with which he ascribed to the conduct of others, even when he could not approve it, the best possible motives.'[40] An example of this occurred in October 1827 when Simeon was staying in Norfolk with the Gurneys and their other guest, Fowell Buxton, hero of the anti-slavery campaign. Apparently Simeon was hurt because Buxton had preferred to go out shooting instead of attending a Jews' Society meeting in Norwich which Simeon had thought all important. A few days afterwards he received a present of game, a peace-offering which Buxton had good reason to know would be very acceptable. Charles Simeon acknowledged it in a long letter, the gist of which was that while he was quite upset at the time, on thinking it over he realised that he would not have wanted his friend to come to the meeting just to please him. So he closes his letter with one of his attempts at light-heartedness: 'Now my dear friend, you see you have shot me flying, and penetrated my heart, and let out, not ill-blood (there is none of that I assure you) but the stream of love which was pent up there.'[41] And as if that was not enough about what was really quite a trivial incident, he has the cheek to ask Buxton for some more game for a party he was planning in a fortnight's time.

Although no one knew better than Simeon that it is not possible really to love people from the pulpit, yet he never hesitated to urge on budding preachers that there is no substitute for love in the heart if a speaker is to win anyone. 'Only speak from *love* to man' he would press upon his young ordinands. He was sad that Henry Martyn on board ship to India, surrounded by his congregation of hardened troops, had wept for them but not with them,[42] and preached them a sermon on hell which got all their backs up. He felt that he should have spoken 'in love and gentleness and from some other text, showing that he only desired to do them good,' and he did not hesitate to use him as a warning to others.

When it came to closer human relationships, Simeon, along with most of his evangelical contemporaries, does not seem to have clearly distinguished between what he termed 'the affections' which were to be encouraged, and 'the passions' which were not. Living the bachelor life that he did, surrounded by men all day long and finding amongst them his closest friends, he was often treading on uncertain ground. What is one to make of Abner Brown's recollections of his effusiveness? 'Who can forget the affectionate brotherly way in which he grasped, and tightly too, a friend's hand in both of his; and if the parting were for a long absence, or under circumstances of sorrow, how he would raise the hand thus doubly grasped, and press it to his lips?' This affectation which would be regarded in most circles today as not just old-fashioned but effeminate, was in Simeon's case an outward expression of an affection both warm and chaste.

Simeon was very conscious, as he told Farington once, that 'in a college life the society of woemen [*sic*] is wanting and men grow splenetick,'[43] but when ladies did appear no one could have shown them more respect and courtesy. Although there is no trace of his ever having had any kind of romantic experience, and Henry Martyn's relations with Lydia may well have discouraged him more than he realised, he did thoroughly enjoy the company of his curates' wives and those of his other friends. We have seen him entertaining them at his houseparties, and in his letters his greetings to the ladies of the house are always warm and cordial, very much so. It gave him special joy when Mrs Dornford, the mother of his colleague Thomas Thomason, took up residence in a house in Pease Hill near the market, where she became one of his most devoted parishioners. From time to time Simeon used to hold house-meetings in her house as a homely alternative to his bachelor quarters in King's. Over a period of thirty years he developed what he called a brotherly relationship with her, the nearest thing he ever came to having a feminine shoulder to lean, or even weep, upon. And his staunch arms were always ready to uphold her in return.

This was particularly so when their dear Thomas sailed for India. Taking his mother under his wing, he wrote to Thomas' wife, 'I hope I love his mother for her own sake, and most of all for her Lord's sake: but I love her also for her son's sake.' His affection for all three of them is quite touching, and letter upon letter after many months' journey to Calcutta by sea, told the young couple that they were daily in his thoughts and prayers as 'if you were only twenty miles off.' In 1813 when Simeon had been having one of his rare patches of bad health, it was with Esther Dornford and her daughter that he spent three happy summer months by the sea 'in quiet retirement' as he told her son. 'If this is wrong,' he went on, 'the fault is yours. You remember your parting charge, "Son, behold thy mother," so that if we obey your commands, you must bear all the blame. Truly, I find her to be a mother to me; nor do I believe it possible for a human being to manifest a maternal spirit to a greater extent towards her own offspring than she does towards me. I pray God I may be permitted in my turn to minister in some measure to her happiness.' Simeon, who could hardly remember his own mother, found Mrs Dornford, though she was only a few years older than him, one who filled a big gap in his life, and provided a feminine touch to his existence from middle-age until within two years of his own death. Her memorial tablet in Holy Trinity church was erected with the loving gratitude of a true son and a grateful brother.

The close links which bound the Thomason family and Charles Simeon together were further strengthened when he was asked to become unofficial guardian to his godson, James Thomason, who in 1814 at the age of six came to England for his schooling, and made his home in the holidays with his grandmother. This young man was to become the distinguished Governor of the North-Western Provinces of India, the chief creator of the 'Punjab System' of government.[44] He was honoured by having one of the houses of his old college, Haileybury, named after him. One cannot help wondering what his reaction would have been if in later life anyone had told him that Simeon had made special arrangements for James' 'flannels to be ready to put on at a moment if wanted', and he was not referring to cricket wear. Simeon welcomed his new charge as giving him something practical he could do to forward the work of God in India by relieving his parents of undue anxiety for their son. He went into raptures about the boy's 'loveliness and sweetness of disposition', his curiosity and enquiring mind, and took great delight in showing him factories and fisheries, castles and stately homes and other interesting holiday attractions. At Cambridge he arranged for him to take up riding every day but he was nearly thrown into a panic to find him, high summer though it was, fishing on the banks of the Cam 'without hat, coat or waistcoat'. He promised his father, 'Every attention which he can have he will, but all tempered with wisdom and discretion.'

And so a new interest broke into the middle-aged don's life, and the man who thought that his sermon outlines were suitable for family prayers began to realise he had a lot to learn about children. He sent James to Matthew Preston's boarding school and thence to the East India Company's college at Haileybury. His progress and reports were followed with the most intense concern by his godfather who impressed upon him that he was 'your loving father in man's stead, your anxious father in God's stead.' James would have appreciated it rather more had Simeon been able to cast this anxiety on the Lord for at one point he got greatly worked up because he thought he detected a decline in his young charge's standards. Noticing that a report stating his conduct had been 'quite regular and correct' was followed by a later one which had dropped the word 'quite', he wrote to the innocent boy in unreasonable distress: 'Beloved James, you have trod a distinguished path: get back to it without delay . . . let me have the supreme delight of sending you off to your father confirmed in all that is good, and laden with the love and applause of all who have the oversight of you.' James Thomason was not unreasonably upset by this somewhat heavy-handed rebuke, and Simeon found he had to write again at once to try and pick up the brick that he had dropped in his exaggerated concern. However, all was forgiven and forgotten and by the time that the young man had reached eminence in the Indian Civil Service he was able to write to his friend Sir Henry Lawrence that it was 'to Charles Simeon I owe all I have in this country.'[45]

Simeon may indeed have been impetuous and intolerant by nature and ready to burst out on occasion, but in fact there were many instances in his life where his patience was quite exceptional. He likened his natural spirit to the bias in bowls which he needed to counteract by going to the other extreme. For instance, when some of his parishioners had provoked him almost beyond bearing, he bore with them for month after month, giving the trouble makers all the time in the world to make amends, when many a man would have tolerated the situation no longer. 'I have been used,' he said, 'to sail in the Pacific; I am now learning to navigate the Red Sea that is full of shoals and rocks, with a very intricate passage. I trust the Lord will carry me safely through; but my former trials have been nothing to this.' In advising an over-zealous and under-patient parson how to deal with difficult church members, speaking out of painful personal experience, he told him a parable: 'Two ships were aground at London Bridge. The proprietors of the one sent for a hundred horses and pulled it to pieces. Proprietors of the other waited for the tide; and with sails and rudder directed it as they pleased.' Many a man would have crumpled up under the provocation that Simeon suffered from time to time, but as Francis Close of Cheltenham, a man of like temperament, said, 'In the discharge of duty to be indifferent alike to the frowns and smiles of his fellow-creatures, what courage, firmness, wisdom and love are needful!'[46]

Simeon was under no illusions about the relationship of faith to temperament. He never expected a man's natural personality to be permanently altered by religious conversion. When he was discussing the meaning of sanctification and the degree of perfection that God might demand of an imperfect person, his common sense and pastoral experience among young and old led him to certain original convictions. At least they were new in his day when it was only too easy for 'enthusiasts' to claim that the grace of God swept away all imperfections and a Christian could expect to be set free from every disfiguring sin once he had surrendered to Christ. Not so, says Simeon.

> Remember, religion does not so alter the character as to leave nothing remaining. An ardent and enthusiastic man, when he becomes religious,

> will still be of the same temperament . . . The timid will be timid still; the person who shuddered at a toad before his conversion, will do the same afterwards. Religion gives, indeed, a new direction and tone to the mind. We are vessels, and religion, when poured into us will taste (as Horace would express it) of the *tan* or the *wood* of our natural dispositions . . . It will eventually and gradually correct our natural failings, but will not obliterate the effects of nervous or constitutional weakness or infirmity.

So spake the Old Apostle in his most sensitive mood knowing the truth of what he said from his own tough experience and from the confidences he had listened to in the seclusion of his rooms in King's.

One is continually struck by the way in which, as Simeon grew older, the common sense which was always such a feature of his personality became more and more marked. By the time he was nearing sixty he admitted 'I am arrived at a time when my views of early habits, particularly in relation to the Ministry, are greatly changed. I see many things in a different light from what I once did, such as the beauty of order, of regularity, and the wisdom of seeking to win souls by kindness, rather than to convert them by harshness and what I once called fidelity. I admire more the idea which I have of our blessed Lord's spirit and ministry than I once did.' This increasing maturity showed itself in much of his correspondence. Commenting on how liable young Christians often are to make great mistakes through excessive enthusiasm, he said 'Of the two, too much zeal is better than too little; but if we can blend zeal with wisdom we do better.' To a heresy-hunting clergyman who wanted Simeon to 'answer and knock down' a certain suspect preacher, he replied 'I know you will forgive me if I say that the very account you give of yourself in relation to controversy is a dissuasive from embarking in it. Let a man once engage in it, and it is surprising how the love of it will grow upon him; and he will both find a hare in every bush, and will follow it with something of a huntsman's feelings.'

Simeon was far more broad-minded than many evangelicals both before and after him. He confessed to having turned down 'one of the holiest men of our age' as unfit for a particular post 'because he wanted elasticity of mind. He could not, I am sure, become all things to all men. It is a Minister's duty to be so.' When he was consulted by someone on how rigidly one should stick to one's principles, Simeon wrote, 'Many think that the opposite to right must be wrong; but the opposite to right may be right. . . . The human mind is very fond of fetters, and is apt to forge them for itself. This is not, however, recommended by Your very affectionate Friend and Brother in the Lord.'[47] Similarly, when the subject was Sunday observance, which is quite falsely considered by many to be an evangelical invention, Simeon showed the breadth of his sympathies and the depth of his insight when he wrote to the enquiring Mary Elliott:

> I think that many Judaize too much, and that they would have joined the Pharisees in condemning our Lord on many occasions. I do not think that they err in acting up to their own principles (there they are right); but that they err in making their own standard a standard for all others. This is a prevailing evil among religious persons. They will in effect argue thus: '*I* do not walk out on a Sabbath day; therefore an artisan may not walk out into the fields for an hour on that day.' They forget that the poor man is confined all the rest of the week, which they are not; and that they themselves will walk in their own garden, when the poor have no garden to walk in . . . To Judaize with Pharisaic strictness is not well; and to condemn others for not acting up to that standard is, I think, very undesireable.

Simeon's common sense gained much of its strength by being linked with a 'perfectly independent mind,' which was one of the requirements that he expected of those who would follow him as Trustees of the churches he later acquired. At a time when Christian men and women were tempted to find an easy security by aligning themselves with some party or 'ism', Simeon maintained a mature independence of what others thought or taught. He cast his net widely and let every Scripture have its say from within its own context from Genesis to Revelation. As the hundred pages of comprehensive index to the later editions of his sermons show, he did not press always on the same points, and so his people could count on hearing something fresh and original on almost every occasion. Thus, together with the increasing stature of character which these extracts have displayed, Simeon retained uncommon and enviable freshness throughout his long life. For over half a century his personal standards never faltered, his zeal remained unabated, his impact gained a sharper cutting edge, and his addresses never palled. Yet he could in 1824 claim in all sincerity 'I am precisely the same that I ever was!' He never spoke a truer word.

CHAPTER ELEVEN

Simeon's School of Thought

Being no one's convert, Charles Simeon became no one's follower. He enjoyed an independence of outlook and adopted an objective attitude to most of those issues over which so many Christians, both before and after his time, have insisted on taking sides and outlawing their opponents. He refused to pigeon-hole his theology or to ally himself with any of the current 'isms' of the day. As he himself liked to express it, in the preface to his *Horae Homileticae,* 'The author is no friend to systematisers in Theology.'[1] For many years he had lived a life of personal isolation unrelieved, so far as we can tell from his writings, by any wide reading. He hardly ever quotes any authority other than the actual text of the Scriptures. He was really never happier than when shut in in his rooms with a chance of uninterrupted Bible study, and it would be from a sense of duty rather than pleasure that he would drag himself away from his open Bible to mix with the outside world. He hardly felt the need to draw on the ancient Fathers or even the Reformation divines for, as he said, he took 'his religion from the Bible and endeavours, as much as possible, to speak as that speaks.' 'He thought for himself,' writes Abner Brown, 'seldom adopting opinions at second-hand, at least without first making them his own, and adding to them the stamp of his own modifications.' 'As for names and parties in religion, he equally disclaims them all'[2], was how the author of the Preface described his own attitude. He would sign on nobody's dotted line, nor would he define his beliefs in any more cut and dried fashion than the creeds of his own church provided. He wanted to feel free to follow the Scriptures wherever they led him, even when one passage might appear to conflict with another. Many of his followers found this a disconcerting attitude but he himself had no doubts that it was the right one for him.

Simeon lived at the time when the Christian public had been driven to take sides between the followers of John Wesley and those of George Whitefield and the Countess of Huntingdon. The Arminian views of Wesley and the Calvinist teaching of his former colleague, had divided the converts of the revival into two camps. Within a few years of his ordination Simeon decided on his own attitude largely as a result of a memorable interview which he had with John Wesley himself. On December 20th, 1784, the up-and-coming young Church of England minister from Cambridge rode over to Hinxworth where the veteran evangelist was conducting meetings. Wesley's journal for that date reads: 'I had the satisfaction of meeting Mr Simeon, Fellow of King's College in Cambridge. He has spent some time with Mr Fletcher at Madeley; two kindred souls, much resembling each other in fervour of spirit and earnestness of their address. He gave me the pleasing information that there are three parish churches in Cambridge (i.e. Holy Trinity, St Edward's and the Round Church) wherein true Scriptural religion is preached, and several young gentlemen who are happy partakers of it.'

Part of the conversation between these two men of God was recorded by Simeon himself and published anonymously in the preface to his printed sermons. It shows the importance that he attached to it as a formative influence on the course he was in future to pursue when faced with occasions of controversy:

> 'Sir, I understand that you are called an Arminian; and I have been sometimes called a Calvinist; and therefore I suppose we are to draw daggers. But before I consent to begin the combat, with your permission I will ask you a few questions, not from impertinent curiosity, but for real instruction . . . Pray Sir, do you feel yourself a depraved creature, so depraved that you would never have thought of turning to God if God had not first put it into your heart?'
>
> 'Yes, I do indeed.'
>
> 'And do you utterly despair of recommending yourself to God by anything you can do; and look for salvation solely through the blood and righteousness of Christ?'
>
> 'Yes, solely through Christ.'
>
> 'But, Sir, supposing you were first saved by Christ, are you not somehow or other to save yourself afterwards by your own works?'
>
> 'No; I must be saved by Christ from first to last.'
>
> 'Allowing then that you were first turned by the grace of God, are you not in some way or other to keep yourself by your own power?'
>
> 'No.'

'What then, are you to be upheld every hour and every moment by God, as much as an infant in its mother's arms?'

'Yes, altogether.'

'And is all your hope in the grace and mercy of God to preserve you unto his heavenly kingdom?'

'Yes, I have no hope but in him.'

'Then, Sir, with your leave, I will put up my dagger again; for this is all my Calvinism; this is my election, my justification by faith, my final perseverance: it is, in substance, all that I hold, and as I hold it: and therefore, if you please, instead of searching out terms and phrases to be a ground of contention between us, we will cordially unite in those things wherein we agree.'[3]

Simeon was clearly delighted with the way the conversation went, or the way in which he succeeded in directing it, and to know that in spite of his apparent brashness, he retained the affection of the great Mr Wesley who was happy to meet him again a few years later.

It would be tedious to try to follow the issues raised in this historic interview any further for the divisions of the church no longer run on these lines. A whole chapter is devoted to the subject in Abner Brown's *Recollections* as it had a full airing from time to time at their conversation parties. With a succinctness which really over-simplified the controversy Simeon maintained that both parties 'are right in all they affirm and wrong in all they deny'. He was glad to know that his beloved Church of England was in no way exclusively associated with one side or the other. Of his own attitude, and of that which he taught the young men whom he wanted to guard from needless disputation, the *Christian Observer* in 1828 had this to say when reviewing the earlier edition of his *Horae Homileticae*: 'We know of no writer living or dead who is more anxious to let every part of Scripture speak its own meaning . . . If there be those who say his trumpet gives an uncertain sound, we may justly reply that it is uncertain only as respects inviting men to enlist themselves under the banner of this or that rival theological chieftain; but it is never uncertain in its summons to them to march under the banner of Christ crucified.'[4] 'I love the simplicity of the Scriptures,' said he who pored over them night and day. 'I wish to receive and inculcate every truth precisely in the way and to the extent that it is set forth in the inspired Volume. Were this the habit of all divines, there would soon be an end of most of the controversies that have agitated and divided the Church of Christ.'[5]

It is possible, by a careful study of the doctrines which lie behind his thousands of sermons, for which there is no room in a work of this kind, to see how consistent Simeon invariably was. His ability to see more than one point of view did not mean that his own teaching varied from one time to another, except in maturity. No one ever accused him of being 'woolly' or indefinite in the theology he passed on to others. He was quite happy as he said, using an analogy of John Newton's,[6] if controversial matters melted into his sermons like sugar in tea, unacceptable in bulk but leaving a recognisable taste. He liked to compare doctrinal mysteries to the working of the moon on the tides or the turning of opposing wheels in the mechanism of a watch.[7] This led him in 1825 to give expression to his much-quoted but only once uttered aphorism: 'The truth is not in the middle, and not in one extreme; but in both extremes.' 'As wheels in a complicated machine may move in opposite directions and yet subserve one common end, so may truths *apparently opposite* be perfectly reconcilable with each other, and equally subserve the purposes of God in the accomplishment of man's salvation.' Simeon nowhere develops to any degree this throwing away of Aristotle's 'golden mean', and perhaps its value has been exaggerated. But at least it did help the clergy of the future whom he was so carefully training from expecting to be able to grasp all required truth in simple capsule form before they had had time to realise what a vast subject they were embarking upon and how wide its ramifications. 'How preposterous would it have been of Columbus,' he told them, 'when he first discovered the New World from his ships, to have immediately set about describing the extent and character of the unknown land.'

Daniel Wilson, distinguished Vicar of Islington who went on to become Bishop of Calcutta, believed that Simeon deliberately planned to create 'a school of Biblicism', but Abner Brown more accurately states that 'his opinions were gradually recognised as a school of Divinity.' It is quite clear that after over fifty years' consecutive training of generations of 'Simeonites' these men in their various spheres did come to represent a definite school of thought in the church, the makings of what Simeon himself least wanted, 'a party'. Sharing the same convictions, taught in the same school, drawing upon the same sole Source-Book, it was inevitable that these evangelical clergy with their congregations should influence the Church of England in a Bible-centred direction. When on one occasion Charles Simeon picked up a small parcel off the table and used it as an illustration about how to handle the Scriptures as a whole, with no extraneous matters intruding, he was in fact demonstrating what evangelicals ever since have tried to maintain, the priority of the Bible and its exclusive authority in matters of faith and doctrine. 'I soon learned that I must take the Scriptures with the simplicity of a little child, and be content to receive as God's testimony what he has revealed, whether I can unravel all the difficulties that may attend it or not. . . . I feel that I cannot even explain how it is that I move my finger, and therefore I am content to be ignorant of innumerable things which exceed not only my wisdom, but the wisdom of the most learned men in the universe.' In this Bible-centred, uncritical simplicity lay much of his strength. We must remember that in his day the critical approach to the Biblical text had hardly begun to dawn.

In accepting the holy Scriptures as the supreme authority Simeon was but being a loyal member of his church which had placed them there at the Reformation. His special contribution was to take them down from the distant pedestal, brush off the dust of over a century's neglect, and open them up. As he did so, the truth of their inspiration became clearly demonstrated by the effect that such Bible exposition had upon those who heard it. As the veracity of the Bible had not yet been called in question, its inspiration had not needed to be defined. Simeon took a very reasonable view about it. He was quite prepared to admit that while 'no error in doctrine or other important matter is allowed; yet there are inexactnesses in reference to philosophical and scientific matters because of its popular style.' He was ready to point out places where no one could be expected to take the text literally, and yet he would yield to none in treating every page with profound respect. Above all, he begged his hearers to realise that 'we cannot understand all now; but hereafter the veil shall be removed, and then we shall understand the whole.' When he was pressed to be more specific, he would distinguish between what he called 'plenary' and 'supervisory' inspiration. The former involved revealing 'those things which man could not know, or which the writer did not know', and the latter, watching over 'the things which the writer did know, to prevent him from going wrong.'

Simeon was much more interested in the interpretation than in the inspiration of the Bible. He started here from the premise that he was 'content to sit as a *learner* at the feet of the holy Apostles', and had 'no ambition to teach them how they ought to have spoken.'[8] To Simeon it was enough, when he opened his Bible, that he was touching something sacred. 'Let persons enter on Scripture as holy ground, putting off their shoes, not leaning on any commentator or expounder,' though many were to lean on him as the years went on. 'Commentators cannot do everything,' he used to say. 'They break the marrow bone, but you must yourself extract what is valuable.' He disapproved of people using the Bible for crystal-gazing or as a bran-tub out of which could be drawn inspiring thoughts totally divorced from their context. 'Scripture is not a collection of precepts, it is a whole.' He would not allow men to misinterpret the Scriptures by making them 'refer to Christ and his salvation when no such object appears to have been in the contemplation of the inspired writer.'[9] For example, he was one who held that neither the Good Samaritan nor Paul's mention of the 'unspeakable gift' in 2 Cor. 9:15 had any direct primary reference to Christ. Yet, when there was clear justification for it, no one could more movingly proclaim Christ as the key to all the Scriptures.[10] In one of his sermons he anticipated a more modern Christian practice, the supply of a regular system of Bible readings for daily personal use: 'If we made a practice of selecting daily some short portion of Scripture for our meditation throughout the day, the most ignorant among us would soon attain a knowledge which at present appears far beyond his reach.'[11] He was a great believer in the lay Christian studying the Bible for himself.

The trouble was that there were far too many homes without Bibles and far too few Bibles printed that were suitable for private reading. No wonder, then, that when in 1803 moves were made by members of the Clapham Sect to form a society for the dissemination of the Bible in this and other countries, Charles Simeon was in the forefront of its supporters. He saw it grow from its original modest purpose of supplying much needed Bibles for Wales until by 1825 it had distributed no less than four and a half million Bibles in all parts of the world. The story of the British and Foreign Bible Society's development is a testimony to the place that the Bible was gaining in public esteem as a result of religious revival coinciding with the increase of literacy in the country. The society, begun as it was on an inter-denominational basis, forged ahead from the start, so much so that Simeon's great opponent, Professor, later Bishop, Herbert Marsh had to admit that 'an attempt to oppose it is like attempting to oppose a torrent of burning lava that issues from Etna or Vesuvius.'[12]

But opposition was strong, and a spate of pamphlets were produced, and duly answered, arguing that the working man could not really be trusted with the Bible. In 1816 one of these stated 'There is a striking difference between not allowing a poor man to read the Bible and not giving him the Bible to read; between taking it from him, and putting it into his hands. The plain practical rule is—neither give him the Bible, nor take it from him . . . The Bible should not be industriously put into his hands because it is too obscure for his rude understanding.'[13] With similar arrogance, complaining that through the activities of this society many congregations were actually being encouraged to follow the lessons and the preacher's text in their new 'pocket' Bibles, 'An Orthodox Churchman' wrote 'How contemptible must the Bible become when thus soiled by the hands of the vulgar.'[14] S. T. Coleridge shared this point of view, but much more politely, on the grounds that handing out the Bible 'without comment' was tantamount to ignoring all the years of patient scholarship that had been devoted to it.[15] Simeon and the evangelicals ignored these objections and carried on their good work regardless.

In 1824, however, the progress of the Bible Society's work was temporarily interrupted by a violent agitation from quite a different direction. When it transpired that copies of the Bible printed for circulation on the continent in Roman Catholic countries included the Apocrypha, Robert Haldane, brother of James who had been such a friend to Simeon on his Scottish tours, opened a virulent attack on the society. In the course of it he took Simeon to task for having supported its action, as he did, on the principle of St. Paul, 'I am made all things to all men that I might by all means save some.' Simeon's reply was quite straightforward: 'I fear not the Apocrypha if the Bible is with it.' He was so anxious to see the Word of God circulating in Europe in any form, and it would not have been acceptable without the Apocrypha bound up with it in Catholic fashion, that he thought the price well worth paying. Not so the fiery Robert Haldane who, quite incorrectly, accused him of 'uncertainty respecting the divine original of particular portions of the Bible.'[16] The *Christian Observer*, as always, stood right behind Simeon, stating its firm belief that 'this most important society . . . has been the instrument of conferring greater benefits on the world than any other institution, ancient or modern.'[17] However, the Committee had to yield to the pressure generated on this particular issue if it was to continue to retain the support of Nonconformists, Presbyterians and Anglicans alike. Its work went forward, and continues to do so to this day. Simeon was disappointed at their decision to drop the Apocrypha because he felt it would so greatly limit their field of operations abroad. But he did not desert them, telling his good friend Samuel Carr, 'The Bible Society will yet do good and still need support. But I do think that the field which they abandon should be occupied.'[18]

For a summary of Simeon's Biblical outlook one cannot do better than look at the sermon he preached before the University on 17th March, 1811, on 'I determined not to know anything among you, save Jesus Christ, and him crucified.'[19] This was the text which he himself chose to appear on his epitaph in Holy Trinity church. The sermon itself, under the title *Evangelical Religion Described*, was printed and distributed after his death to everyone in the parish according to a clause in his will. He begins his address by acknowledging that God can speak and has spoken to man in various ways in the past, but it is mainly through the written word expounded by authorised teachers that men can come to recognise the will of God. When he came to deal with the crucifixion, he points out how much more Paul dwells on the doctrine about the cross than on the event itself. The death of Christ, he explains, is firstly the ground of all our hopes and secondly the motive of our obedience. There is no other way in which sinful men could be reconciled to a holy God, and it is the love of Christ in dying for us which is the driving force that leads a man to forsake sin and seek forgiveness. This, says Simeon, is the heart of the Gospel, the evangel, and it is when 'viewing its transcendent excellency we must rejoice and glory in it ourselves, and show forth its fruits in a life of entire devotedness to God; we must call upon our hearers also to rejoice and glory in it, and to display sanctifying effects in the whole of their life and conversation. Thus to preach, and thus to live, would characterise a person and his ministry as evangelical in the eyes of the Apostle.' He closed the address, as one might expect, with an urgent appeal to his listeners to get to know Christ for themselves and to give him first place in their lives.

Simeon's views, of course, were those shared by all divines who called themselves evangelical. Samuel Thodey, one of the Dissenting Ministers in Cambridge, in an obituary tribute to his Church of England brother with whom he was spiritually and theologically so much at one, said how 'He laid great stress in his preaching upon the depravity of human nature, the divinity and atonement of Christ, the justification of a sinner exclusively through the merits and righteousness of the Redeemer, the necessity of the agency of the Holy Spirit to restore the divine image, and final perseverance.'[20] Simeon had come to believe all this not because it happened to be the correct corpus of faith for an evangelical, but because, like Hugh Latimer of St Edward's church, John Wesley of Epworth, Henry Venn of Huddersfield and hundreds of others, he had found it all in his Bible, and it fully answered his need. He could never forget what it had meant to him as a young man to learn of the way of forgiveness through the sacrificial death of Jesus Christ at Calvary. That was the 'ground of his own hopes' and 'the subject of all his ministrations' as his memorial tablet records. Right to the end of his life he found his assurance, as he said during his last illness, 'in the *sovereignty* of God in choosing such a one—and the *mercy* of God in pardoning such a one—and the *patience* of God in bearing with such a one—and the *faithfulness* of God in perfecting his work and performing all his promises to such a one.' He needed no further inner security than these 'certain truths of which I never would be unconscious at any moment: 1st. I am a creature—a mere worm; 2nd. I am a sinner, whose guilt exceeds all that can be expressed or conceived; 3rd. I am redeemed by the blood of God's only dear Son, and completely reconciled to my God and Father.' And so he would urge upon men and women in sermon, in letter and by word of mouth, their 'need of a dying Saviour to atone for you by his blood, and a living Saviour to renew you by the influence of his Spirit.'

Simeon was, throughout his long life, the complete Anglican. This comes out particularly when we examine his teaching on the sacraments of the Gospel. He did not deliver many sermons on Baptism or Holy Communion for the simple reason that he had committed himself to preaching on a different passage each time in order eventually to cover the whole Bible, with a view to the publication of his outlines. Consequently he seldom repeated himself, and as texts about the sacraments are not many, sermons on these subjects were infrequent. But we must remember that he supplemented his pulpit with instruction in the Parish Room for his own people and in his college rooms for ordinands and other students. On these occasions he could and did tackle sacramental doctrine.

Baptism was more of a controversial matter in those days than Communion. Simeon stood between the Dissenters who rejected infant baptism and those considerable number of Church of England clergy who taught the baptismal regeneration of infants. The Reformers' term, 'regeneration', he declared was never intended to be synonymous with the new birth: 'They use it for the beginning of that process by which we are changed, and not for the change as if effected at once.' On the other hand, Simeon certainly believed that where parents had true faith their prayers for the child would be answered and they could well look upon Holy Baptism as the occasion when the Holy Spirit begins his work in the heart. In his university sermon, *An Appeal to Men of Wisdom and Candour*, he stated: 'Great, exceeding great, benefit accrues to the soul from baptism. In many instances, where the ordinance is really attended upon in faith, and prayer is offered up to God in faith, we do believe that God bestows a peculiar blessing on the child.'[21] Simeon did not, however, adopt a rigorous attitude to those nominal church members who wished that their children might be baptised, on the grounds that, like the Jewish rite of circumcision in Old Testament times, it is the sign of membership of the community of God's own people, and not lightly to be denied to anyone.

Confirmation, at which the readiness to renew baptismal vows as an indication of Christian maturity normally preceded admittance to Holy Communion, in Simeon's early days had suffered from the general decay in the activity of the Church of England. Horrific stories are told of the chaos associated with the ordinance when, owing to the fact that bishops only held confirmations every four years in any one place, numbers were often unmanageable. Even as late as 1833 the confirmation in Cambridge, lasting from ten thirty to five in the afternoon, was accompanied by the most unseemly noise and laughter. The luckless William Cecil, son of Richard Cecil, minister of St John's, Bedford Row, who was Vicar of Long Stanton near Cambridge, after five hours waiting in church with his candidates who had had nothing to eat since seven a.m., was not only hit on the head by boisterous youths in the pew behind during the ceremony, but had his gown and coat so torn in the crush that he hardly dared return home in them. He immediately published a strongly worded, noble and courageous protest to Bishop Sparke of Ely complaining of the 'disorder and profaneness exhibited at the Parish Church of St Michael's, Cambridge, on the occasion of the Confirmation held there, June 20th 1833.[22] The scene must have tried Simeon sorely, and even more his friend and former curate, Professor Scholefield, who was minister of the church concerned and had protested about a similar scene at the previous confirmation in 1829. Admission on these occasions was by ticket and Simeon was insistent that they only be given to candidates who had attended classes regularly. In Holy Trinity he prepared his young people by giving them 'lectures' twice a week and on Sunday afternoons. The course had to be concentrated because bishops had a way of only giving a few weeks' notice of an impending confirmation. On the Sunday afterwards Simeon used to preach specially to the confirmees, reminding them how solemnly they had renewed their baptismal vows, and how committed they now were to 'a total surrender of yourselves to God at the table of the Lord'.[23]

We have already seen something of Simeon's deep appreciation of 'the Lord's Supper', as he always used to term it. It had been the means of his conversion, and it was always the medium of his own regular self-surrender to God. His teaching on the subject is coloured by his own experience, especially in its frequent references to the Passover and the Old Testament sacrificial system. He seldom used the word 'Communion'. Though he uses the plural whenever speaking of it, he does tend to treat the sacrament as an intensely personal interview between the believer and his Lord rather than as a family fellowship meal in which the church meets as the body of Christ and the members share together their common sinnerhood at the foot of the cross. It was to fall to others from the sister university to recall the Church of England to a less individualistic understanding of the nature of Holy Communion. Meanwhile, Simeon taught his people faithfully what he personally believed about the Lord's Supper: 'There we see Christ crucified, as it were, before our eyes: there we contemplate the most stupendous mysteries: there we commemorate the greatest of all mercies: there we are admitted to most familiar fellowship with God.' And again, 'It is a memorial to the death of Christ, and a medium of communion with Christ, whose body and blood we feed upon in the sacred elements, and by whom we are strengthened for all holy obedience.' 'It is by an actual fellowship with Christ in his death, and by that alone, that we can ever become partakers of the benefits which it has procured for us.' 'He truly, though spiritually, feasts with us when we are assembled around the table of the Lord.'[24]

When Simeon was asked about the process of new birth, regeneration and conversion, his comment was: 'Conversion is contrary to the course of nature, and only brought about by God's almighty power . . . Before conversion, his heart and mind and soul flow rapidly downwards—away from his Creator, by its natural tendency—towards destruction. After conversion, all its tendencies are changed, and it flows upwards from destruction, back again towards its Creator. Is this due to human agency? All the inhabitants of the globe could not do it. It is done by an invisible power, by a way of which we know nothing but the name and effects. Tell the worldling (who knows nothing of this power) these truths, and he will ridicule the whole idea, and you for entertaining it.'

Simeon's own experience was so inexplicable on any other grounds than that it was God working in his heart, that we are not surprised to find how much emphasis he put on the person and work of God the Holy Spirit. He did this at a time when the Church as a whole had almost entirely overlooked the existence of a third Person in the Trinity. Public fear of Methodist 'enthusiasm' in the late eighteenth century, followed by the dissension to which Edward Irving's extremist views gave rise in the second quarter of the nineteenth, made the whole subject suspect. Anything, whether it be charismatic manifestations or evangelistic zeal, which might disturb the comfortable complacency of the ecclesiastical establishment, was anathema to the hierarchy. When the Archbishop of Canterbury, Dr Manners Sutton, proposed the health of the newly consecrated first Bishop of Calcutta, he said, 'Remember, my Lord Bishop, that your Primate on the day of your consecration defined your duty for you: that duty is to put down enthusiasm and to preach the gospel.'[25]

The dreaded word 'enthusiasm' could clearly be misunderstood. Simeon used it frequently but cautiously. No one was in fact more enthusiastic in his calling than the 'earnest' Mr Simeon. He believed that 'lukewarmness in religion is as odious to God as an utter neglect of it.'[26] Yet he gave his *imprimatur* to his gifted curate Thomas Thomason's Norrisian Prize essay which was on the theme that 'The holy Scriptures, rightly understood, do not give encouragement to enthusiasm or superstition.' In the course of his argument Thomason wrote 'Enthusiasm is as pointedly reprobated as superstition. Our religion must be reasonable, consistent, uniform; our faith must stand on a solid foundation that can bear the severest scrutiny; it must be confirmed by the fullest conviction of our judgment.'[27] Clearly he was making an attempt here to forestall the accusation that the religious revival that was beginning to emerge through the work at Holy Trinity, Cambridge, was in any way unbalanced or unduly emotional.

Certainly Charles Simeon, whose heart was easily warmed and who gave vent to his personal feelings without much encouragement, never allowed the hysteria or other strange phenomena which accompanied some of Wesley's and much of both Whitefield's and Irving's evangelism, to creep into his own ministry. He was particularly worried about the teaching of Edward Irving which was beginning to affect evangelical congregations. Charlotte Elisabeth, 'the little lady with blue eyes and fair complexion' as Joseph Romilly remembered her,[28] has left a telling description of the Old Apostle struggling with his feelings in the matter at a public meeting in London:

> I saw and spoke to Mr Simeon. He recognised me in a meeting, not very large, held in a room in Regent Street, for the Irish Educational Society. He ran to me, seated himself near me, and I shall not soon forget the sequel. At that time Mr Irving had not long been led to propound his fearful heresy respecting the human nature of our spotless Immanuel; but he had done enough to startle all thinking Christians; and I suppose the various errors and delusions set forth by him and his followers never had a more determinate, uncompromising enemy than in Simeon. Contrary to all expectation, Mr Irving chose to address the meeting, and in the midst of his speech proposed prayer. All were taken by surprise. But the expression of Simeon's countenance who can

portray? He rested his elbows on his knees, firmly clasped his hands together, and placed his chin against his knuckles. Every line in his face, where the lines were neither few nor faintly marked, bespoke a fixed resolve to say Amen to nothing that he had not well sifted and deliberately approved . . . I never more beheld Mr Simeon, but I shall hope never to forget his look that day. There was in it as much of sober reproof, exhortation and caution as a look could convey![29]

When it came to Irving's teaching on what are today termed charismatic gifts, Simeon, in a sermon on the subject, made his position perfectly clear: 'Are we all to possess the power of "working miracles, and speaking divers kinds of tongues"? No; the time for such things is long since passed . . . no such power exists at this day, except in the conceit of a few brain-sick enthusiasts.'[30] This last phrase which Simeon seems to have borrowed from Wilberforce's *Practical View*,[31] a book he must have read and admired though he never mentioned it, betrays the degree of his anxiety. Perhaps if there had been rather less aggressiveness on the part of the Irvingites he might have expressed himself less strongly. But he wished to establish an essential truth—that God the Holy Spirit works normally through the usual channels of the ministry and liturgies of a church, and that excesses of one kind or another are no indication that less demonstrative Christian activity is devoid of his power. Simeon believed that to have the Spirit is to have not 'those miraculous powers which were given in the apostolic age . . . but . . . those special influences of the Spirit whereby men are enlightened and transformed into the divine image.'[32]

At this time when many Christian people were giving rein to their feelings at the expense of such poise as Thomason had commended in his essay on enthusiasm, Simeon decided in November 1831 to devote four University sermons to the subject.[33] They were listened to we are told 'with mute attention' by a vast congregation. In these addresses he presented his answer to the claims of scepticism on one hand and fanaticism on the other. When they were published the *Christian Observer* congratulated 'this much venerated Christian instructor to whom so many successions of students have looked up with reverence and affection, and who has effected more, under the blessing of the Holy Spirit of whom he writes, towards promoting truly scriptural piety in the Church of England than, perhaps, any man now living.'[34]

These sermons are indeed a masterly exposition of the Biblical doctrine of the Holy Spirit, particularly in his work in the individual soul which was the point at issue, rather than in his wider working within the church as a whole, or in the world at large. In the first sermon he begins by disarming his critics who might think that the subject is an 'enthusiastic conceit.' He then proceeds to establish that the main function of the Holy Spirit is to make Christ real which he does by indwelling the believer. With typical courage the preacher used the opportunity provided by the large academic congregation crowded into Great St Mary's, in challenging them right at the start of these four addresses: 'I must declare, from Almighty God, that whatever any man may think of his attainments or his virtues, he is not a Christian truly if his soul be not a temple of the Holy Ghost.' His closing five minutes were spent in driving this point home with reiterated emphasis. The three remaining addresses similarly, as was his wont, combined a carefully expressed exposition of this teaching with a pointed application to the daily lives of his hearers.

To turn to another Christian doctrine about which the Vicar of Holy Trinity was much consulted, there was in the second quarter of the nineteenth century a marked revival of interest in eschatology. Possibly the upheavals of the Napoleonic wars and the prophecies of doom associated with them may have played their part in this. Then on top of that came the impact of Irving and his views on the second coming of Christ. The Irvingites became quite a considerable force among the faithful, and Christians found themselves being pressed into one or other of two camps, those who dogmatically asserted that Christ would come and set up his reign on earth for a thousand years, the 'premillennialists', and those who looked for his coming at the final end of all human history without an earthly millenium intervening. Simeon sided with the latter, believing that the future reign of the Messiah with his saints was meant to be understood spiritually and not literally.[35] But he did so with due humility saying that Christians must be allowed to differ on a matter which could not be convincingly proven from Scripture either way. Eschatology is a subject about which Christian people have been notoriously liable to lose their balance, and even the steady Simeon, as we shall see, became somewhat obsessed when it came to the destiny of the Jews. But as he once said, 'Who ever rode a favourite hobby without going now and then a little too fast!'

On the whole Simeon adopted a very sensible stance. When one of his clerical correspondents said that he had now 'got views of prophecy relating to the Second Advent' and was 'unfolding them' to his congregation, Simeon wrote and begged him not to be diverted from preaching 'not Jesus Christ and him *reigning* on earth, but Jesus Christ and him *crucified*'. Similarly, anxious that his friends should realise 'the great scope' of the divine revelation, and not be sidetracked from it, he wrote to Ellen Elliott, granddaughter of old Henry Venn, who was becoming caught up in the new fascination for premillennialism: 'I have no objection to your believing the personal reign of Christ and his saints: I object to the prominence given it, and to its *thrusting into the background* all the wonders of redeeming love.' In a strongly worded letter to Samuel Carr at Colchester written in 1829, he urged him to restrain those of his flock who were affected by 'doubtful disputations', and not to get involved in argument with them.[36] 'I do not object to their thinking as they please, provided they do not thrust their opinions down people's throats and disturb the simple Christian,' he told one of his conversation parties.

Closely linked with Simeon's belief in the return of Christ was the question of the future of God's people, the Jews. Society was beginning to become conscious of their existence, of their business acumen, of their distinctive culture and close sense of community, and of the social problems created by the less fortunate members of their race. The evangelicals, in so far as they thought out the socio-political aspect of this, solved the issue in their own minds by seeking to convert them to Christianity. Simeon himself went further, believing that if the Scriptures could be circulated to the Jewish community at home and abroad, they would be sure to recognise their Messiah, become Christians in large numbers and then be a great evangelistic force to the Gentile world. In 1810 he was invited to become a corresponding member of the London Society for Promoting Christianity among the Jews which had been founded the year before by a number of evangelicals known to him. With great enthusiasm he threw himself into the work, going on deputation tours on the society's behalf, and speaking at most of their Annual Meetings for the next twenty years. At one of these he was sitting on the platform next to Edward Bickersteth of the Church Missionary Society. Jealous on behalf of his own society's work, Bickersteth wrote on a slip of paper which he handed to his brother, '6 million of Jews and 6 hundred millions of Gentiles—which is most important?' The reply was not long in coming: 'But if the conversion of the six is to be the life from the dead to the 600,000,000, what then?'[37]

Simeon was so convinced of the importance of this work that he found the funds himself for the purchase of a chapel in Amsterdam where an Anglican ministry among the 30,000 Jews there could develop, and some kind of headquarters be established for work on the continent. In 1818 he himself spent over two months at the chapel pending the arrival of an appointed chaplain. When an evangelical layman, Lewis Way, came unexpectedly into a very substantial fortune and decided to devote it all to the evangelisation of the Jews through the newly organised and now exclusively Church of England Society,[38] Simeon saw this as divine guidance to go ahead. Mr Way himself spent some time in Europe and 'had repeated interviews with the Emperor of Russia who conversed with him as a Christian and a Brother', as Simeon reported to Thomason in great excitement. Mr Way even attended the Congress at Aix-la-Chapelle where he had remarkable success in persuading the five united powers to agree to promote 'the civil and religious advancement of the Jews in their several dominions.' A protocol to that effect dated 21st November, 1818, appeared over the impressive signatures of Prince Metternich of Austria, the duc de Richelieu for France, Lord Castlereagh and the Duke of Wellington for Great Britain, Prince Hardenburgh and Count Bernstoff of Prussia, and Counts Nesselrode and Capo d'Istria of Russia.[39]

Although the Society had a Committee, it seems to have been Charles Simeon personally who from time to time was consulted in the many problems that arose in those early days, such as how converted Jews should be taught, and what amount of financial help, if any, should be given when they became Christians at the cost of losing their jobs and becoming destitute. Simeon was to learn the hard way that evangelising the Jews meant calling on them, when baptised, to pay a higher price than he had anticipated when he first enthused about the Mission. In a University sermon devoted to the subject in 1820 he said, 'I acknowledge that the difficulty of the work is great; and that the efforts which have already been made have not succeeded so far as might have been wished, or so far as persons of a sanguine temperament and unacquainted with the difficulty of the undertaking were induced at first to expect . . .' He went on to suggest, on the controversial point of how much relief should be given to Jews who claimed to be converted, that 'it may well be doubted whether we have not thereby rendered the gate of heaven more strait than God ever designed it to be.'[40]

Simeon became more deeply involved when a certain Joseph Wolff crossed his path. Wolff was the son of a Jewish rabbi, born in Vienna in 1795. He became a Roman Catholic but soon gave that up and drifted to England. After being introduced to him, and finding that now he seemed to have been truly converted, Simeon arranged that he should come to Cambridge. There he studied Persian, Arabic, Chaldean and Syriac under Samuel Lee, studies to which he devoted some fourteen hours a day rising at two a.m. The hope was that he might become a missionary under the auspices of the society who paid his expenses while at college. He shared lodgings in King's College with Simeon who discovered that it fell to him to teach this most unpractical of all his acquaintances, some of the basic essentials of civilised living. He gave him a new umbrella which he forthwith went and lost; when asked to make tea at Mrs Dornford's house, Wolff put the hot kettle down on her beautiful polished table and ruined it; and finally, when Simeon tried to show him how to use and sharpen a razor, he promptly went and cut the strop in half to Simeon's extreme exasperation.[41] Notwithstanding his uncouthness, Joseph Wolff had the most remarkable career. In 1826 he startled society by announcing that he was about to marry none other than Lady Georgiana Walpole, daughter of the Earl of Orford, 'his darling angel in human shape'. Simeon officiated at the wedding, but could never quite make Wolff out, although he greatly admired the courage with which he set forth and proclaimed Christ in Turkey, Persia, Turkestan, Afghanistan, Kashmir, India and the Middle East, often at the greatest risk to life and limb, and frequently accompanied on his hair-raising expeditions by his intrepid wife.

There were undoubtedly times when his friends found Simeon's enthusiasm for all this activity on behalf of God's chosen people a bit much. One of these, the Vicar of Oakington near Cambridge, who was responsible for organising local support for the Church Missionary Society, in enclosing a generous contribution complained to the Secretary that 'Our valued friend Simeon is so Jew mad that he interferes very much with our plans without intending it.'[42] This great interest was the nearest that Simeon ever came to losing his balance, but in due course he got even this enthusiasm sorted out into its true perspective. But the Church's Ministry among the Jews very much regard him as one of their most respected founding fathers.

CHAPTER TWELVE

Charles Simeon and the World

We have already seen that Charles Simeon was the most loyal member of the Church of England, breathing a sigh of relief when he got back from his travels to the familiar territory of the Book of Common Prayer. He was said to have raised his hand on crossing the border after one of his trips to Scotland and exclaimed 'Thank God we have a Liturgy!' But as he showed in his support of the Bible Society, and the Jews' Society in its earlier days, he was always happy to share in a movement which included dissenters. As Trevelyan has pointed out, it was the Evangelicals of the Established Church, of which Simeon was an acknowledged leader, who formed the only real bridge across to the Nonconforming denominations.[1] In Cambridge many of their members were glad to sit at Simeon's feet where they found so much that was familiar to them, and little if anything to offend. In his early and excitable days, Simeon envied the open Bible study and prayer meetings which the dissenters held, and wondered how he could incorporate something of that kind into his church life. One evening he decided to examine one of their gatherings at first hand and quietly gate-crashed a meeting at which about ten people were present in a small room dimly lit by candles. No one recognised him in the dark corner he chose. When it was all over he got quite carried away and could not stop himself from calling out 'Let us sing, Praise God from whom all blessings flow!' At first they thought he must be joking, but when they realised how sincerely he meant it, everyone joined in heartily in the doxology.[2] Assuming that Simeon's limited musical ability enabled him to start on the right note, the Old Hundredth can have seldom sounded so sweet.

Simeon developed the happiest relationship with a dissenting character of the name of John Stittle who, in company with 'Mr Simeon, the very bully of beliefs and castigator of good works,' found his way into Byron's

Notes on Hints from Horace. A native of Madingley, he was by occupation a hedger and thrasher. After being converted through John Berridge of Everton he took up lay preaching, but being unable to write had to speak without notes. He started a meeting in Green Street in a little room which he enlarged by knocking down the partition walls and then cutting away the floor of the bedroom above to leave an improvised and somewhat precarious gallery all round. Simeon was said to have helped him pay for these alterations. When, in one of his University sermons, Simeon disappointed some of the local dissenters who had attached themselves to him by not preaching Calvinism strongly enough, it was to Johnny Stittle's meeting place that the dissidents went. Simeon, far from resenting this, actually made Stittle a generous quarterly allowance which, as he playfully expressed it, 'was for shepherding my stray sheep.'[2]

When he began to establish weekday meetings in the parish and discovered that objections were raised on the grounds that a church building was the only proper place to hold them, Simeon felt greatly frustrated. He always maintained that if a Church of England clergyman was to be fully faithful to his ordination vows, he must try to keep in close touch with his flock by meeting them other than always in church. Otherwise, as he put it, 'the clergyman beats the bush and the dissenters catch the game.' He was always thankful that, unlike his nonconforming brethren, he had liberty to preach without having to account to the laity for what he said or how he did it. He realised how much they had to watch their step. 'No Dissenter,' he once said gratefully, 'dares to preach as I do, one day Calvinist, another day Arminian, just as the text happens to be, for his people would take offence.' Churchman that he was, he believed that 'dissent is an evil' and 'schism is an evil', but he was too much of a realist not to acknowledge that divisions in the church were not likely to disappear in a hurry, and that there was indeed room enough for all. When it came to his own parish he regarded everyone, Dissenters and Roman Catholics included, as those for whom he held the care and 'cure' of souls. Though when he was younger he had occasionally spoken in a nonconforming chapel, or even in a barn, he soon felt that in loyalty to his own church he must refuse such invitations. This decision set a precedent and example to other earnest evangelical Anglicans of his day and went a long way to retaining within the established church much of the new enthusiasm.

Simeon did this out of his sense of what was right and proper, but no doubt his attitude was influenced by one or two unfortunate experiences that he had with neighbouring Baptist ministers. When he first began to introduce an evening lecture at Holy Trinity his people thought he had gone all 'Methodist' and complained to his bishop. Hearing of this, one evening after church in a great state of tension, and still dressed in his full clerical robes, young Simeon left Holy Trinity and hurried off to the Baptist chapel in St Andrew's Street where he burst in on the minister in his vestry. He told him that he was threatened with a prohibition of his lectures by the bishop on the grounds that they led to acts of immorality. He asked the minister, Robert Robinson, if he had found his own evening meeting ran any such risk. Robinson's answer was that Mr Simeon should 'come out from the ungodly', in other words leave a church that laid such ecclesiastical restrictions on the preaching of the gospel, and join the dissenters. 'The young divine departed,' the record states, 'exclaiming as he left the room, "The Lord will provide".'[4] He did indeed.

Robinson's successor was even less helpful to Simeon. The year was 1795, and the vicar of Holy Trinity had been preaching on behalf of the 8000 emigrant clergy who had escaped from France to England and were in dire straits. In the course of his sermon he assured these refugees that the Lord was fighting for their cause against the new paganism of the French revolutionaries, and would in time assuredly restore them to their work. Robert Hall really went to town when he heard about this and wrote an open letter to the local press accusing Simeon of entertaining 'Your hearers with more politics in one sermon than most dissenting ministers have done during their whole lives.' He also complained of him 'circulating an inflammatory prayer for success in the present war.'[5] Simeon wisely ignored this letter realising, perhaps, that Mr Hall was not quite himself when he wrote it for he suffered from some instability and recurrent depression. Anyway, the baptist's reference to Simeon preaching politics must have made him smile for, as we have reason to show, this was one thing he said he would never do. 'Many men,' he reminded James Haldane, 'whose piety we cannot reasonably doubt, have sadly hurt their own spirit by dabbling in politics.'[6]

By nature Simeon recoiled from controversy, but when he believed that it was an inevitable sequel to his trying to apply Bible exposition to important occasions, he would not shirk it. We look, however, in vain among the mass of his addresses, many of them printed and published for a wider audience, for anything approaching a specifically political theme. He had his own decided views in these matters, and had little personal sympathy with the politics which he believed lay behind the utterances of some of the local dissenters. But the pulpit he treated as sacrosanct and neutral in concerns about which convinced Christians took opposing attitudes. Other evangelical preachers such as John Overton of York and Simeon's friend Miles Atkinson of Leeds who had invited him in 1797 to set aside Friday evenings for prayer for the nation, seem to have been more at ease than he was in applying the action of providence to national and international affairs.[7] Another of his friends whom we have already met, Thomas Jones of Creaton, who incidentally as a young man had suffered the indignity of being hit on the head with a stick by his rural dean in an attempt to cure him of his evangelical views, felt able to declare that 'God has a quarrel with us as a guilty nation.'[8] But this type of prophetic declaration did not appeal to Simeon who preferred to be politically quiescent, no doubt lest he should be distracted from the primary task of preaching the gospel. But he was by no means indifferent to the state of the nation. He was greatly disturbed for instance by the activities of the radicals of Cato Street in 1820, and wrote to his former colleague Thomas Thomason in some concern, 'I never touch on news or politics; but the nation is in a most dreadful state. You will have heard of the conspiracy to destroy all the King's Ministers.'

When he got a chance to do so, Simeon would fearlessly face a wider audience than his normal parish provided and press home what he believed to be God's message for the occasion. As an example of this, when invited to preach the Assize Sermon before His Majesty's Judges in August 1797, he expressed his 'sense of the important connexion with the welfare of the state and the wise administration of public justice', and the truths of the gospel. His text was 1 Samuel 2:25. In a very rare excursion on to the fringe of political comment, with the patriotic instincts of a true Tory colouring his address, he let himself go on the situation brought about by the French Revolution. 'We have witnessed the destruction of all constituted authorities, and the utter annihilation of all established laws. We have beheld licentiousness stalking with the cap of liberty, and ferocious despotism, under the name of Equality, spreading desolation with an undiscriminating hand. But, blessed be God, it is not thus with Britain; I pray God it never may be . . . If the necessary restraints be violated by presumptuous demagogues, we have magistrates that will call the offenders to trial; juries that will bring in their verdict with conscientious truth; and judges that while they declare the sentence of the law with firmness, know how to temper judgement with mercy.' After an able discourse in which the place of the law of God in human affairs was clearly stated, the evangelist in Simeon rounded upon his distinguished congregation with a potent reminder that at the final judgment a criminal who implored mercy through the blood of Jesus would stand as a monument of redeeming grace; while the judge who condemned him, if dying impenitent, would be doomed to 'the second death in the lake burning with fire and brimstone.'[9] After this we may be surprised to learn that he was invited to preach an assize sermon a second time. This was in July 1803 when he urged his learned hearers to 'flee from the wrath to come'. It was his last such invitation.

In June 1818, engaged in the concerns of the Jews on the continent in whose welfare Simeon was so deeply interested, it fell to him to preach in Amsterdam at an anniversary service of thanksgiving for the victory of Waterloo. In the course of this he allowed himself the liberty of saying, 'If any event ever deserved repeated annual commemoration, it is that which has freed the world from the most grievous tyranny that it ever endured. Of the bitter cup which was put into the hands of every nation in Europe, this nation (the Netherlands) drank very deeply: and the change which it has experienced in the restoration of their rightful monarch, and in the establishment of a free constitution, calls for their devoutest acknowledgement to Almighty God. Doubtless we may with justice pay some tribute of honour to those who by their counsels and their arms effected the overthrow of the usurper: but it is God alone who giveth victory to kings, and to whom the glory of this great victory must be primarily ascribed.'[10] On the other hand, preaching in Cambridge in 1812 on the somewhat abstruse subject of the king of Moab sacrificing his son (2 Kings 3:27), Simeon commented, 'How great are the calamities of war!' Then referring to the burning of Moscow by the Russians in advance of Napoleon's approach, he said 'Let us learn to sympathise even with our enemies, and to moderate our joy at the victories we obtain by feelings of compassion for the miseries we inflict.'[11] That was about as far as he would go in reference to the contemporary military scene.

Simeon preached in his own church in February 1820 at a service to observe the accession of George IV, his sermon being subsequently published. Turning a conveniently blind eye on the character of the new king who was described in *The Examiner* as 'a violator of his word, a libertine over head and ears in disgrace, a despiser of domestic ties, the companion of gamblers and demi-reps,'[12] Simeon proclaimed the traditional doctrine of the divine right of kings to rule with authority from on high. 'Religion and loyalty', he said, 'are inseparable', and 'to inquire whether any or what circumstances would justify a departure from this rule (that the powers that be are ordained of God and are to be obeyed), is no part of the author's design: it is ground which a minister of the Prince of peace is not called to occupy.'[13]

In 1827 when Parliamentary Reform was very much in the air the repeal of the Test Acts discriminating against Roman Catholics and nonconformists was impending, and even Catholic emancipation was being talked about, Simeon told a questioner, 'I do not think clergymen have much to do with politics.' Like William Cowper who was horrified to think of 'the symbols of atoning grace' being made 'an office-key, a picklock to a place', Simeon viewed the practice of using Holy Communion as a test for the holding of a public post as 'a horrible abuse.'[14] He maintained that ministers of religion 'had better attend more to the politics of eternity and the care of souls. I used once to avoid all politics, for I had enough to do without them. But now I rather attend a little to them, because I have so many friends that my opinion is often asked, and it becomes a duty to have my mind clear on subjects such as the present, that I may give my reasons.' On another occasion he said, 'Politics in general have very little to do with religion, because politics are seldom founded upon truth.' He went on to illustrate this by referring to the way in which Pitt justified the rearmament programme on the grounds of Russia increasing its power in the Black Sea whereas the true purpose of it was to prevent the dismemberment of Poland as planned by Russia, Austria and Prussia. It would have been interesting if Simeon had been pressed to enlarge on this theme, but it seems he was not.

Much as he wanted to keep clear of the subject, at least during the first half of his ministry, Simeon could not help betraying his own views from time to time. His chief objection to dissent was not on theological grounds, but from the fear that they were in no way tied to the status quo and might even hold within themselves the seeds of revolution or at least of reform. He wrote to William Carus in 1835 on the occasion of a new nonconformist chapel being opened in Cambridge, saying 'I am thankful that they can and will accommodate themselves.' But he had to go on, 'My fear, however, is that they will contract sentiments and habits unfavourable to good government and to all the established institutions of the land.'[15] He was a patriot if ever there was one. In a sermon preached after the assault on the Prince Regent when various conspiracies had come to light in 1817, he declared: 'It is generally agreed by those who have studied the constitution of Britain, that it is the most perfect of any upon earth. In no other state under heaven is there a greater measure of liberty combined with the same measure of security and strength. The extent of our civil and religious liberties is justly the boast of all who have the happiness to live in our favoured land.'[16] For Simeon good government normally meant Tory government. When he wrote a bread-and-butter letter to Thomas Fowell Buxton in January 1820 after staying in his happy home ('I do not expect to see in this world a brighter image of heaven'), he pulled his leg about his political views: 'I do not know that I shall not thrash you for supporting the radicals.' But he went on, 'I look to you, under God, to be an instrument of great good in the House of Commons . . . I am no politician, but I feel a regard for you . . . so you must bear with this impudent letter.'[17]

This 'great good' Simeon realised would fall short of full Christian activity for he was sufficiently realistic to accept that governments would only 'rule by strict Christian principles when they have those only to rule over or contend with who are strictly Christians, but hardly before, I fear.' However, this did not stop him praying for and encouraging the increasing number of committed Christian men who at that time were finding their way into Parliament. At the 1827 elections, when Simeon was faced with a candidate, Robert Grant, who supported Catholic emancipation, he said he would have to abstain from voting even though the candidate's father, Charles, had been for many years so close a personal friend. 'Gladly would I give to Catholics every privilege that could conduce to their happiness:' was his view on this crucial issue; 'but to endanger the Protestant ascendancy and stability is a sacrifice which I am not prepared to make.' In 1832 with the Reform Bill very much in everyone's thoughts, he wrote to Samuel Carr, 'I shall vote for Capt Yorke who is a Tory' – and went on, 'and for Mr Adeane because, though a Whig, he would not go the whole length of that party . . . This is the kind of man we want and must have, one who will not be the delegate of a mob, but will think for himself,'[18] which is exactly what Simeon himself always did.

In saying that he treated his parliamentary vote 'not as a *right* but as a *trust*, to be used conscientiously for the good of the whole kingdom', Simeon was establishing a principle of great importance to Christian people living as they were in his lifetime in a slowly evolving democracy. Although with William Wilberforce he believed that 'the problems with our age should be regarded as moral and spiritual rather than political and economic', he took his responsibilities as a citizen seriously and taught his followers to do the same. It did not trouble him that in the Church of England there were some who thought differently and voted differently from him, but he did regard the Methodists and other dissenters, probably rightly, as leaning much further than he himself would in the direction of reform. Benjamin Flower, left-wing editor of the *Cambridge Intelligencer*, a fervent supporter of the French Revolution and opponent of England's involvement in war with France, tried to exploit Baptist Hall's critical letter to Simeon mentioned above in the interests of radical politics. He printed it twice over in full under the heading *National Sins Considered.*[19] He was clearly hoping to diminish Simeon's standing in the town and expected that some members of the established church would join his supporters among the dissenters in the cause of reform. But no one rose to the bait, no correspondence ensued, and he had to acknowledge in the end that Simeon's people had remained loyal to him. Simeon told his bishop that he would ignore it all, passing it by 'in silent contempt.' Two days later he had overcome his very natural resentment about it and entered in his diary 'I began to pray for . . . Mr Flower.'

Evangelicals, and most certainly Charles Simeon, gave very little support to reformers largely because they pinned their hopes for the future on 'the favour of heaven' granted to the nation for 'possessing more religious and moral worth than in this sinful age is to be found elsewhere,'[20] a difficult point to prove. They had no faith in the mob, and were terrified of disturbing the stability of a society whose tranquillity had made it possible for them to carry on their work and witness unhindered by civil strife or commotion. Simeon does not seem to have regarded party politics as in any way a dirty game, nor did he see any great need for change in the electoral system. Bribery was so much an acknowledged part of an election that it failed to appear reprehensible. When in 1805 someone told a prospective candidate 'You need not ask me, my Lord, who I votes for: I always vote for Mr Most,' he was speaking for all his fellow-voters. Wilberforce, though he later came to think differently, took it for granted that his first election would cost him between eight and nine thousand pounds.[21] Society had never known the hustings without violence and corruption, but the evangelicals were really too taken up with 'heavenly' matters to put their mind to reform in such quarters as these.

When he was asked at a conversation party for his views about why his much loved Jews should be denied the franchise, Simeon produced no argument. He simply stated: 'On one hand, all good subjects who pay taxes ought (theoretically) to have a share in the privileges of the government; yet, on the other hand, all do not have that share, because the public good is better served by keeping them without power. Thus women have not all the privileges of British subjects.' He really was dodging the issue, but his mind was on what he felt were higher things most of the time. As far as the British constitution was concerned no one could have been happier than he. In one of his rare inroads into the subject in a sermon he said, 'Under the whole heavens there never was a country where the laws were more equitably, more impartially dispensed . . . The peace and security which we of this happy land enjoy, under the domination of the laws, are not exceeded by any people under heaven, and are equalled by very few.'[22] The nearest that Simeon seems personally to have got to associating himself with the Reform movement was when in 1831 he wrote to congratulate Lord Harrowby on a speech he had made which was described by Greville as 'amazing fine and delivered with great effect.'[23] In five long pages Simeon, admittedly somewhat with his tongue in his cheek, pretends to argue the point. Though himself an anti-Reformer, it was King Mob that he feared rather than the modest changes proposed. When in the end the Reform Bill became law, this leader of the most active part of the established church of the land let pass without comment one of the great turning points in our country's history.

Exactly the same thing happened with the abolition of the slave-trade. Simeon was a contemporary of William Wilberforce, shared his Christian convictions, became a personal friend, met and corresponded with him on a number of occasions, but nowhere and nowhen does he seem to have made any mention of the burning question which occupied fifty years of the great reformer's life. We do not find any praising of the Lord in King's College or Holy Trinity in the fateful summer of 1833 as we do at Cadogan Place where the crusader was dying happy with his work at last completed, slavery itself having been finally outlawed. It is difficult to understand Simeon's total silence. In 1788 Robert Robinson, the Baptist Minister, drew up what was probably the earliest of many petitions to the Commons against the slave-trade from 'the gentry, clergy, freeholders and others in the county of Cambridge,'[24] and we hope Simeon's signature was on it, but it was not he that had taken the initiative. When he visited Wilberforce on March 11th, 1807, he mentions in his diary the 'sweetly solemnising effect' of their prayer together, but not a word does he say about the tense anxiety through which his friend was then passing as the Bill for the Abolition of the Slave-Trade was edging its way at last through Parliament, coming up for its third reading only five days later. All we really know about Simeon's concern for the great work of liberation to which Wilberforce devoted his life was that he gave an annual subscription of £10 to the African Institution. Judged by his normal standards of giving, this is not the gift of an enthusiast. Simeon does not seem to have shared John Wesley's view expressed in 1772 that slavery was 'that execrable sum of all villainies.'

Matters of this sort, and the need for reform of the criminal code at a time when one hundred and sixty crimes, many of them trivial, still carried the death penalty, and the degrading spectacle of public hangings continued,[25] Simeon left to be dealt with by Christian laymen. He was in close touch with his friends of the Clapham Sect under the spiritual leadership of his one-time friend, John Venn, vicar of Clapham. The record of these men's activities, supported no doubt by the prayers of Simeon and his congregation when they were awakened to the state of society around them, has been admirably summarised by Dr Howse:

> The Clapham Sect, the leading evangelicals of their day, did not divorce religion from life. They linked religion to life. They linked it to hunted negroes on the coast of Africa, on the high seas, and in the plantations of the West Indies. They linked it to standards of political conduct, to the corrupt manners of society, and to the debauched mobs of their time. They linked it to the wretches condemned by game laws, and oppressed in filthy prisons. They linked it to the ragged children condemned otherwise to ignorance, and by philanthropic and benefit societies they linked it to the improvident and unfortunate poor. Their efforts were sometimes casual and their methods were often awry, but at every point at which they did touch life, it was their religion that led them to the contact. The religion may, indeed, have been other-worldly centred, but the circumference of its action embraced a weltering area of humanity, of which most contemporary religion was comfortably oblivious.[26]

Does the answer to the mystery of Simeon's apparent lack of concern for such vitally important matters as these perhaps lie in his words to Mary Elliott: 'I have no imagination – I never had.' Certainly this would account for some of his limitations in aesthetic appreciation. How else can one explain how a don of one of Cambridge's most distinguished colleges could stand beside one of England's leading artists, look up at

> that branching roof
> Self-poised, and scooped into ten thousand cells,
> Where light and shade repose, where music dwells
> Lingering – and wandering on as loth to die;

and then turn to his friend Joseph Farington with the sole comment that Noah's Ark was twice the length and twice the breadth and two-third's the height of King's College Chapel?[27] When, on a visit to Paris, Simeon was taken by Lady William Bentinck to view an art collection, his remarks on the pictures were those of a preacher, a little out of his element. Of the 'Return of the Prodigal' he said, 'Most persons would think that the father expresses too little joy; but to me, he says to his son, "Drop that subject; you pain me by your confessions"; and this I consider to be more suited to the occasion than an expression of great joy; joy alone might have become a brother or a sister; but this mixed feeling became a father.' Of its kind, it was fair comment – but was it a good picture? As for most evangelicals, Simeon's concern for the Fine Arts was coloured by a puritanism which regarded such things at best as 'the icing on the cake, the jam on the bread and butter,'[28] optional extras. He never dared to allow himself the pleasure of studying English literature, and, fearing lest they should be led astray, he warned his young undergraduate friends to 'use it cautiously, and step as with your toes in mud.' Dr Johnson's writings he admitted to admiring, and he certainly knew his Gibbon,[29] while on the musical side he confessed to approving of Handel. But that seems about the limit of his sophistication. There was only a very small field comparatively free of mud into which he was prepared to venture outside the strictly 'serious' subjects which occupied so much of his time.

We are not surprised to find the same element of puritanism in Simeon's attitude to the world, particularly the life of high society in which he had a number of significant friends, but where he himself was never really at home. This, however, he said was no excuse for keeping aloof: 'Had our blessed Lord acted like the Pharisees, who kept all others at a distance, he would never have been called the friend of publicans and sinners. The point for you to judge of is this: What is my motive? . . . The very instant you find pleasure in worldly company you are got off from Christian ground . . . I would be the Christian everywhere: and though I would not lug in religion neck and shoulders, I would never leave anyone to doubt for a moment whose I am and whom alone I serve.' He fully realised that this kind of withdrawal might justly lead to people saying that he was standoffish and considered himself spiritually a cut above worldly men. To this his reply, as far as a clergyman was concerned, was 'The minister must come out from the world, and yet he may be sinning in doing so, if he act from a sense of being holier than the rest, or, as the Scripture phrase is, lest he should smell "the smoke under his nose" (Isaiah 65:5).'

Simeon did not like the smell, but was more concerned about those he would wish to influence than about any possible effect on himself. He pointed out to his congregation how under the worldlings' superfical vanity lay many a troubled soul: 'The gaiety which is exhibited in worldly company is often assumed, for the purpose of concealing the real feelings of the heart. They who appear so delighted to see each other, have frequently no mutual affection . . . their pride, their envy, their jealousy, their private piques, their domestic troubles, their worldly cares, make them inwardly sigh, so that they can with difficulty prevent the discovery of the imposture they are practising.'[30] But he could never bring himself to condemn the worldly man or call such to account. Rightly or wrongly, he felt that that was not his metier, though R. M. Beverley thought he should certainly have reproved from the pulpit those members of the university who lived dissolute lives.[31] Simeon's answer was 'Jesus went into the society of Pharisees and sinners to do them good. He reproved them. I cannot do this, for I am not a prophet. I may endeavour to check, but not with authority. I must remember who and what I am – my own nothingness. I have no extraordinary commission out of my own line of duty.'

No one ever doubted where Simeon stood, but what was so unusual was the degree of common sense and balance with which he gave such advice as that quoted above to the clergymen and others who turned to him for guidance. He told them what it would cost. 'If any man will live as faithfully as he preaches, if in his life, as in his sermons, he will utterly condemn the world, he will not get much favour from the world . . . he will lose his popularity with the upper classes, and will get no Bishopric.' Simeon knew what he was talking about. George Pryme, who later became Professor of Political Economy and Member of Parliament for the borough, lived in Simeon's parish in Sidney Street, and used to attend Holy Trinity. He tells in his *Recollections*: 'I ventured to differ from Charles Simeon as to the impropriety of theatrical entertainments and card-playing, which latter was then (1820) still a general custom. He candidly argued the matter with me; I maintained them to be objectionable only in their abuse, when the play was immoral or the stakes were high.'[32] But to Simeon no half-measures would do.

Evangelicals at that time had not yet hardened into the attitude which marked the second half of the century, when every form of entertainment or pleasure that could not be shown to be wholly innocent was condemned. Wilberforce admitted that he 'felt awkward about cards, though I did not make a point of conscience of not playing', but others regarded them as quite untouchable, 'the Devil's Prayer Book' in fact.[33] Shakespeare was banned in some homes, even after Bowdler had had his way with him, and there are no signs that Simeon ever allowed himself the luxury of reading any of his plays. But it was the theatre and dancing that caused the greatest heart-searching among those who in increasing numbers were newly become Christians. When Charlotte Sophia, sixth Duchess of Beaufort, sister-in-law of Lord Harrowby, first saw the light she succeeded in introducing family prayers into her home, using a handbook by Jenks which Simeon had edited and republished. So when the problem arose about her Christian duty in the world of social entertainment in which she was inevitably involved, it was to Charles Simeon that she turned for guidance. He did his best to help her to see the difference between Christian liberty and Christian duty. As far as his own personal experience was concerned, he said 'I feel, and have ever felt, that I have no talents for the world, no taste for the world, no time for the world; and therefore, except as an Ambassador from the Lord, I have had for forty-four years almost as little to do with the world as if I had not been in the world.'

He made no bones about being unsociable and not feeling at ease amongst ungodly people however classy, and he would advise young clergymen, 'Let your rule be – go into the world as a doctor into an hospital, in the path of duty; not liking the place, not lingering long in it, but glad when you can get out and breathe pure air again.' This sounds very like an echo from John Newton who used to say that 'a Christian in the world is like a man transacting his affairs in the rain; he will not suddenly leave his client because it rains, but the moment the business is done he is off.'[34] For Simeon personally the matter was quite straight-forward, the issues were black and white. 'I was tinder,' he said referring to his younger days, 'and did not like to go near sparks.'

But he realised that the position of Christians in high society of whom there were an increasing number as a result of the ministries of Hannah More and William Wilberforce in particular, was very different. Accepting this, he laid down a general principle which those who find it difficult to think in 'shades of grey' have too often and too easily overlooked. Writing to the Duchess of Beaufort he said: 'What would be wrong in one person, would not be so in another; and what would be wrong under some circumstances, would not be so under other circumstances. What would be wrong if done from choice, might not be wrong if done for fear of offending others, or of casting a stumbling-block before them, or with a view to win them.' Inspired by this advice the Duchess we are told came to the decision that 'in things sinful in themselves, such as the theatre and races, to request the duke to excuse the attendance of herself and their daughters; but as to balls etc. she and they were ready to go whenever he wished it, though they would feel very grateful to be exempted from attending them.'[35]

Although Simeon felt it necessary to be extremely cautious in discussing the world of fashion and society lest its influence took the edge off the Christian's commitment to Christ, yet he readily accepted the world of God's creation as existing for man's enjoyment. He told his young friends not to be afraid of God's blessings and reject them like Jews or monks, but to 'serve God in your recreations and enjoy him . . . Our rule should be to enjoy God in everything; to feel the delight of affluence, science, friends, recreations, children, in fact of everything, as coming to us from God.' And in a sermon on 'All is vanity' he modified the world-rejection of the writer of Ecclesiastes by reminding his congregation that in their attitude to the good things of life 'there are but two lessons for the Christian to learn: the one is, to enjoy God in every thing; the other is, to enjoy every thing in God.'[36]

CHAPTER THIRTEEN

The Old Apostle's Legacy

'It becomes us, not to sit wishing for the spoils of victory, but to continue fighting till God shall call us to put off our armour.'[1] After over fifty years' active service, during the first thirty of which Simeon was subjected to every kind of discouragement and intermittent opposition, he could preach about the patience of Job with much fellow-feeling, and his people were by then well aware that he knew what he was talking about. The sheer resilience of the man who survived the earlier attacks on his ministry, and went on in spite of everything for so much longer than most modern clergymen are content to stay in one living, is quite remarkable. His last quarter of a century of cooperation, fellowship and profound respect were welcome relief and well deserved reward for a faithfulness that can only be described as out of this world. In 1826 he made a touching reference in a short memorandum to the visit of three bishops who wanted to consult with him: 'I am not conscious that I am one atom less faithful to my God than in former days, or more desirous of human favour; yet God is pleased thus graciously to honour me. In former years I should as soon have expected a visit from three crowned heads, as from three persons wearing a mitre.' But times had changed, and the evangelical outlook which had been so novel when the Venns, Milner and Farish were standing up with Simeon for what they believed the gospel demanded, had by the end of his life become very widely adopted. 'The sun and the moon are scarcely more different from each other', he wrote joyfully to Thomason in 1824, 'than Cambridge is from what it was when I was first minister of Trinity Church; and the same change has taken place through almost the whole land.'

In his controversial open letter to the Duke of Gloucester as Chancellor of the university written in 1833, R. M. Beverley pays this tribute to the work of Charles Simeon:

> I come now to speak of the only semblance of real religion in the university. I need not tell your Royal Highness that this part of my subject has brought me to speak of Mr Simeon, and that powerful party which his long Christian labours have raised up in the university. This venerable man was for years the only beacon in days when the darkness might be felt. He began his Christian struggle, and a very severe struggle it was, without a friend to help him; he was shamefully persecuted, insulted and outraged, directly by the undergraduates, and indirectly, but still more severely, by many unprincipled persons in authority. Long and laborious was his trial, and all his Christian patience was fully elicited; but at last his perseverance in good deeds and the excellent instructions which he delivered from the pulpit were blessed with an ample return of sincere and zealous converts. Thus, whilst the university was pouring forth floods of immoral, licentious and mischievous men in all parts of the kingdom, and in every rank of life, Mr Simeon was a fountain in a small and humble way indeed, issuing forth in pure streams far and wide for the blessing of many a benighted parish. He has sent forth pious clergymen into every county; he has named faithful preachers of the gospel in many most important stations; he has encouraged the poor and neglected clergy; drawn out the diffident; instructed the ignorant, and upheld the persecuted; and by the largesses of a bountiful purse, as well as by his advice and example, has fostered the cause of evangelical religion in the Church of England till now it can bear his departure, and not sink down extinguished when his torch shall be burnt out.[2]

Simeon may well have felt embarrassed when he read this. Although he was just as conscious as Beverley of the decadence of the student world and the lax control of the university authorities which were the main themes of the pamphlet (and were probably greatly exaggerated), it was not his way to scold the ungodly or tirade against those who neglected their duties. He preferred a more positive approach. For example, he would never, he said, had he been a missionary, 'speak against idolatry' for the straightforward reason that it would do no good, and might well so antagonise his hearers as fatally to hinder the work. Similarly he begged earnest young ministers not to try to commend themselves to God by the vehemence with which they presented what they believed to be God's whole truth, but rather to 'be gentle among your people' as a mother with her family.

This did not mean that he was indifferent to or unmoved by the wickedness of others. Indeed, earlier in his ministry he wrote to a fellow clergyman severely taking him to task for his behaviour and conversation which had so disturbed him that he could not forget it. He wrote anonymously, no doubt to give himself peace of mind for not having rebuked him at the time, but it is not clear why he waited so long to communicate with the offending brother. Simeon's letter ran:

> Rev. Sir, I happened to spend a day in company with you in the year 1782. Your conversation then shocked me, as being the most obscene and profane I ever heard, neither have I during the ten years I have spent since been witness to anything like it – the impression it made upon me was so deep that I never can forget your name, your manner and your words and I never recollect them without horror. I would hope that you have since deeply repented and that you no longer possess that polluted disposition from which as from a corrupt fountain so copious a stream of iniquity flowed . . . You are besides a Clergyman, the Ambassador of God, the reprover of sin, the pattern of holiness whose heart ought to be pure, whose eye chaste and whose mouth a fountain of holy conversation.[3]

Simeon was a great one for anniversaries. We have already seen how he celebrated each birthday as a day of humiliation and heartsearching. His fortieth year in the ministry led to his writing a memorandum on his inner life from which we have already quoted. 1829, however, marked fifty years since he entered King's College and became a Christian. In January of that year he was due to become once more Dean of Divinity, and he recorded with excusable enthusiasm, 'at the very hour on which I was first admitted, will the whole college of above forty members meet to elect me Dean'. He arranged a dinner party for a group of his friends to celebrate the occasion, followed the next morning by a Bible reading and prayer meeting at which John Sargent and Daniel Wilson were among those who took part. William Wilberforce had been invited but had to decline as he did not feel up to travelling so far. He wrote warmly to wish his distinguished colleague in the cause of Christ every blessing: 'I shall not forget to return my humble thanksgivings to the Giver of all good for having enabled you "to continue unto this day", (how much is contained in that brief though compendious expression!). The degree in which, without any sacrifice of principle, you have been enabled to overcome, and if I may so term it, *to live down* the prejudices of many of our higher ecclesiastical authorities, is certainly a phenomenon

I never expected to witness.'

Three years later Simeon organised another Jubilee celebration, this time to mark the fiftieth anniversary of his ministry at Holy Trinity. Wilberforce wrote to him on this occasion also, saying how marvellous it was going to be for him to have among his forty clerical guests a number of his own converts. It was indeed, and we are not surprised to read that it moved them once more to tears. A warmth of love and respect for their 'beloved friend and father' as William Carus expressed it, surrounded him as John Sargent, William Jowett, Edward Bickersteth, William Marsh, Francis Close, Robert Hankinson, John Cunningham, William Farish, Edward Edwards, George Hodson, Samuel Wilberforce, James Scholefield, the young John Williamson and others found their way up the well-known 'H' staircase of King's, to meet together in grateful fellowship with the old apostle. For three days they prayed and talked and studied the Bible, sharing their problems of the present and hopes for the future. Amongst other things discussed was the very relevant topic of reform, not so much in the world of politics as in the Church of England. Apart from the burning question of appointments to livings, they came to the conclusion that there was nothing in particular that they were called upon to do, for neither the liturgy nor the established order of their church seemed to them to be lacking in any essentials.[4]

In addition to this coming together of his special friends, Simeon marked the Jubilee in the parish by providing a dinner for two hundred and fifty of his poorer churchgoers whom he managed to squeeze into the King Street schoolroom. The churchwardens took the opportunity to present to him, on behalf of the congregation, two handsome pieces of plate which with the silver inkstand from his brother clergy were to be treasured memorials of a memorable occasion. There was, of course, a special service to crown the proceedings, when he took as his text 2 Peter 1:12-15, 'I think it meet, as long as I am in this tabernacle, to stir you up . . . that ye may be able after my decease to have these things always in remembrance.' He said, 'I can appeal to all who have ever known me, that to proclaim a suffering and triumphant Messiah, as revealed to us by Moses and the prophets, has been *the one object of my life, without any variation* as arising from the persons addressed (who might equally have been a crowded Easter congregation, a restless group of prisoners in Newgate, or a highbrow college Founder's Day audience) . . . and *without ever turning aside* after novelties, or fond conceits, or matters of doubtful disputation. From the beginning "I determined" like that blessed Apostle, "to know nothing amongst you save Jesus Christ and him crucified".'[5]

It was a declaration no one could dispute, and it gave Simeon great joy to be able to make this modest boast. His cup was, indeed, overflowing, not only because of the kindness of his many friends and the affection of his now happy parish, but also because he could see light at the end of the long tunnel in the completion at last of his twenty-one volumes of 'Skeletons' which were almost ready for publication. On top of this, Holy Trinity church was undergoing a face-lift, by way of the rebuilding of the east end. This meant, we are told, eighty-five additional seats in the new chancel, all of them free and unappropriated which was how he liked them to be. No wonder his diary, kept so spasmodically throughout his life, bursts out now in a note of ecstasy:

> Nov. 4th. 1873. What wonderful things have I been spared to behold!
> 1 Union and harmony and love throughout my whole parish, together with an increased attention to religion.
> 2 My Jubilee completed, and kept with such devout affection.
> 3 My entire Work out, presented and as far as I know, approved.
> 4 My Church, enlarging so as to hold 1100 persons, and so beautiful as to be the ornament, instead of the disgrace of the town . . .
> Never did I long more to spend and be spent for the Lord than at this moment. Blessed be God!

All this excitement took place when Simeon was seventy-three. Apart from one or two false alarms, when he was so tired that, as he put it, 'I am scarcely able to walk to the vestry, but totter and stagger like a drunken man,' he was in reasonably good health. Gout was his great enemy. In February 1833 he suffered from it for some twelve weeks being often unable to move even in bed without assistance. When recovering from this attack he insisted on going out even though it meant his being carried down and up the two flights of stairs, and 'put into and taken out of my carriage like a log of wood'. But as he assured his lady correspondent, he would most certainly be in his pulpit next Sunday even if he had to be helped in. He had become very conscious of his age by now and often referred to the fact that his time could not be far off. There was of course never any suggestion of his giving up his work. If Newton, Romaine and Wesley died in harness, he said he could and would also.

The nearest that Simeon ever came to admitting that he might be failing in any way was far back in 1816 when with the first twinges of gout beginning to bother him, he saw a red light. This meant, sad news,

'I am rather inclined to think that the time is now approaching when I must descend from my horse to a carriage.' And he went on, 'If so, I consider it as a very long step towards the eternal world.' He had, in fact, twenty of his most active and happy years before him, but even then the next world was almost as real to him as this one, and every year he seems to have felt to be equidistant from eternity. 'It has for many years,' he told Thomason, 'been my delight to contemplate death as close at hand: and the more my mind is familiarised with death now, the more tranquil, I trust, it will be when the closing scene of life shall have actually arrived.' There was nothing morbid in such an attitude. Simeon was a realist and ready to face facts. With mortality what it was in the first quarter of the nineteenth century, death was a very familiar experience in every family, and of course to every minister. There was something delightfully cheering for members of a congregation to know how ready their parson knew himself to be for the time of his departure 'to be with Christ which is far better.' Young Alfred Tennyson, who like most serious-minded undergraduates no doubt attended Holy Trinity Church from time to time when he was at college, being deeply affected by the death of his godly mother, 'moved from beneath with doubt and fear', in 1830 wrote his '*Supposed Confessions of a Second-rate Sensitive Mind not in unity with itself*.' It almost seems that it was with a glance up at the aged but serene figure of Charles Simeon that the thought came to him

How sweet to have a common faith!
To hold a common scorn of death!

One of Simeon's visitors in his old age was Charles McIlvaine, the young Bishop of Ohio, whose impressions of his two visits, one in 1830 and the other five years later, show him to have been quite swept off his feet in admiration of 'that holy man of God' who 'belonged a great deal more to the heavenly world than to this.' The bishop was a sentimental man, judging from his letters to his wife, but allowing for this his description of the old apostle helps us to envisage the tenor of his closing years. 'I found him lying upon his sofa, from which he rose to receive me. The sweet, affectionate expression of his face, and the welcoming tone of his voice, united with the great softness and childlike simplicity of his manners, instantly made me feel as if I was in the presence of a father . . . When Mr Simeon ascended the pulpit his countenance was heavenly. He seemed perfectly absorbed in devotional meditation. His whole appearance was a sermon to me on the solemnity and responsibility of a minister's work . . . He seemed as young and fresh in mind as if the joys of religion were new every day, and every step towards the grave were revealing to his eyes some new beauty of the heavenly inheritance.'[6]

With his Jubilee behind him and the re-opening of his enlarged church in the good hands of William Carus as lecturer, Simeon decided that as he was now feeling pretty well and 'preaching at seventy-six with all the energy of youth', he ought to make a grand tour of as many of the churches as possible where his special men were holding down important spheres of work. Travelling by coach was still a tedious and exhausting business, and this journey was going to take some eight weeks and cover five hundred miles. But he looked forward to it with childlike enthusiasm and on June 13th 1836 he set off. His first port of call was Cheltenham where he was warmly welcomed by Francis Close. 'Here at Cheltenham', he wrote excitedly, 'I have almost had a heaven upon earth. The churches so capacious and so filled; the schools so large; so numerous, so beneficial; the people so full of love; the ministers such laborious and energetic men; and God himself so graciously with me in my exertions; in truth I can scarcely conceive any higher happiness on earth than I am now privileged to enjoy.' From there he moved on to Hereford where his friend John Venn's grandson was for nearly forty years incumbent of St Peter's, a parish where he displayed an unusually practical turn for an evangelical by providing a corn-mill driven by steam for the benefit of the poor. Simeon then travelled on to Birmingham, Darlaston, Newcastle-under-Lyme, Lichfield and Derby, enjoying every minute of what was a strenuous and demanding tour, yet looking forward as it drew to a close to 'getting every hour nearer and nearer to my dear people and my blessed home.'

In August he returned to his beloved church in Cambridge. In a very unsteady hand he wrote in the diary he had kept of this journey, 'Sunday, Aug. 7th. 1836 – We had 245 at the Lord's Table.'[7] It was almost his last entry and one of his happiest. His affectionate family had welcomed him back as their presiding minister in the service which he chiefly loved to conduct for them. He was a very tired man, but he threw himself once more into his parish duties in a deceptively euphoric state. 'I never remember to have had greater energy for work than at this time' was how he felt just then. On September 18th he preached a powerful sermon on 2 Kings 10:16, 'Come with me and see my zeal for the Lord,' calling on his hearers to serve the Lord with ardent love and wise enthusiasm.[8] It was to be his last sermon. No theme could have been more appropriate.

In his zeal for his Master Simeon felt it his duty as one of the senior clergy in the diocese, to pay a courtesy call of welcome on the newly appointed Bishop of Ely, Joseph Allen. September 21st proved a cold and blustery day and Ely Cathedral where they met was a very bleak place. He consequently caught a severe chill and in a few days a feverish illness developed from which he was not to recover. This he soon realised and began quite contentedly and full of 'praise for countless, endless mercies', to prepare to die. His servants moved his 'beautiful French-polished bedstead' about which his bedmaker told Marianne Thornton 'it made him so unhappy if they weren't careful of it', into the more spacious dining-room with its outlook on the front court.[9] Here he could more easily welcome the many callers who wanted to express in person something of their regard and affection for him.

Simeon retained his faculties to the end, and made a great impression on his physician, Dr Haviland, not only by his serenity and quiet confidence, but also by those occasional sparkles of wit which lightened the solemnity of the death-bed scene from time to time. Romilly, a friend of the doctor, records in his diary how Simeon once asked Dr Haviland, 'Were you ever in Bedlam? Well, if I succeed in a plan of mine you'll find me tomorrow jumping and dancing about my bed just like a maniac.' The doctor duly called next morning and remarked 'You are decidedly better today.' 'Yes,' said Simeon, 'but it's all owing to that glass of brandy I took.'[10] When Dr Haviland raised his eyebrows at this, Simeon showed him a letter that his nephew, Sir Richard, had just read for him from the Bishop of Ely appointing his trusted colleague, William Carus, to succeed him as incumbent of Trinity Church. It was the fulfilment of his last wish and prayer. He could now die without a care on his mind.

One day when the doctor suggested to Simeon that it might be possible to prolong his life if he went through an operation, he flatly refused. 'He felt he was dying and that he did not wish life to be supported by artificial means; that he would be glad to see Dr Haviland as a friend, but begged he would send him no more medicine,'[11] a request the doctor said no patient had ever made to him before. Simeon had an absolute horror of those long drawn out sentimental death-bed scenes which the evangelical tract writers of that era so delighted to portray. Once when the nurse, three servants, one doctor and two curates all happened to be present in his room at the same time, he spoke out quite sharply: 'You are all on a wrong scent, and are all in a wrong spirit; you want to see what is called a *dying scene*. That I abhor from my inmost soul. I wish to be *alone*, with my God, and to lie before him as a poor, wretched, hell-deserving sinner . . . but I would also look to him as my all-forgiving God . . . don't let people come round to get up a scene.' 'If I am admitted, as I hope to be, to heaven', he said a week or two later, 'then, if there be one that will sing louder than the rest, I think I shall be that one. But while I am here I am a sinner – a redeemed sinner; that is my style; and as such I would lie here to the last, at the foot of the cross, looking unto Jesus; and go as such into the presence of my God.'[12]

It is notable how Simeon remained inspired to the very end of his life by those same truths which, away back at Easter time, 1779, had first brought peace to his soul. When at the advanced age of seventy-six he was invited once more to be Select Preacher to the university, he prepared a series of four sermons on the ceremonial of Old Testament sacrifices and their fulfilment in the death of Christ. In these he stated his own eternal hopes by comparing the Christian believer to a Jew who 'if interrogated how he was to obtain mercy at God's hands, might without a moment's hesitation answer, "By sacrifice to be sure, and by means of a victim dying in my stead". '[13] When on Sunday, November 13th 1836 the bells of Great St Mary's were ringing out for the university sermon which he had hoped to be delivering himself, Charles Simeon died – within sight of the university church where his special contributions had been always so well received, and within a few minutes' walk of the parish church where he had laboured for fifty-four faithful years.

But it was in the world-famous chapel of the college of which he had been so distinguished a member all these years that, as he hoped, he was buried, in a vault marked to this day by the modest inscription, 'C.S. 1836'. Simeon's funeral was probably the most remarkable that Cambridge has ever seen. The town recognised the occasion, in spite of it being market-day, by closing its shops, the university by suspending all lectures. The entire nave of the chapel was filled by eight hundred members of the parish of Holy Trinity who had been issued with tickets at Simeon's special request. Another eight hundred or so, members of the university, assembled at the college hall. A contemporary engraving shows how the procession stretched from there right round the river side of the great Court, and then up to the west door of the chapel.[14] Four senior Fellows walked each side of the coffin which was followed by his nephew, Sir Richard Simeon, as chief mourner. Behind him came members of the Simeon Trust, his curates and the clergy, eight masters of colleges, doctors and professors, MAs and BAs and undergraduates, four abreast, wearing their college 'squares' with black mourning ribbons hanging down from each corner. The vast congregation of town and gown led by a choir famous even in those days, with the organist giving Handel's Dead March a memorably impressive rendering, all combined to make the occasion one of which men were to speak in awed terms for many a year to come. The one who had often been spoken against as 'the arch-enemy of the church' and against whom undergraduates were warned to beware even as late as 1817,[15] was receiving a tribute the like of which has not been recorded of anyone else's funeral in Cambridge before or since.

Every bell of each college chapel being tolled to mark the moment of interment was testimony enough to the truth of the rector of Fulbourn's contention, written in 1834 on the basis of twenty-four years' association with the university, that 'so great a change has taken place in men's hearts that at this moment there is not a more popular man in the whole university than the venerable minister of Holy Trinity Church; and when he preaches before the university, there is not a master of a college, nor a master of arts, nor a professor, nor an undergraduate absent who can possibly be present.'[16] That is high testimony indeed. No one would have been more surprised or more humbled than the old apostle himself at the last tribute being paid him, but who deserved the honours more than he? No one had done so much for so long under such difficult circumstances for the town and university of Cambridge.

But if Simeon had been asked where his chief loyalty lay, his answer would have been – not to the university or the town, nor even to his own parish of Holy Trinity; it was to his beloved Church of England as a whole. Archbishop Ramsey has testified that in addition to the extremes to which he used to go in abasing himself before his crucified Saviour, Charles Simeon drew no limits in his devotion to the church.[17] He was 'a faithful and devoted son of the Church of England', content with the Thirty-Nine Articles of Religion, happy with Morning and Evening Prayer and the Litany, and always enraptured by Cranmer's Service of Holy Communion, preparation for which had been the turning point in his life. Not blind to his church's faults, he regarded them as no more than 'spots upon the sun's disk'. As for reform of the prayer book, he was quite sure that it would result 'in greater evils than those which you wish to remedy'. He even went so far as to say 'no other human work is so free from faults as it is.' He took a particularly poor view of home-made prayers such as free church ministers composed. In comparison with them he 'felt the prayers of our church as marrow to my soul', as he stated when returning from his travels north of the border. 'If all men could pray at all times as some men can sometimes, then indeed we might prefer extempore to precomposed prayers,' was his general verdict.[18]

No one could have been more loyal to his bishop, as witness his last visit to Ely. The fact that Bishop Allen was not a man of any special eminence or spirituality (of his sermons when published the *Christian Observer* commented 'We are unable to discover a single reason why they should have been dug out of their obscurity')[19] in no way lessened Simeon's respect for his office. No one did more than he to retain within the established church those evangelical enthusiasts whose zeal for preaching the gospel tempted them at times to ignore its rules and regulations. It was his love of his own church, his satisfaction with its liturgy, and his belief that the reformers in the 16th century had faithfully brought it back to the Bible, that led Simeon to pray that his own *magnum opus* might be used 'not to strengthen a party in the church, but to promote the good of the whole.' His enthusiastic loyalty was so infectious that most of the 'serious' young men who gathered round him, and who could so easily have been carried away by the extremists of the day, were retained to make their full contribution to the very needy national church.

Whereas John Henry Newman in the 1830s was rushing the Oxford Movement forward faster than the church was able to accept, Charles Simeon in his old age remained a restraining influence upon the 'seriousness' of younger churchmen. Indeed, James Stephen, distinguished author of *Essays in Ecclesiastical Biography*, whose comments on Simeon's personality we have already quoted, said that when it came to 'touching other men's hearts and influencing their conduct . . . Charles Simeon is worth a legion of Newmans.' Newman, when he heard this modestly accepted the verdict saying 'Doubtless Mr Simeon is ten thousand times more attractive than I, but not than the church I serve.'[20] Simeon would have equally modestly upheld the prior claims of the church he loved and served as loyally as any Newman. 'There is every reason to believe,' wrote the biographer of Rowland Hill, 'that the observance of *order*, which has been so judiciously regarded by Mr Simeon and his followers at Cambridge, has tended greatly to promote the influence of numbers of the zealous clergy who are now so vigilantly and successfully defending the best interests of the church.'[21]

This is not the place to try to assess the general condition of the Church of England in Simeon's day. Enough has been hinted at already to suggest that it was far from healthy. It was bad enough for John Byng, who dearly loved a really bright service when he could find one in the course of his many journeys, to have to record sadly in his diary for June 26th, 1791, 'The day must come when this country will be convulsed by interior commotions, on the claims and oppressions of the clergy, their non-residence and their neglect of duty.' Eight years after he wrote this, out of 11,194 parishes in the country, 7,358 had no resident parson.[22]

The absentee rectors, often holding and receiving the emoluments of several churches sometimes far apart, left the work in the hands of pathetic impoverished curates who had no possible hopes of preferment, and no other means of support except by taking a few pupils when such could be found.

In such a situation, what were the chances of Simeon's young men, whom he was gradually feeding into the system, finding a worth-while job? Being the type of men they were, and committed to the self-denying principles which were part of Simeon's way of life, the church which needed them so much was not geared to receive them. In 1821 Simeon wrote to the Prime Minister complaining that evangelicals such as his men were being overlooked and kept down 'by the highest authorities in the church.'[23] Such men were not prepared to pull strings or push themselves in any way, nor to compromise their principles in order to get the right side of some potential patron. Not for them the advice of Tennyson's churchwarden to the curate that 'if tha wants to git forrards a bit' it would be fatal to 'speak plaain out' like his 'serious' rector. 'Creep along the hedge-bottoms, an' thou'll be a Bishop yet', was his most un-Simeonlike recommendation. This unassuming spirit was what James Bean so much admired in evangelicals: 'We see them, with talents sufficiently popular to carry the prize of emolument or honour . . . sacrificing such prospects by honestly refusing to accommodate themselves to the taste of their times; making a stand against what they think wrong in those who have favours to bestow, though fully aware that inferiority of rank and straitness of income are the certain consequences of their fidelity.'[24]

Few evangelical or 'serious' clergy were in fact known to the upper crust of society where so much of the patronage lay. The vested interests of the well-to-do were disturbed as George Eliot pointed out, by 'Evangelicalism . . . invading the very drawing rooms, mingling itself with the comfortable fumes of port-wine and brandy, threatening to deaden with its murky breath all the splendour of the ostrich feathers' of the glamorous ladies in the front pews of the church.[25] The result was that time and again Cambridge men who had been brought to Christ through Simeon and then been privileged to sit at his feet to learn the secrets of a faithful ministry and be trained for their work according to his school of thought, often had to be – and indeed were – content with the limited sphere of some out of the way villages with populations around two or three hundred, where they could be destined to remain for a lifetime. In this way Samuel Settle was vicar of Winterbourne-Stoke in Wiltshire and Dr Fearon rector of Ore for thirty years, John Williamson was forty years at Theale, Somerset, and John Sargent at Graffham in Sussex for twenty-eight years. Simeon's nominee as tutor to the small Gladstone boy, William Rawson, was at Seaforth for no less than fifty-seven years. Not only were livings hard to come by, but there was the real danger that if the incumbent, after a faithful and effective ministry, were to move to another church, his successor might very well be someone totally out of sympathy with what he had been doing, as happened when Henry Venn left Huddersfield for Yelling. The resulting disturbance among the parishioners who, if this took place, would have nowhere else to go but to the dissenting chapel, can be imagined. 'What else can they do? If they have tasted of manna and hunger for it, they cannot feed on heathen chaff, nor yet on legal crusts, though baked by some staunch Pharisee quite up to perfection,' was how the unique John Berridge uniquely expressed it to Lady Huntingdon.[26]

There was only one really practical answer, and it is no surprise to discover that Charles Simeon was soon on to it. This was to purchase the right of presentation to as many churches as possible from any patrons who could be persuaded to dispose of them. It might be a kindness to any free church reader of these pages to explain the strange situation which made it possible for Simeon to influence the future of the Church of England not only through the example he set and the great number of men and churches that he helped, but also in his buying for cash these 'advowsons' as they are called. The origin of the right to present a clergyman to a benefice lay in the action of a godfearing landlord, way back in the middle ages, not only in building a church for his village, but also, rather naturally, seeing that there was a parson to minister there. This gradually became a much valued privilege and the villagers were perfectly happy that their squire should have the responsibility of providing their minister, and seeing that his son continued the good work. In time the right of presentation came to be regarded as a piece of property to be handed down from father to son, or disposed of by gift or sale. As the Brontës and Jane Austen described in their novels, when these livings were worth something, favoured sons and nephews came to aspire to them as the best means of marrying with security, the more so as the work could be done with the minimum of effort. No wonder Simeon took all this to heart, writing at one point to the Bishop of Oxford to say how he felt that 'the greatest reform that the church needs is an improvement in the method of appointing to the cure of souls.' 'Some of the most efficient and godly clergy in the church remain unbeneficed whilst utterly worthless and useless idlers were able to secure important livings for the sake of the loaves and fishes,' he so rightly complained.[27]

Customs dying slowly in this country, many churches have remained in the hands of lay patrons, local squires or colleges, as well as the Crown, the dioceses and various societies of one kind or another. Patronage of this sort may not long survive in the national church, but in those days there was nothing specially outrageous in the idea of cornering some of the appointments in the interests of ensuring that evangelical clergy should have somewhere to go and could know that they would be followed by men of similar convictions. The first to purchase such advowsons was John Thornton, a very rich London merchant whose son Henry of the Clapham Sect, followed suit. Simeon first got drawn into it by being made one of the Trustees in John Venn's place to administer the Thornton livings on Henry's death. He immediately saw the possibilities of developing the system and it was not long before he became the moving spirit.

Simeon took his responsibilities as an appointing trustee with the utmost seriousness, and was soon urging on his fellow-trustees certain basic principles on which to work. In the earlier days one of these was that, all things being equal, special consideration should be given to whichever of a number of possible candidates happened to be in the most straitened circumstances. But later this emphasis was subordinated to the supreme issue as to who would suit the parish best. 'Why have I bought these livings? Not to present a good man to each, but to fill them with men who shall prove great and leading characters of commanding influence in the Church of God.'[28] He was prepared to stand up to anyone in the matter of only choosing the best possible man. If there was any doubt about someone he would drop him at once. In 1816 the great Isaac Milner, then Dean of Carlisle, wrote to Simeon for advice when he was being pressed by a friend to appoint a man to a living whom he honestly did not feel was really up to it. Simeon's reply was short and to the point: 'Were – my own father and wanting bread, I could not do it. – I would not do it,' and he went on to enlarge on his reasons.[29] On one occasion, in setting aside a name recommended by none other than Mrs Wilberforce, he explained that 'to obtain a fit person will not satisfy my conscience. I must, in order to approve myself to God, have the fittest person I can possibly find.'[30] He told Samuel Carr that in one case he had received two petitions, one signed by 400 and the other by 700 persons. He complied with neither but sent them someone they did not know, and 'within six months I received a letter of thanks signed by forty of the heads of both parties saying that I had provided infinitely better for them than they would have provided for themselves.'[31]

Simeon's motive all along was to try to ensure that worthy men had worthy jobs to go to. He had his eye on churches in strategic centres such as Cheltenham where in 1817 for £3000 he secured the parish church of a town which was reaching the peak of its popularity.[32] In Bradford he got what is now the Cathedral of a city whose population rose between 1801 and 1841 from 29,754 to 105,259.[33] Colchester, Newcastle-under-Lyme, Drypool, Darlaston, Clifton, Hereford, Northampton, Ipswich and Chichester came one by one into his net. And in his appointment to the churches in these centres for which he became responsible, the principle on which he worked was always the same: 'The securing of a faithful ministry in influential places would justify any outlay of money that could be expended on it – I purchase *spheres* wherein the prosperity of the established church and the kingdom of our blessed Lord may be advanced; and not for a season only, but if it please God, in perpetuity also.'

When the possibility of securing such a church arose, he would take the plunge at once without waiting for any committee or consultation, or even until the money was forthcoming, so as to be sure of getting there first. He was only very occasionally thwarted. 'My plan is first to leap into the mire, and then to say to my friends, "If you choose to give me a helping hand, I will take a few more leaps"; but my efforts must of necessity be bounded by my means. I do not first ask, then act; but first act and then ask, and leave it to the Lord to send friends to my assistance or not, as it shall please him.' The system worked, and over the years after Simeon had devoted the greater part of his brother's legacy to the fund, gifts flowed in from all directions, many of them substantial contributions of £10,000, £9000, £8000, £4000 and so on. 'Shall I on account of these assistances spare myself?' he argued. 'God forbid. No. I will, with God's help, proceed and rather increase than diminish my own efforts in proportion as God stirs up his people to help me. And I record this . . . as a pledge to Thee, my God and Father, that with thy help I will proceed to serve Thee with my own property as well as with the property of others which may be entrusted to me.' To the end of his life this became one of his great preoccupations, and one of the last things he did was to alter his will so that all that was left of his property which, after a few personal legacies, came to about £5000, was entirely devoted to this one great object.[34] By the time of his death he was responsible for some forty livings.

The Municipal Corporations Act of 1835 which had laid down that all boroughs must rid themselves of any church patronage, led to a number of important churches coming on the market. Simeon and his colleagues wasted no time in negotiating for such places as Bath Abbey (which cost them £6330),[35] Bridlington Priory, Derby Parish Church, St Michael, Macclesfield and Beverley Minster, all of which were acquired. In the case of the last Simeon just beat the Duke of Northumberland to the post. When asked to surrender it to him, Simeon of course refused, in spite of the worthy Duke's family connection with the Minster. 'What are Dukes or Kings in comparison of fidelity to God?' was his comment on the situation.[36]

In 1833 Charles Simeon formally created a Patronage Trust and bequeathed to his successors, who are now responsible for about a hundred and forty livings, the marching orders by which they examine their faithfulness to the founder's intentions. When the centenary of Simeon's death was being celebrated in 1936 at Holy Trinity, Cambridge, the then Archbishop of Canterbury, Dr Lang, a man of somewhat different churchmanship to Simeon but with wide experience of patronage problems, gave it as his opinion that 'no better manual for all patrons of Benefices could be found than the Deed which declared his Trust. I am bound to add,' he went on, 'that in my experience his trustees have been loyal to the spirit of this Trust.'[37] Archbishop Michael Ramsey has shown similar sympathy with Simeon's actions in writing: 'The original aim and the original result was to strengthen the parochial system by bringing within it an apostolic zeal which might otherwise have been apart from it.'[38]

The terms of the Trust are notable for their freedom from any partisan spirit. There is no mention of a 'party' interest, nor is any attention drawn to what the word 'evangelical' stands for. Simeon felt that his charge, which is read by every new trustee on his appointment, was sufficiently spiritual in tone to ensure that a succession of faithful men would be sent to those churches which the generosity of the laity had thus saved from all private or unworthy influences. It runs as follows:

IN THE NAME AND IN THE PRESENCE OF ALMIGHTY GOD I give the following Charge to all my Trustees and to all who shall succeed them in the Trust to the remotest ages. I implore them for the Lord Jesus Christ's sake, and I charge them also before that adorable Saviour who will call them into Judgment for their execution of the Trust:

First, that they be very careful, whenever they shall be called upon to fill up a vacancy in this Trust, which they must invariably do within three months of a vacancy occurring, that they elect no one who is not a truly pious and devoted man, a man of God in deed and in truth, who with his piety combines a solid judgment and a perfectly independent mind. I place this first, because a failure in this one particular would utterly defeat, and that in perpetuity too, all that I have sought to do for God and for immortal souls.

Secondly, that when they shall be called upon to appoint to a living, they consult nothing but the welfare of the people for whom they are to provide and whose eternal interests have been confided in them. They must on no account be influenced by any solicitation of the great and powerful, or by any partiality towards any one on account of the largeness of his family or the smallness of his income. They must be particularly on their guard against petitions from the Parishes to be provided for, whether on behalf of a Curate that has laboured among them, or of any other individual. They must examine carefully, and judge as before God, how far any person possesses the qualification suited to the particular Parish, and by that consideration *alone* must they be determined in their appointment of him.

Signed by me this 18th day of March in the year of our Lord one thousand eight hundred and thirty-three.

CHARLES SIMEON

This was the man who for fifty-four years devoted himself not only to the winning of souls, but also to training and teaching one generation after another of young men to do the same when the opportunity provided by their ordination made it possible. The result of his life's labours locally was that he lived 'to see all Cambridge filled with the belief and love of the truth which he preached; every parish church therein occupied with a ministry of kindred spirit,' as Bishop McIlvaine wrote in an article *On the State of the Church of England* in the *New York Review* in 1838.[39] Not only so, but Bishop Welldon on October 24th 1936 wrote to *The Times* to say that his friend John Willis Clark, who as registrar of the university for many years had every reason to know, told him 'that the moral regeneration of Cambridge dates from Charles Simeon'.[40]

His influence was not confined to Cambridge. As one of the recognised leaders of the evangelical wing of the national church, Simeon had a formative part to play in the rise of that vital Christianity of which the historian W. H. Lecky had this to say: 'They gradually changed the whole spirit of the English church. They infused into it a new fire and passion of devotion, kindled a spirit of fervent philanthropy, raised the standard of clerical duty, and completely altered the whole tone and tendency of the preaching of its ministers. Before the close of the century the evangelical movement had become dominant in England.'[41] This verdict was borne out by Gladstone who, though no longer of that way of thinking himself, had been greatly influenced by 'the evangelical gospel which he believed as a baptised and converted member of the Catholic church,'[42] and was ready to give credit where credit was due. He wrote in 1879,

> They preached Christ largely and fervently where, as a rule, he was but little and but coldly preached before. And who is there that will not say from his heart, 'I therein do rejoice, yea, and will rejoice.' . . . The pith and life of the evangelical teaching, as it consists in the re-introduction of Christ our Lord to be the woof and warp of preaching, was the great gift of the movement to the teaching church, and has now penetrated and possessed it on a scale so general that it may be considered as pervading the whole mass.[43]

Charles Smyth who believes that Simeon 'more than any other inspired and promoted the evangelical revival in the second and third generation of its course,'[44] has also stated it as his conviction that 'More than any other single factor, the evangelical movement in the Church of England transformed the whole character of English society and imparted to the Victorian Age that moral earnestness which was its distinguishing characteristic.'[45]

The acts of the old apostle lived after him. To this day his life is remembered with gratitude in the chapel of King's College, Cambridge, by the saying of this prayer every 13th day of November, the anniversary of his death:

> Almighty and everlasting God, who by thy holy servant, Charles Simeon, didst mould the lives of many that they might go forth and teach others also; mercifully grant that as through evil report and good report he ceased not to preach thy saving Word, so we may never be ashamed of the Gospel of Jesus Christ our Lord, who with Thee and the Holy Spirit liveth and reigneth one God world without end.

References

Chapter One INTRODUCTION TO CAMBRIDGE

1. W. H. Tucker, *Eton of Old* (1892), p.27.
2. A. D. Coleridge, *Eton in the Forties* (1896), p.9.
3. W. H. Tucker, op.cit., pp.20, 51.
4. C. Hollis, *Eton* (1960), p.174.
5. *The Farington Diary*, 7.10.1814.
6. J. S. Watson, *The Life of Richard Porson* (1861), p.21.
7. C. Smyth, *Simeon and Church Order* (Cambridge 1940), p.79.
8. J. Morley, *The Life of William Ewart Gladstone* (1903), i, 28.
9. A. C. Benson, *Fasti Etonenses* (1899), p.242.
10. C. Hollis, op.cit., pp.188, 234.
11. W. H. Tucker, op.cit., p.42.
12. Byron, *Hints from Horace*, 27.
13. *Autobiographical Recollections of George Pryme* (Cambridge 1870), p.46.
14. C. Carlyon, *Early Years and Late Reflections* (1856), iii, 80.
15. R. Willis and J. W. Clark, *The Architectural History of the University of Cambridge* (Cambridge 1886), i, 573.
16. J. A. Venn, *Statistical Chart to illustrate Entries in the University of Cambridge, 1544–1907.*
    T. Harwood, *Alumni Etonenses* (1797).
17. *Alma Mater or Seven Years at the University of Cambridge by a Trinity-Man* (J. M. F. Wright) (1827), i, 83.
18. C. Wordsworth, *Social Life at the English Universities in the Eighteenth Century* (Cambridge 1874), p.129.
19. *The Torrington Diaries*, 29.5.1794.
20. J. M. F. Wright, op.cit., i, 61.
21. J. Saltmarsh in *Victoria History of Cambridgeshire and the Isle of Ely* (1967), iii, 398.
22. C. Wordsworth, op.cit., p.84.
23. H. C. G. Moule, *Charles Simeon* (1892), p.6.
24. D. A. Winstanley, *Unreformed Cambridge* (Cambridge 1935), p.53.
25. *A Frenchman in England*, trans. S. C. Roberts (Cambridge 1933), p.222.

26. R. Coupland, *Wilberforce* (1945), p.10.
27. D. A. Winstanley, op.cit., p.210.
28. A. B. Gray, *Cambridge Revisited* (Cambridge 1921), p.77.
29. M. Milner, *The Life of Isaac Milner* (1842), p.399.
30. J. Williamson, *A Brief Memoir of the Rev Charles Simeon* (1848), p.13.
31. A. C. Benson, op.cit., p.250.

Chapter Two A CHRISTIAN AT KING'S

1. J. M. F. Wright, *Alma Mater*, i, 31, 33.
2. *Memoirs of the Life of Gilbert Wakefield* (1792), p.148.
3. Quoted in C. Smyth, *Simeon and Church Order*, p.115.
4. D. A. Winstanley, *Early Victorian Cambridge* (Cambridge 1955), p.91.
5. *Anecdotes of the Life of Richard Watson, Bishop of Llandaff* (1817), pp.29, 37, 149.
6. D. A. Winstanley, *Unreformed Cambridge*, p.108.
7. W. H. Tucker, *King's Old Court*, p.5.
8. G. Tyerman, *The Life of George Whitefield* (1890), i, 360.
9. R. Southey, *The Life of William Cowper* (1854), i, 81.
10. James Boswell, *Life of Doctor Johnson* (1791), i, 29.
11. Thomas Carlyle, *Oliver Cromwell's Letters and Speeches* (1845), i, 76
12. F. Close, *Occasional Sermons* (1844), p.203.
13. R. Southey, *The Remains of Henry Kirke White* (1821), i, 209.
14. Charles Simeon, *Horae Homileticae* (1833), Sermon 1346.
15. R. M. Beverley, op.cit., p.8.
16. *Jane Austen's Letters* ed. R. W. Chapman (Oxford 1932), pp.298, 256, 410.
17. M. M. Preston, *Memoranda of the Rev Charles Simeon* (1840), p.3.
18. H. Venn, *The Life and Letters of the late Rev Henry Venn* (1834), p.345.
19. Ibid.
20. R. Whittingham, *The Works of the Rev John Berridge* (1838), p.418.
21. H. C. G. Moule, *Charles Simeon*, p.29.

Chapter Three MINISTER OF HOLY TRINITY CHURCH

1. J. Bean, *Zeal without Innovation*(1808), p.149.
2. A. B. Grosart, *Works of Richard Sibbes* (Edinburgh 1973), xxxvi, cxi.
3. The Rev J. Barton, *Notes on the History of Holy Trinity Church.*
4. Simeon Trust Papers.
5. Quoted in Sykes, *Church and State in England in the XVIIIth Century* (1934), p.240.
6. Ridley Hall Papers.
7. *Cambridge General Advertiser*, 6.3.1839.
8. *Cambridge Intelligencer*, 12.10.1793.
9. D. A. Winstanley, *Unreformed Cambridge*, p.142.
10. *Journals and Letters of the Rev Henry Martyn*, ed. S. Wilberforce (1837), i, 132.
11. Charles Simeon, *Horae Homileticae*, Sermon 395.

12. H. C. G. Moule, *Charles Simeon,* p.108.
13. J. Venn, *Annals of a Clerical Family* (1904), p.196.
14. J. and J. H. Pratt, *Memoirs of the Rev Josiah Pratt* (1849), p.5.
15. J. Williamson, *A Brief Memoir of the Rev Charles Simeon,* p.49.
16. Charles Simeon, op.cit., Sermon 333.
17. H. C. G. Moule, op.cit., pp.42, 43.
18. Parish Vestry Minutes.
19. Venn MSS. C.22.
20. E. Sidney, *The Life of the Rev Rowland Hill* (1834), p. 161.
21. J. King, *Memoirs of the Rev Thomas Dykes* (1849), p.8.
22. *Cambridge Chronicle,* 22.12.1792.
23. *Eclectic Notes,* ed. J. H. Pratt (1865), p.496.
24. M. M. Preston, *Memoranda of the Rev Charles Simeon,* p.36.
25. Charles Simeon, op.cit., Sermon 2036.
26. P. H. Ditchfield, *The Parish Clerk* (1907), p.15.
27. H. Gunning, *Reminiscences of the University, Town and County of Cambridge* (1854), ii, 149.
28. M. M. Preston, op.cit., p.37.
29. Quoted in C. Smyth, *Simeon and Church Order,* p.275.
30. *Cambridge Intelligencer,* 17.1.1795.
31. G. F. A. Best, *Temporal Pillars* (Cambridge 1964), p.141.
32. Charles Simeon, op.cit., Sermon 767.
33. Ibid. Sermon 826.
34. Ibid. Sermon 1539.
35. *Memoirs of the Life of Elisabeth Fry* (1847), ed. K. F. and R. E. C., i, 132.
36. H. Gunning, op.cit., ii, 121.
37. *The Autobiography of Arthur Young* (1898), ed. M. Betham-Edwards, p.369.
38. H. Venn, *The Life and Letters of the late Rev Henry Venn,* p.377.
39. Venn MSS. C.22.

Chapter Four SIMEON IN THE PULPIT

1. Ridley Hall Papers.
2. J. Stephen, *Essays in Ecclesiastical Biography* (1907), ii, 238.
3. Venn MSS. C.16.
4. J. Downey, *The Eighteenth-Century Pulpit* (Oxford 1969), p.5.
5. N. Sykes in *Theology,* February 1939, p.98.
6. J. Downey, op.cit., p.24.
7. Charles Simeon, *Preface to Horae Homileticae* (1832), xxvii.
8. F. Close, *Occasional Sermons,* p.185.
9. C. Smyth, *The Art of Preaching* (1940), p.175.
10. Charles Simeon, *Horae Homileticae,* Vol. xxi, p.294.
11. *British Critic,* April 1797, p.435.
12. Charles Simeon, op.cit., p.291.

13. Ibid., p.398 (see The Apocrypha, *Bel and the Dragon*).
14. Ibid., p.406.
15. *The Farington Diary*, 7.7.1807.
16. A. T. Hart, *The Eighteenth-Century Parson* (1955), p.44.
17. M. Seeley, *The Later Evangelical Fathers* (1879), p.270.
18. J. Farington, op.cit., 31.1.1805.
19. *Tracts relating to Cambridge* (C.U. Library).
20. C. Smyth, op.cit., pp.175, 208.
21. Quoted in *Evangelicalism 1785–1835* (Hulsean Prize Essay 1962, H. Wilmer), pp.30, 36.
22. *Eclectic Review*, July 1820, p.77.
23. Charles Simeon, *Preface*, xxi.
24. C. Buxton, *Memoirs of Sir Thomas Fowell Buxton* (1848), p.263.
25. J. Jerram, *Memoirs of the late Rev Charles Jerram* (1855), p.131, 132.
26. J. Williamson, *A Brief Memoir of the Rev Charles Simeon*, pp.49, 50.
27. Ridley Hall Papers.
28. J. Jerram, op.cit., p.86.
29. J. Williamson, op.cit., p.51.
30. Ridley Hall Papers.
31. Quoted in C. Smyth, *Simeon and Church Order*, p.277.
32. *Christian Observer*, March 1821, p.154.
33. *The Autobiography of Arthur Young*, ed. M. Betham-Edwards, p.398.
34. J. Stoughton, *Religion in England 1800–1850* (1884), i. 124.
35. M. M. Preston, *Memoranda of the Rev Charles Simeon*, p.49.
36. H. C. G. Moule, *Charles Simeon*, p.95.
37. F. Close, op.cit., p.187.
38. W. R. Fremantle, *Memoir of the Rev Spencer Thornton* (1850), p.53.
39. J. Farington, op.cit., 18.5.1806.
40. C. Smyth in the *Church Times*, 13.9.1936.
41. Charles Simeon, op.cit., Sermon 1951.

Chapter Five IN THE ACADEMIC WORLD

1. J. Noble, *A Memoir of the Rev R. T. Noble* (1867), p.46.
2. M. D. George, *Hogarth to Cruickshank: Social Change in Graphic Satire* (New York 1967), pp.88, 89.
3. D. A. Winstanley, *Unreformed Cambridge*, p.316 ff.
4. C. Wordsworth, *Social Life at the English Universities in the Eighteenth Century*, pp.442, 446.
5. A. A. Leigh, *King's College* (1899), p.218.
6. Ibid., p.242.
7. D. A. Winstanley, op.cit., p.258.
8. W. H. Tucker, *King's Old Court*, p.14.
9. H. Gunning, *Reminiscences of the University, Town and County of Cambridge*, ii, 64.

10. A. A. Leigh, op.cit., p.255.
11. Ibid., p.250.
12. Ibid., p.219.
13. C. Smyth, *Simeon and Church Order,* p.134.
14. J. Jerram, *Memoirs of the late Rev Charles Jerram,* p.85.
15. *Christian Observer,* May 1811, p.309.
16. *Memoirs of the Life of Gilbert Wakefield,* p.145.
17. H. C. G. Moule, *Charles Simeon,* p.95.
18. Charles Simeon, *Horae Homileticae,* Sermons 2174, 1948.
19. Ibid., Sermon 908.
20. Ibid., Sermon 1973.
21. Edmund Burke, *Reflections on the Revolution in France* (1790), p.14.
22. Charles Simeon, op.cit., Sermon 2000.
23. G. O. Trevelyan, *The Life and Letters of Lord Macaulay* (1876), i, 50.
24. Charles Simeon, op.cit., Sermons 191–194.
25. *Edinburgh Review,* November 1822, p.434.
26. M. Milner, *The Life of Isaac Milner,* 463ff.
27. D. A. Winstanley, *Early Victorian Cambridge,* p.20.
28. C. Smyth, op.cit., p.294*n*.
29. J. Williamson, *A Brief Memoir of the Rev Charles Simeon,* p.34.
30. Ridley Hall Papers.
31. J. Williamson, op.cit., p.72.
32. W. Selwyn, *Memoirs of the late Rev James Scholefield* (1855), p.27.
33. Harrowby MSS. cxii, 151.

Chapter Six WITH MEN FOR THE MINISTRY

1. *Works of the late Joseph Milner,* ed. I. Milner (1810), viii, 279.
2. M. Milner, *The Life of Isaac Milner,* p.100.
3. J. Bean, *Zeal without Innovation,* pp.38, 40.
4. H. Venn, *The Life and Letters of the late Rev Henry Venn,* p.375.
5. M. Hennell, *John Venn and the Clapham Sect* (1958), p.277.
6. J. Lock and W. T. Dixon, *A Man of Sorrow* (1965), p.20.
7. *Charles Simeon (1759–1836),* ed. A. Pollard and M. Hennell (1959), p.166.
8. C. Smyth, *Simeon and Church Order,* p. 243*n*.
9. Quoted in *The Yorkshire Evangelicals in the 18th Century,* Ph.D. dissertation, J. D. Walsh (1956), p.267.
10. M. Hennell, op.cit., p.278.
11. J. Bateman, *The Life of the Rev H. V. Elliott* (1868), p.121.
12. F. W. Cornish, *The English Church in the Nineteenth Century* (1910), i, 23.
13. J. and J. H. Pratt, *Memoirs of the Rev Josiah Pratt,* pp.252, 326.
14. W. R. Fremantle, *Memoirs of the Rev Spencer Thornton,* p.61.
15. T. Hervey, *Life of the Rev S. Settle* (1881), p.39.

16. J. Bateman, op.cit., pp.19, 104.
17. Charles Simeon, *Horae Homileticae*, Sermon 1948.
18. Parish Vestry Minutes, 15.6.1825.
19. C. Whibley, *In Cap and Gown* (1889), p.109.
20. J. W. Clark, *Cambridge* (1908), p.133.
21. E. K. Purnell, *Magdalene College* (1904), p.180.
22. W. W. Rouse Ball, *A History of the First Trinity Boat Club* (1908), p.12.
23. *MS Diary of Romaine Hervey*, (1795–1797).
24. T. Hervey, op.cit., p.52.
25. S. Meacham, *Henry Thornton of Clapham* (Harvard 1964), p.55.
26. J. M. F. Wright, *Alma Mater*, i, 56.
27. J. H. Overton, *The English Church in the Nineteenth Century* (1894), p.60.
28. Adeney Papers.
29. C. A. Jones, *A History of the Jesus Lane Sunday School* (1864), p.22.
30. Eugene Stock, *History of the Church Missionary Society* (1899), ii, 62*n*.

Chapter Seven A BAND OF BROTHERS

1. *Evangelicalism and English Public Life*, p.11.
2. H. C. G. Moule, *Charles Simeon*, p.58.
3. R. Lloyd, *Memoirs of the Rev Thomas Lloyd* (1830), pp.19, 29.
4. *Christian Observer*, December 1837, p.799.
5. J. Sargent, *The Life of the Rev T. T. Thomason* (1833), p.83.
6. J. R. Elder, *Letters and Journals of Samuel Marsden* (1932), p.529*n*.
7. *Cambridge Review*, 2.12.1937.
8. J. Venn, *Annals of a Clerical Family*, p.118.
9. Ibid., p.100.
10. H. Venn, *The Life and Letters of the late Rev Henry Venn*, p.54.
11. J. Venn, op.cit., p.119*n*.
12. H. C. G. Moule, op.cit., p.45.
13. E. Sidney, *The Life of the Rev Rowland Hill*, p.159.
14. Venn MSS., C.22.
15. E. Sidney, op.cit., p.161.
16. H. Venn, op.cit., pp.473, 481.
17. C. Smyth, *Simeon and Church Order*, p.271.
18. Venn MSS., C.22.
19. M. Hennell, *John Venn and the Clapham Sect*, pp.60, 65.
20. Ibid., pp.92–94.
21. Ibid., p.104.
22. W. Knight, *Memoirs of Henry Venn* (1882), p.24.
23. J. Venn, op.cit., p.187.
24. *Christian Observer*, November 1837, p.738.
25. J. Venn. op.cit., p.189.
26. *Christian Observer*, September 1837, p.613.

27. Ibid., October 1837, p.675.
28. *Magdalene College Magazine*, December 1937; *William Farish 1759–1937*, C. Smyth.
29. *Cambridge Intelligencer*, 28.2.1795.
30. J. Owen, *Memoir of the Rev Thomas Jones* (1851), pp.144, 268.
31. *Cambridge Intelligencer*, 21.8.1794.
32. R. A. Willmott, *Conversations at Cambridge* (1836), p. 257.
33. M. M. Preston, *Memoranda of the Rev Charles Simeon*, p.66.
34. Carr Correspondence.
35. M. M. Preston, op.cit., p.66.
36. J. Sargent, op.cit., p.38.
37. Ibid., p.102.
38. Ibid., p.141.
39. C. Marsh, *The Life of the Rev William Marsh* (1867), p.50.
40. P. Brontë, *The Maid of Killarney* (1818), p.13.
41. J. Venn, *Alumni Cantabrigenses*.
42. A. M. Lee, *A Scholar of a Past Generation* (1896), p.vii.
43. F. W. B. Bullock, *The History of Ridley Hall, Cambridge* (Cambridge 1941), i, 99.
44. W. Selwyn, *Memoirs of the late Rev James Scholefield*, pp.19, 28.
45. Carr Correspondence.

Chapter Eight REACHING BEYOND CAMBRIDGE

1. J. T. Coleridge, *A Memoir of the Rev John Keble* (1869), p.176.
2. G. O. Trevelyan, *The Life and Letters of Lord Macaulay* (1876), i, 68*n*.
3. Charles Simeon, *Horae Homileticae*, Sermon 359.
4. W. Hanna, *Memoirs of the Life and Writings of Thomas Chalmers* (Edinburgh 1850), ii, 20, 287.
5. H. C. G. Moule, *Charles Simeon*, p.155.
6. G. R. Balleine, *A History of the Evangelical Party* (1908), p.122.
7. M. Hennell, *John Venn and the Clapham Sect*, p.85.
8. *Church Quarterly Review*, 1958, p.387. A. Pollard on *Evangelical Parish Clergy 1820–1840*.
9. J. Sargent, *The Life of the Rev T. T. Thomason*, p.39.
10. M. Hennell, op.cit., p.221.
11. *Eclectic Notes*, ed. J. H. Pratt, pp.211, 295, 404.
12. Ridley Hall Papers.
13. A. Rees, *The Cyclopaedia* (1819), Vol. ix.
14. F. K. Brown, *Fathers of the Victorians* (Cambridge 1961), p.356.
15. *The Greville Memoirs 1814–1860*, ed. L. Strachey and R. Fulford (1938), ii, 276, 290; iii, 7; vi, 2.
16. Harrowby MSS. xvi, 116, 117.
17. Ibid., xvi, 120.
18. Ibid. xviii, 324.

19. Ibid., xvi, 122.
20. Charles Simeon, op.cit., Sermons 452, 484.
21. B. Fawcett, *Observations on the Nature, Causes and Cure of Melancholy* (1780), p.49.
22. Ibid., pp.3, 5, 19, 48.
23. Simeon Trust Papers.
24. H. C. G. Moule, op.cit., p.182.
25. Charles Simeon, op.cit., Sermon 1952.

Chapter Nine WITH THE WIDER CHURCH

1. C. Wordsworth, *Social Life at the English Universities in the Eighteenth Century*, p.688*n*.
2. A. Haldane, *Memoirs of the Lives of Robert Haldane of Airthrey and James Alexander Haldane* (1852), p.138.
3. W. Carus, *Memorials of Charles McIlvaine* (1882), p.161.
4. J. Sargent, *The Life of the Rev T. T. Thomason*, p.163.
5. A. Haldane, op.cit., pp.142, 149.
6. M. M. Preston, *Memoranda of the Rev Charles Simeon*, p.44.
7. G. Smith, *The Life of Alexander Duff* (1881), pp.1, 6, 175.
8. A. Haldane, op.cit., p.134.
9. Simeon Trust Papers.
10. A. Haldane, op.cit., p.197.
11. E. Stock, *History of the Church Missionary Society*, i, 59.
12. A. Mayhew, *Christianity and the Government of India* (1929), p.28.
13. Charles Simeon, *Memorial Sketches of the Rev David Brown* (1816), pp.4, 31, 102, 236.
14. H. Morris, *The Life of Charles Grant* (1904), pp.109–112.
15. Ibid., pp.122, 189.
16. H. Pearson, *Memoirs of the Life and Writings of the Rev C. Buchanan* (Oxford 1817), i, 63, 79, 82.
17. *Evangelicalism and English Public Life* (1962), Ian S. Rennie, pp.343, 346.
18. J. Sargent, *Memoirs of the Rev Henry Martyn* (1825), pp.15, 16.
19. *Journals and Letters of the Rev Henry Martyn*, ed. S. Wilberforce, i, 38, 30, 57, 66, 108, 171, 184.
20. J. Sargent, op.cit., p.45.
21. S. Wilberforce, op.cit., i, 245.
22. J. Sargent, op.cit., p.90.
23. G. Smith, *Henry Martyn* (1892), p.192.
24. J. B. Braithwaite, *Memoirs of Joseph John Gurney* (1854), i, 446.
25. *Memoirs of the Rt Rev Daniel Corrie* by his Brothers (1847), p.200.
26. G. Smith, op.cit., p.545.
27. D. Corrie, op.cit., pp.2–3, 13.
28. Charles Simeon, op.cit., p.xiii.
29. C. Hole, *The Early History of the Church Missionary Society* (1896), pp.62, 79.
30. Charles Simeon, *Horae Homileticae*, Sermon 394.

31. *Church Missionary Intelligencer*, September 1887, p.251; C. Hole, *Early Days of the C.M.S. in Cambridge*.
32. Charles Simeon, op.cit., Sermon 2145.

Chapter Ten THE MAN HIMSELF

1. Y. Brilioth, *Evangelicalism and the Oxford Movement* (1934), p.5.
2. J. Jerram, *The Memoirs of the late Rev Charles Jerram*, p.124.
3. J. Morley, *The Life of William Ewart Gladstone* (1908), i, 9.
4. J. Stephen, *Essays in Ecclesiastical Biography*, ii, 239.
5. F. Close, *Occasional Sermons*, p.204.
6. J. Owen, *Memoirs of the Rev Thomas Jones*, p.76.
7. W. Dealtry, Sermon in *The Pulpit*, xxix. 739, p.191.
8. *The Farington Diary*, 19.5.1806.
9. Carr Correspondence.
10. C. R. Fay, *King's College* (1907), p.99.
11. *The Standard* (London), 19.3.1895.
12. G. W. E. Russell, *The Household of Faith* (1902), p.234.
13. *The Autobiography of Arthur Young*, ed. M. Betham-Edwards, p.399.
14. F. Close, op.cit., p.202.
15. H. Morris, *The Life of Charles Grant*, p.313.
16. F. K. Brown, *Fathers of the Victorians*, p.429.
17. C. H. Cooper, *Annals of Cambridge* (1862), iv, 478.
18. J. Farington, op.cit., 16.5.1806.
19. J. Stephen, op.cit., ii, 97.
    J. Scott, *The Life of the Rev Thomas Scott* (1823), p.425.
20. H. C. G. Moule, *Charles Simeon*, p.179.
21. Ridley Hall Papers.
22. J. Bateman, *The Life of the Rt Rev Daniel Wilson* (1860), i, 169.
23. Venn MSS. C.22.
24. Carr Correspondence.
25. J. Farington, op.cit., 15.3.1808.
26. Ibid., 13.9.1805.
27. M. Betham-Edwards, op.cit., p.400.
28. H. C. G. Moule, op.cit., p.179.
29. Harrowby MSS., xvi, 118; xviii, 321.
30. J. Clark and T. Hughes, *The Life and Letters of Adam Sedgewick* (Cambridge 1890), i, 469.
31. E. M. Forster, *Marianne Thornton* (1956), p.82.
32. J. Farington, op.cit., 11.7.1813.
33. M. M. Preston, *Memoranda of the Rev Charles Simeon*, p.40.
34. M.Warren, *Charles Simeon* (Great Churchmen series), p.12.
35. J. Jerram, op.cit., p.124.
36. H. Venn, *The Life and Letters of the late Rev Henry Venn*, pp.473, 481.

37. J. Stephen, op.cit., pp.239, 240, 242.
38. R. F. Housman, *The Life and Remains of the Rev Robert Housman* (1841), p.ccx.
39. Lady Louisa Finch, *A Sketch of the Character of a Beloved Mother* (1861), p.144.
40. W. Dealtry, op.cit., p.191.
41. C. Buxton, *Memoirs of Sir Thomas Fowell Buxton*, p.198.
42. J. W. Kaye, *Christianity in India* (1859), p.189.
43. J. Farington, op.cit., 13.9.1805.
44. I. Bradley, *The Call to Seriousness* (1976), p.92.
45. D. Awasthi, *Dawn of Modern Administration in India* (New Delhi 1972), p.3.
46. F. Close, op.cit., p.183.
47. H. C. G. Moule, op.cit., p.188.

Chapter Eleven SIMEON'S SCHOOL OF THOUGHT

1. Charles Simeon, *Preface to Horae Homileticae*, p.xxiii.
2. Ibid., p.xiv.
3. Ibid., p.xvii*n*.
4. *Christian Observer*, December 1828, p.778.
5. H. C. G. Moule, *Charles Simeon*, p.96.
6. J. Scott, *The Life of the Rev Thomas Scott*, p.446.
7. Charles Simeon, op.cit., p.xxiii.
8. Ibid., p.xxiv.
9. Ibid., p.xxv.
10. Charles Simeon, *Horae Homileticae*, Sermons 1516, 2036, 2011.
11. Ibid, Sermon 2187.
12. J. Owen, *History of the Bible Society* (1816), ii, 560.
13. *Thoughts on the Tendency of Bible Societies* (1816), A. O'Callaghan, p.21.
14. *The Danger of Disseminating the Scriptures without note or comment* (1818), p.34.
15. J. H. Overton, *The English Church in the Nineteenth Century* (1894), p.292.
16. *Evangelicalism and English Public Life*, I. S. Rennie, p.50.
17. *Christian Observer*, July 1827, p.438.
18. Carr Correspondence.
19. Charles Simeon, op.cit., Sermon 1933.
20. S. Thodey, *Sermon at Downing Street Meeting House* (1836), p.37.
21. Charles Simeon, op.cit., Sermon 1975.
22. William Cecil, *A Solemn Appeal to the Rt Rev the Bishop and to the Reverend the Clergy of the Diocese of Ely* (1833), pp.6, 9–22, 82.
23. Charles Simeon, op.cit., Sermon 595.
24. Ibid., Sermons 1980, 1401.
25. S. C. Carpenter, *Church and People 1789–1889* (1933), p.28.
26. Charles Simeon, op.cit., Sermon 811.
27. J. Sargent, *The Life of the Rev T. T. Thomason*, pp.59, 61.
28. *Joseph Romilly's Diary*, 5.7.1840.

29. J. Williamson, *A Brief Memoir of the Rev Charles Simeon*, p.109.
30. Charles Simeon, op.cit., Sermon 1863.
31. William Wilberforce, *A Practical View* (1797), p.78.
32. Charles Simeon, op.cit., Sermon 1862.
33. Ibid., Sermons 1863–1866.
34. *Christian Observer*, January 1832, p.49.
35. M. M. Preston, *Memoranda of the Rev Charles Simeon*, p.77.
36. Carr Correspondence.
37. T. R. Birks, *A Memoir of the Rev Edward Bickersteth* (1852), ii, 61.
38. W. T. Gidney, *A History of the London Society for Promoting Christianity amongst the Jews* (1908), p.47.
39 Charles Simeon, op.cit., Sermon 1262*n*.
40. Ibid.
41. H. P. Palmer, *Joseph Wolff* (1935) pp.99, 100, 102.
42. C.M.S. Archives, G/AC3.

Chapter Twelve CHARLES SIMEON AND THE WORLD

1. G. M. Trevelyan, *English Social History* (1944), p.494.
2. J. Williamson, *A Brief Memoir of the Rev Charles Simeon*, p.55.
3. A. Gray, *Cambridge Revisited*, p.98.
4. *Diary, Reminiscences and Correspondence of Henry Crabb Robinson* (1869), ed. T. Sadler, iii, 272.
5. *Cambridge Intelligencer*, 8.8.1795.
6. A. Haldane, *Memoirs of the Lives of Robert and James Haldane*, p.146.
7. *The Yorkshire Evangelicals*, Ph.D. dissertation, J. D. Walsh, pp.355–358.
8. J. Owen, *Memoirs of the Rev. Thomas Jones*, pp.46, 115.
9. Charles Simeon, *Horae Homileticae*, Sermon 283.
10. Ibid., Sermon 408.
11. Ibid., Sermon 361
12. Quoted in M. Jaegar, *Before Victoria* (1956), p.73.
13. Charles Simeon, op.cit., Sermon 434 and note.
14. Ibid., Sermon 1761.
15. Ridley Hall Papers.
16. Charles Simeon, op.cit., Sermon 1911.
17. C. Buxton, *Memoirs of Sir Thomas Fowell Buxton*, p.96.
18. Carr Correspondence.
19. *Cambridge Intelligencer*, 7.8.1795.
20. *The Farington Diary*, 5.9.1807.
21. W. C. Sydney, *England and the English in the Eighteenth Century* (1891), ii, 175.
22. Charles Simeon, op.cit., Sermon 291.
23. *The Greville Memoirs*, ii, 205.
24. G. Dyer, *Memoirs of the Life and Writings of Robert Robinson* (1796), p.195.

25. W. C. Sydney, op.cit., ii, 269, 294.
26. E. M. Howse, *Saints in Politics* (1953), p.134.
27. J. Farington, op.cit., 13.9.1805.
28. J. Marlowe, *The Puritan Tradition in English Life* (1956), p.102.
29. Charles Simeon, *Appendix to Dr Marsh's Fact* (1813), p.4.
30. Charles Simeon, op.cit., Sermon 785.
31. R. M. Beverley, *A Letter to His Royal Highness the Duke of Gloucester*, p.28.
32. *Autobiographical Recollections of George Pryme*, p.141.
33. G. W. E. Russell, *A Short History of the Evangelical Movement* (1915), pp.74, 75.
34. J. Bull, *John Newton* (1868), p.371.
35. G. W. E. Russell, op.cit., p.73.
36. Charles Simeon, op.cit., Sermon 827.

Chapter Thirteen THE OLD APOSTLE'S LEGACY

1. Charles Simeon, *Horae Homileticae*, Sermon 460.
2. R. M. Beverley, *A Letter to His Royal Highness the Duke of Gloucester*, p.27.
3. Venn MSS. C.22.
4. T. R. Birks, *The Life of the Rev E. Bickersteth*, ii, 37.
5. Charles Simeon, op.cit., Sermon 2421.
6. W. Carus, *Memorials of Bishop McIlvaine*, *pp*.55, 109.
7. Simeon Trust Papers.
8. Charles Simeon, op.cit., Sermon 372.
9. E. M. Forster, *Marianne Thornton*, p.167.
10. *Joseph Romilly's Diary*, 21.11.1836.
11. Ibid.
12. M. M. Preston, *Memoranda of the Rev Charles Simeon*, p.82.
13. H. C. G. Moule, *Charles Simeon*, p.256.
14. T. H. Case, *Memoirs of a King's College Chorister* (1899), p.9.
15. H. C. G. Moule, *The Evangelical School in the Church of England* (1901), p.8.
16. *A Letter to R. M. Beverley Esq.*, (1834), F. R. Hall, p.36.
17. A. M. Ramsey, *Canterbury Essays and Addresses* (1964), p.111.
18. H. C. G. Moule, *Charles Simeon*, p.166.
19. *Christian Observer*, August 1858, p.663.
20. Quoted in D. Newsome, *The Parting of Friends* (1966), p.182.
21. E. Sidney, *The Life of the Rev. Rowland Hill*, p.161.
22. N. Sykes, *Church and State in England in the Eighteenth Century*, p.217.
23. *The Journal of Theological Studies*, New series, Vol. x. (1959); G. F. A. Best, *The Evangelicals and the Established Church in the early 19th Century*, p.68*n*.
24. J. Bean, *Zeal without Innovation*, p.163.
25. George Eliot, *Scenes of Clerical Life: Janet's Repentance* ch.ii.
26. Quoted in C. Smyth, *Simeon and Church Order*, p.238.
27. *Charles Simeon: An Interpretation* (1936), p.92.
28. Carr Correspondence.

29. M. Milner, *The Life of Isaac Milner*, p.635.
30. Simeon Trust Papers.
31. Carr Correspondence.
32. M. Milner, op.cit., p.636.
33. *Charles Simeon 1759–1836*, ed. A. Pollard and M. Hennell (1959), p.177.
34. H. C. G. Moule, op.cit., p.265.
35. O. Chadwick, *The Victorian Church* (1960), i, 110.
36. Simeon Trust Papers.
37. *Charles Simeon: An Interpretation*, p.100.
38. A. M. Ramsey, op.cit., p.109.
39. *Christian Observer*, January 1839, p.55.
40. Quoted in M. Warren, *Charles Simeon*, p.33.
41. W. H. Lecky, *A History of England in the Eighteenth Century* (1878), ii, 627.
42. D. L. Edwards, *Leaders of the Church of England* (1971), p.181.
43. W. E. Gladstone, *Gleanings of Past Years* (1879), vii, 207, 224.
44. C. Smyth, op.cit., p.18.
45. *Ideas and Beliefs of the Victorians* (1949), ed. H. Grisewood: C. Smyth, *The Evangelical Discipline*, p.98.

For Further Reading

In addition to the books quoted above the following have proved relevant and valuable to the writer:

These were his Gifts, F. D. Coggan (Exeter 1974).

The Archbishop of Canterbury devotes one of his Bishop John Prideaux Lectures to Charles Simeon and his significance for the Church of today.

Ideas of Revelation, H. D. McDonald (1959).

Contains a useful chapter on the theological outlook of Charles Simeon.

Cambridge and the Evangelical Succession, Marcus Loane (1952).

Includes short biographies of William Grimshaw, John Berridge, Henry Venn and Henry Martyn as well as of Simeon.

Religion at Oxford and Cambridge, V. H. H. Green (1964).

Covers the religious foundation and development of Oxford as well as Cambridge down to the present day.

The Making of Victorian England, G. Kitson Clark (1962).

The classic book on the subject.

Victorian Prelude, M. J. Quinlan (1941).

A fascinating 'History of English Manners 1700–1830'.

The Magdalene Evangelicals, J. D. Walsh (Church Quarterly Review, clix. 499).

Entertaining glimpses of the Elland Society grantees at college.

Evangelicalism and the French Revolution, V. Kiernan (Past and Present, i, Feb. 1952).

Surveys religio-political trends in which Wilberforce and the Clapham Sect were prominent.

English Evangelical Eschatology 1790–1850, S. C. Orchard (Ph.D. thesis 1969).

Comprehensive study of a controversial subject.

Index